TRADER'S GUIDE TO FINANCIAL MARKETS AND TECHNICAL ANALYSIS

Jitender Yadav

www.visionbooksindia.com

www.visionbooksindia.com

Disclaimer

The author and the publisher disclaim all legal or other responsibilities for any losses which investors may suffer by investing or trading using the methods described in this book. Readers are advised to seek professional guidance before making any specific investments.

First Published 2012
Reprinted 2020, 2022, 2023

ISBN 10: 81-7094-851-7
ISBN 13: 978-81-7094-851-3

A Vision Books Original

Published by
Vision Books Pvt. Ltd.
(Incorporating Orient Paperbacks and CARING Imprints)
24 Feroze Gandhi Road, Lajpat Nagar 3
New Delhi-110024, India.
Phone: (+91-11) 2984 0821 / 22
e-mail: visionbooks@gmail.com

Printed at
Thomson Press
B-315, Okhla Industrial Area, Phase 1
New Delhi 110020, India.

Contents

Preface

"If a man empties his purse into his head, no man can take it away from him. An investment in knowledge always pays the best interest." — *Benjamin Franklin*

IN 1988, I HAD JUST FINISHED MY HIGH SCHOOL and was looking to get admission into a good college. As luck would have it, I was not one of those bright students and so could not get admission into a regular college. Since I had plenty of time, I took up part time jobs and earned more than I needed. It was then that I first ventured into the financial markets and started trading in stocks occasionally. In the next few years I made average profits in stocks. Then, in early 1990's, I was introduced to the currency market. Anybody who is a currency trader would understand that I was completely impressed by this new market. At that time, I was full of confidence and my track record in stocks got me some clients. My first currency trade was in the Swiss franc. I bought Swiss franc because I had seen US dollar weakening all along. It was an exciting moment as I waited to make a huge profit. Within ten minutes of the trade, all my confidence was shattered as I saw the market go against me at a speed that I had never before experienced. I could not think or act as this was not what I had anticipated. I had a margin call within fifteen minutes of the trade.

What I felt at that moment is hard to explain as multiple emotions rocked me, but those fifteen minutes changed my whole outlook towards the markets. I was at a stage where I had to make a career choice and this loss did not make things easier. However, I decided to stay rather than quit and find out why things went wrong. I came to the conclusion that if there was anybody to blame, it was me. The markets will move as they have always done and it was up to me to make the right entry and exit. In my overconfidence, I had not devoted time to fully understand the currency market. I had no trading plan and so was completely clueless when the position went into a loss. There were many other aspects which I should have taken care of. Anyway, I learnt from my mistakes and life went on. I tried everything to make my trades profitable. This was the time I dived deep into technical analysis and became a hardcore fan. Fundamental analysis was something that did not impress me. It does not mean that I ignored fundamental analysis, but I only used it as a supporting tool, not for primary analysis.

I never saw my entry price again in Swiss franc and forgot all about it as time passed. In early 2008, I finally saw those levels of Swiss franc after fourteen years and remembered my first trade. If at that time I had been stubborn and not accepted that I needed to change, then no matter how big my account was, it would have finished.

Trading in financial markets is no less than war — you fight with every trade. Once you have taken a position, you have to fight for winning the money from someone else and at the same time keep your own money safe. A soldier who goes unprepared to the battleground is doomed to end up as a loser. Similarly, an unprepared trader is destined to lose.

If you plan to be a trader, or are already one, this book will prepare you to stay on the winning side.

This book is specifically written for both present and aspiring traders for whom the sole purpose of trading in financial markets is to make profit. It is a combination of my trading and teaching experience. The book is divided into two parts. Although the main objective of this book is to impart knowledge of technical analysis, part one has been devoted to providing a basic knowledge of financial markets. The question "What are financial markets?" is tackled in an easy way and specific markets like stock, commodity, forex, etc., are explained. After going through these chapters, a reader would be able to clearly understand these markets and their functioning. The approach throughout the book is practical and the explanations simple.

No matter whether you are a day trader or a long-term investor, whether you trade in stocks, commodities or currencies, whether you trade cash or derivatives, technical analysis is your indispensable knowledge resource. Technical analysis will make you capable of spotting the right entry and exit points. It's a must know for every speculator and trader. At the same time, it is also helpful for occasional investors who will learn when to exit their investments and when to enter the market again.

An equally important aspect of trading, other than knowing when to enter and exit, is money management. There is a full chapter on money management that will help you to understand what, why and how things go wrong before and after a trade is made and what needs to be done to become a perfect trader. My advice to all readers is to go through the money management chapter thoroughly and you will then never make any of the mistakes that most traders do.

The prevailing myth is that making money in financial markets is very difficult. I hope that this book breaks the myth and turns every reader, no matter what his or her background is, into a trader for whom profit is just another daily routine.

All the best!

JITENDER YADAV

Introduction

Answers to Some Common Questions

What are the Different Ways of Analysing the Markets?

The analysis of financial markets or, in simple terms figuring at what to buy and what to sell, can be done through two methods, fundamental and technical.

Fundamental analysis is all about interpreting financial data such as revenues, expenses, assets, liabilities, etc. Financial statements like balance sheet, cash flow statements, income statement, etc., are studied and the financial health of an entity is judged. The future prospects of a company are analysed based on such analysis. This analysis is commonly known as quantitative analysis. Fundamental analysis also includes qualitative aspects that are difficult to quantify, such as the quality of management, a company's business model, threat from competition, etc. In the case of commodities, supply and demand figures (present and projected) form the basis of analysis whereas in the case of currencies, factors like interest rates, political situation and economy are looked into.

Technical analysis uses the past traded price and volume data to predict future market movement. Technical analysis does not look into the actual nature of the market, company, currency or commodity; it is based solely on historical price and volume information. This price data is plotted on a chart and analysed. For example, if you have to trade in Google as a technical analyst, the only thing you would require is the past traded prices of Google on the stock exchange. You do not need to look into Google's revenues, sales, debt, etc., to make a decision. So, if you have the price history of anything, be it a stock, a commodity or currency, you can analyse it with equal ease using technical analysis.

It is evident that these two tools are completely distinct. Fundamental analysis uses financial facts and figures whereas technical analysis uses past price data. Fundamental analysis enjoys universal acceptance and respect that technical analysis has yet to achieve, which is unfortunate. Time and again we have seen big corporate houses collapse even though they were supposedly fundamentally sound. Fundamental analysts could not foresee the credit crisis in the US that led to the end of some of the biggest investment banks. At every step of the market decline through 2008, investors had been told one thing; stocks are cheap fundamentally. Yet shares continued to fall. The subsequent rise of global equities in 2009 left them equally surprised. The technical *versus* fundamental debate has been going on for long and it may never end, but my personal view is that both have their own place and neither should be looked down upon. However, one big advantage that technical analysis has over fundamental analysis is the flexibility of analysis. As a technical analyst, you can analyse any market, the only thing required is a price chart. Long-term investors may decide whether they want to use technical analysis alone or in combination with fundamental analysis. However, for a trader, technical analysis is the only option, as fundamental analysis does not reveal what may happen in the next few hours or days.

Apart from these, there is astrology which is not accepted as an analysis tool at all but is nevertheless used by many, especially commodity traders.

Why Be a Trader?

1. The foremost reason is to make money — and lots of it. Trading gives you liberty to use the money you have and earn much more than is possible anywhere else. Trading is the only vocation which gives you an opportunity to start with a very small amount and earn accordingly. High returns in trading come with high risk. Some of you may like to challenge this premise as a trader by trying out new methods to reduce risk — and there is no reason why you should not.
2. The second reason is that trading gives you instant results. Once a position is taken, you will know in a matter of minutes or hours if you are making profit or loss. Nowhere else is this possible, except of

course gambling, and that is why many people mistakenly see trading as a form of gambling.

3. The third reason is that it gives you flexibility of operations. As a trader, you are your own master and you have a choice of working when you want and where you want.
4. You do not need any significant infrastructure for trading. You can start trading whenever you decide and leave it with equal ease without any botheration of winding up.
5. The fifth reason is if you are not able to find a job anywhere. This may not sound good but sometimes trading can be your destiny. However, utmost caution is required in such a case as trading is a stressful job and you cannot afford to have other psychological pressures while trading.

When Not to Be a Trader?

1. A prerequisite for being a trader is to trade with money you can afford to lose. If your trading account is coming from cutting down on your necessities, don't even think of becoming a trader. It does not mean that trading is a losing game; on the contrary, it can be very profitable if done rightly. However, the fact is that most people lose money in trading because of multiple reasons. Therefore, if any aspect of your life is dependent on the money that you are planning to trade with, then better not do it.
2. Understand the limitations of trading. If trading can give you instant profits, it also gives instant losses. You can lose within minutes what you have earned in years. If you are not comfortable with this risk, then don't become a trader.
3. Don't be a trader if you get thrill out of market moves. When you start to look at trading as a thing of enjoyment and not take it as work to be done seriously, then forget about being a trader. Addiction to the market is much more devastating than drug addiction.
4. Don't become a trader just because your friends are.
5. Don't be a trader if you have not properly educated yourself and acquired in-depth knowledge about the market you are going to enter.
6. Don't become a trader if you think that you can take big risks since you are young. This notion is responsible for ruining many lives. If

you are young, see that as an opportunity — you have plenty of time to prepare yourself for becoming a trader rather than taking unwarranted risk. You have spent years on getting a formal education, so don't think that you can make instant money without having to spend time on learning about trading.

Why Spend Time Learning How to Trade or Invest by Yourself?

The truth is we tend to take the easy way. For those of us who are busy and have money to invest, the easy way is to look for options like mutual funds, etc. And the easy way for traders is to be on the look-out for tips or news and become a slave of the markets rather than learning to analyse the markets. Most people start trading at a stage in their lives when spending time on reading books seems cumbersome. Nevertheless, remember that there is no substitute to your own knowledge. The only hindrance to gaining knowledge is the time required and the difficulty of the subject.

Fortunately, technical analysis is one of the easiest subjects and can be learnt in a short duration. Anyone can learn technical analysis and make money in the markets. It's as simple as that. The biggest advantage of learning technical analysis is that it will make you independent and capable of taking your own investment decisions. The moment you start learning technical analysis, it will start complementing your trading and give you a new insight into financial markets. Even if you have hired a professional to take care of your investments, it is worthwhile to gain this knowledge. Of course, for traders it is an absolute must to learn technical analysis. Traders need to realise that the tip that they get is a way for someone else to come out of his positions. Why would anyone give you something for free? Moreover, if you pay for the services, how can you be sure that you cannot be better than the other person in a few months?

Once you have learnt technical analysis, you will realise that it is enormously rewarding in every possible way.

Is Speculation the Same as Gambling?

No market is made for speculators but no market can do without them. Why, then, is speculation a dirty word? Is it because it is taken as gambling? We like to call ourselves jobbers, traders, etc., but nobody likes to be called a speculator, and this is strange because ultimately we are speculating even when we invest for the long term.

It is a fact that both gambling and speculation are risk dependent. Although speculation in financial markets is sometimes referred to as gambling, this is an inaccurate reference. The difference between gambling and speculation is that in gambling new risks are created whereas in speculation the existent risk is merely transferred from one person to another. Gambling has no contribution to the general economic well-being of a system, whereas in speculation there is an assumption of risk that exists which is a necessary part of the economy. Gambling in a casino is no more than entertainment of a few people. On the other hand, speculation in commodity trading, for example, performs the economic function of establishing a market price for the commodity, supported by an enforceable, legal contract providing for delivery of a cash commodity. Whether the commodity is finally delivered, or whether the futures contract is subsequently cancelled by an offsetting purchase or sale, is of no real consequence. The main point is that someone has taken a risk which a farmer may not wish to take and so in a way has helped the farmer. Speculation in currency market, on the other hand, is more close to gambling but even here trades are based on some parameters and not merely left to chance. Of course, a speculator has complete freedom of choice and at no time is there any reason to assume a risk that he does not think is a good one. One's skill in selecting good risks and avoiding poor risks is what determines one's success or failure as a speculator in the financial markets.

PART 1

Financial Markets

People have different views on what financial markets are. Some people may refer to the stock market as the financial market, yet others may refer to the commodity market while defining a financial market. Such confusion about financial markets arises because too many terms are associated with it. In fact, the stock market, the commodity market, the bond market, the currency market are all constituents of the financial market. These are the markets where large numbers of buyers and sellers meet on a single platform and carry out financial transaction primarily to help businesses grow and make money for investors. The flow chart as shown in Figure 1 (Overleaf) explains the different components of a financial market. Each market is then individually explained in the chapters that follow. These are written for traders and investors and are not designed for the academic reader.

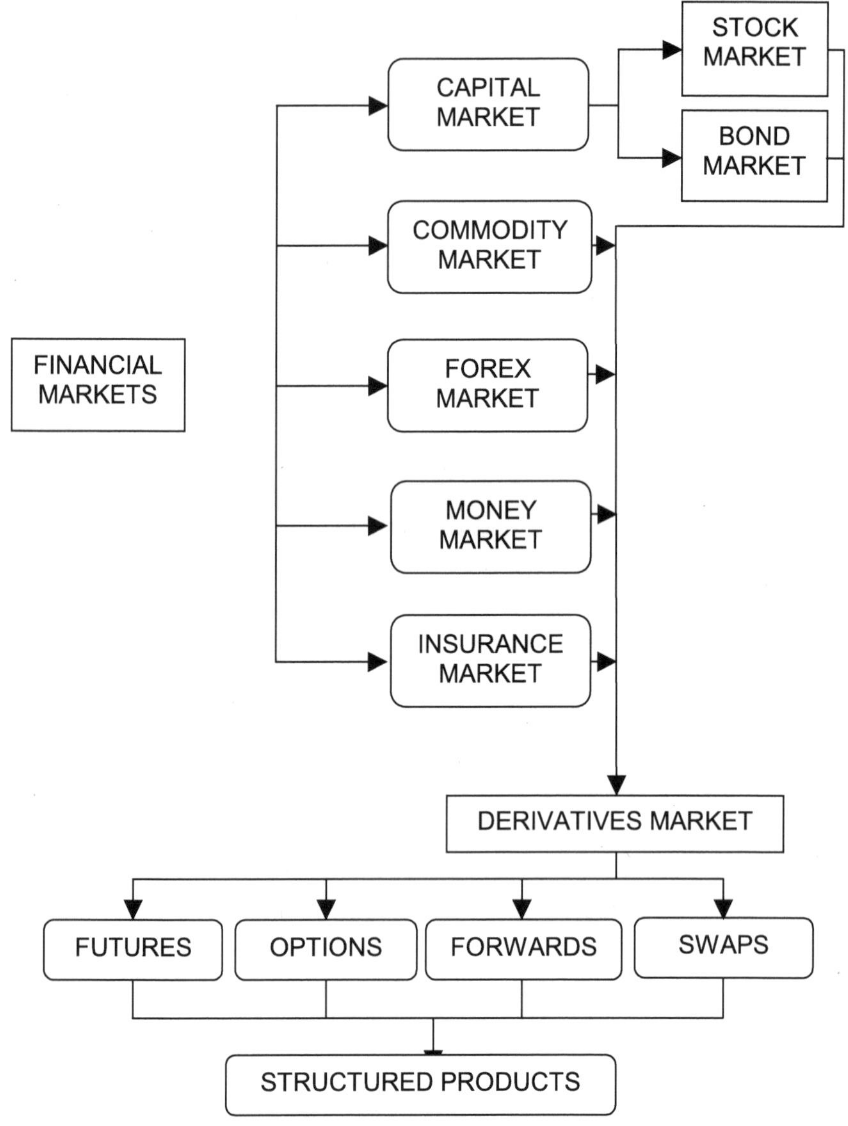

Some or all types of derivatives are present in all financial markets.

Structured products are generally derivatives based investment instruments.

Figure 1: **Flowchart**

Chapter 1

The Capital Market

BEFORE VENTURING INTO THE CAPITAL MARKET, let us first understand the term capital. If you plan to start a restaurant, you would need money to invest in property, equipments, raw material, furniture, etc. The money that you need to invest to start a business is called capital. Capital may be required by corporates, governments and individuals to start a new business, fund a new project, expand a running business, or for any other purpose related to a business. The required capital can be raised in two ways:

1. By issuing shares (i.e., certificates of partial ownership in the company) to people who may be interested to be a part of the business venture in return for a proportional share in its ownership and the profits that the company might generate. This is done through equity or stock markets.
2. By taking a loan or borrowing money that will need to be paid back with interest. This is done through the debt or bond market.

Capital markets assist transfer of money from people with excess funds, i.e. those who spend less than they earn, to those who have a shortage of funds, i.e. people who spend more than they earn. We all go through this cycle of excess and shortage. Therefore, capital markets may be defined as markets where people, companies and governments with more money than they need transfer it to people, companies or governments who have a shortage of funds. Stock and bond markets are two major constituents of the capital market.

Capital markets thus play an important part in the economic development of any country by channelling money from non-productive to productive use.

Let us take an example. If you earn ₹ 10,000 a month and spend ₹ 7,000, your net savings are ₹ 3,000 and you decide to put your savings in mutual funds. What you have done is given the excess money to companies who have issued stocks or bonds because they need it and can put it to some productive use. The company which has received the money will now be able to implement its business plans and you would get better returns. This is direct financing. However, even if you keep the money in your bank account, the bank will lend the money to companies that require funds. In this case, the bank acts as a financial intermediary between you as the saver and the company as the borrower. This is indirect financing. A capital market makes all these transactions easy and quick, thereby helping economic growth.

Primary and Secondary Capital Markets

Capital markets — both stock and bond markets — have primary and secondary markets.

The primary market is where new securities, such as stocks and bonds, are issued. The corporation or government agency that needs funds issues securities to purchasers in the primary market. The term "securities" is used for a broad range of investment instruments. Investors have essentially two broad categories of securities available to them: equity securities, which represent part ownership of a company, and debt securities, which represent a loan from the investor to a company or government entity.

Big banks and financial institutions assist in this issuing process. The banks underwrite the securities, i.e., they guarantee a minimum price for a business's securities and sell them to the public. In case of a new stock issue, the sale is known as initial public offering, or IPO. Since the primary market is limited only to issuing new securities, it is of lesser importance for a trader.

Once the securities are issued, they are traded in secondary markets. Stock exchanges like NSE, Dow Jones, Hang Seng, etc. are secondary markets where trading of previously issued securities takes place. The majority of capital transactions take place in the secondary market making these markets suitable for traders.

Stock is the most recognised form of equity security. When investors buy stock, they become owners of a “share” of a company’s assets and earnings. If a company is doing well, the stock price will go up and if the company is not able to grow, or runs into losses, its stock may fall in value and shareholders can lose money. Stock prices are also subject to both general economic and industry-specific market factors.

On the other hand, investors who purchase debt instruments are creditors. The most common example of a debt instrument is a bond. In this case, investors give a loan to the company and don’t take a share in it as is the case in equity. When investors buy bonds, they are lending their money to the issuers of the bonds. In return, they will receive interest payments, usually at a fixed rate, for the life of the bond and receive the principal back when the bond expires. Many types of institutions, such as big corporates, governments, municipal agencies, etc., sell bonds to raise money.

Chapter 2

The Stock Market

THE STOCK MARKET IS THE MOST POPULAR AVENUE for investors. However, despite being a part of everyone's life directly or indirectly, it is often not completely understood. In the last few years the participation in stock market has been growing at the fastest pace ever because of technological development, but most equity investments are still done on pure hearsay. Most people have yet to realise the down side of investing in the stock market. The irony is that we haggle over the price of relatively low priced products, but make huge investments in the stock market based merely on hearsay or tips. Therefore, it is very important for you to be thoroughly aware of the market you are entering if you have to be a long-term player and make profits.

Before proceeding further, let us first see the different ways a business can be carried out.

Suppose you want to start a business and have enough money to start on your own without any partners or stockholders, you are said to be a sole proprietor. You bear all the costs and keep all the profits. As a sole proprietor, you are responsible for all the business's debts and other liabilities.

However, instead of starting on your own, you may wish to pool money and expertise with friends or relatives. In such a case, you can form a partnership. The partnership agreement will set out how management decisions are to be made and the proportion of profits each partner is entitled to. The partners then pay personal income tax on their share of these profits. Partners, like sole proprietors, have the disadvantage of unlimited liability. Nevertheless, many professional businesses are organized as partnerships. These include the large accounting, legal, and management consulting firms. Many well-known companies, such as

Microsoft and Apple, started life as partnerships and the same goes for most large investment banks such as Morgan Stanley and Goldman Sachs.

As your firm grows, you may need more funds for expansion to cater to the growing demand. Your personal resources may not be able to cover the large amount of funds required. In such a case, you may decide to raise capital by incorporating your firm and issuing shares to the public. By this process, you have partially diluted your ownership but have generated the required funds. The people who have bought the shares become a part owners in your firm. When you issue shares to raise money, it is known as equity financing.

The other way a business can raise finance is by taking a loan or by issuing bonds. This is known as debt financing. Now, why would a company part with its profit if it can get money without doing so by way of debt financing? The answer is that debt financing requires regular payments in the form of interest until the full amount is repaid and the interest payment may become a problem in case business slows down. The shareholders take this risk with a view that, in future, the value of their share will be much more than what they had paid to acquire it.

The corporation is owned by its shareholders and they get to vote on important matters. Unlike proprietorships or partnerships, corporations have limited liability, which means that the stockholders cannot be held personally responsible for the liabilities of the firm. The most a shareholder can lose is the amount he or she invested in the stock. While the stockholders of a corporation own the firm, they do not usually manage it. Instead, they elect a board of directors which, in turn, appoints the top managers. The board is the representative of shareholders and is supposed to ensure that the firm's management acts in their best interests. This separation of ownership and management is one distinctive feature of corporations.

There is one more type of business entity which is known as limited liability partnership or LLP. It has all the advantages of a partnership; at the same time the partners have only limited liability. LLP can be considered as fusion between a partnership and a private limited company.

All public limited companies are not necessarily listed but all listed companies who have issued shares to the public are essentially incorporated. A sole proprietor, partnership, LLP and private limited firms cannot be listed or traded on stock exchanges.

Before any company can raise capital from the general public by issuing shares, it must fulfil certain conditions laid down by the respective regulator, such as the Securities and Exchange Commission (SEC) in the US or SEBI in India. After complying with all the required formalities, the company issues shares in the primary market. When shares are issued for the first time by a company, it is known as initial public offering or IPO. Each stock issue is limited to a certain number of shares which when issued, they are given a par value. The market will then adjust that par value according to the strength of the company and its growth potential.

You can buy shares either in the primary market or in the secondary market. The primary market is basically like a birth place of new securities. When a company raises money from public for the first time, it has to go to the primary market through the IPO route. Once the shares are issued, they can be freely traded in the secondary market through stock exchange like BSE, NSE, FTSE, NYSE, etc. In secondary market, the issuing company has no role in the trading of its stock. When people talk about the stock market, it is usually the secondary market they are referring to.

Important Points about Stock Markets for Traders

Since it is in the secondary market, or the stock market where actual trading happens, it is important to understand all aspects of a stock market before you venture into it.

Thousands of companies are listed on stock exchanges and the listed shares are classified according to many different factors. Let us consider the important ones.

Market Capitalisation

This is the most important classification of stocks. Market capitalisation simply means the value of the company in the market. It is calculated by multiplying the current price of the company's share with the total number of outstanding shares of the company.

Market capitalisation = (Current stock price) × (Total outstanding shares)

Stock are typically classified into three categories by market capitalisation:

1. **Large Cap:** These are stocks with the highest market capitalisation. They are also typically the most actively traded stocks; in other words the most liquid.

   Traders should always concentrate on large caps as it is very easy to enter and exit without getting into the risk of being stuck with a position. These companies usually pay good dividends and are held by most of the big institutions and fund houses.
2. **Mid Cap:** These stocks fall in the middle range by market capital value. These are stocks of companies which are on a growth path and whose business model is working in the right direction. Some of these companies eventually become large cap. Since they require funds for growth, the dividend payout is usually less than those of the large cap stocks.

   Traders should be careful while entering in these stocks as they are not as liquid as large caps and are prone to large price swings that can wipe out your entire trading account.

   Mid cap stocks are, however, very important for investors as they offer chances of huge returns in the long term.
3. **Small Cap:** These are stocks with the lowest range of market capital value. They are risky for both traders as well as investors.

   Traders, in particular, should keep away from this category as not much of an analysis is possible in the case of small caps. It is also difficult to trade in huge quantities in small caps as their liquidity is very low. Small cap companies rarely ever pay any dividends. Many small cap companies go out of business instead of gradually moving to a higher cap category.

   Investors can select some small caps but the risk is high.

No matter whether you are a trader or an investor, it is very important to understand the detailed business profile of the company that you are considering to invest in. Some people confuse market cap with the share price. Higher share price does not mean bigger market cap. A company with stock price of ₹ 100 may be small cap and one with ₹ 50 may be large cap.

Blue Chips

Blue chip stocks represent some of the largest and best established companies. These companies usually have very high earnings year after year, and have a record of stability and exceptional corporate management. These companies have great financial strength, and often pay quarterly dividends.

Sectoral Stocks

Stocks can also be grouped on the basis of the type of business they are into. For example, all companies in power generation are clubbed in the power sector. There are many different sectors, such as banking, steel, power, consumer goods, IT and so on.

Defensive Stocks

Defensive stocks are companies that are generally stable all year round as they provide important goods and services that are required irrespective of the general economic conditions. That means their products and services enjoy steady demand in the market throughout the year and do not depend on the business cycles and overall market conditions. Traditional defensive stock sectors have been pharmaceutical and FMCG or fast moving consumer goods.

Growth Stocks

Growth stocks represent companies whose earnings are expected to grow more relative to the market. The returns on equity of growth stocks are much higher and these are the companies that can create fortunes for investors. Generally, growth stocks are not to be found in the traditional, well-known sectors but in new and upcoming fields, such as nano technology, biotechnology, computers, telecommunications and health care. These companies usually do not pay any dividends.

Cyclical Stocks

These represent companies whose sales and profits fluctuate according to business cycles.

Penny Stocks or Speculative Stocks

These are the stocks, which are priced so low that you can buy them in loads with small investments. They exist only for speculators' interest as they never pay dividends, trade below par value for most of their lives, and have poor managements who are sometimes themselves involved in stock manipulation. Penny stocks become active at the height of a bull market frenzy and many people lose their hard-earned money by investing in them. These stocks eventually get delisted, so even if you buy them at throwaway prices, you are still likely to suffer loss. It is best to keep away from these stocks.

Index

The most common word in the stock market is index. When people talk of stock market going up or down, they are actually referring to the index. Index is a group of stocks which are selected based on factors such as market capitalisation, liquidity, floating stock, etc. These stocks are usually market leaders, mostly large cap and blue chip stocks, and reflect the general direction of the economy and market sentiments.

There are different ways to calculate the value of an index. The first stock index was the DJIA or Dow Jones Industrial Average, created in 1896. It consisted of twelve of the largest public companies in the US at that time and the index was price based. The price of all the twelve stocks were added together and divided by 12 making it a simple average of stock prices. Today, most index values are based on market capitalisation. For example, if a company's market cap is ₹ 100, and the total value of all the stocks in the index is ₹ 1,000, then the weight of that company in the index will be 10%. That is why sometimes a major move in even one stock of the index which has a high weight, leads to a major move in the index even though other stocks may not have moved at all.

The most common indices like Nifty, DJIA, S&P500, Hang Seng, Nikkei 225, FTSE 100, and BSE Sensex are all broad based indices. It means that stocks from all sectors are present in these indices. There are also sector specific indices, like the Bank index, which consists only of bank stocks, and the indices based on market cap, like a mid cap or a small cap index.

It is important to know that you can also trade in an index. You can buy or sell an index just like any other stock but cannot take delivery of an index as it is a notional thing. You can only trade in index derivatives and the profit or loss is all cash settled at the expiry of the contract.

Before Starting a Trade

Before you start trading, you must understand the market, the stocks or the index you are going to trade. The decision to buy or sell should be based on your own judgement. It will not be difficult once you are familiar with all aspects of the stock market.

Choose one right broker; the broker's credentials should be well established and he should have an unblemished record of servicing clients. You may think that a broker's role is only limited to executing your orders but the broker's ability to manage risk and margin money at his end is very crucial. In a sudden market fall, brokers who have not exercised proper risk management may not be able to place your order and you may lose good opportunities.

Some important points to keep in mind before selecting a broker are:

1. **Online or Local Broker:** Most trading companies nowadays offer online trading services which have great advantages. Remember, however that online trading is prone to minor hitches due to many reasons. Therefore, if you are a fast trader or a scalper, it is better to have a local broker.
2. **Brokerage:** It is very important to get the best possible brokerage rates, especially for traders. Talk to several brokers and select the one with the lowest brokerage without any conditions like minimum trade, etc. Low brokerage increases the chances of profitable trades to a great extent. Of course, this aspect does not matter too much for long-term investors.

3. **Services:** Most online stockbrokers provide their clients with a range of online technical and fundamental tools that help them make their investment decisions or trading calls. Look for services that you would be using and who can provide them best.
4. **Speed of Order Execution:** In any stock market trade, timing is critical. Prices may move sharply within seconds and it is important that the stockbroker has the capacity to execute orders speedily and get the rates the client desires.
5. **Calm and Quiet Approach:** Your broker should be calm even in major market moves. The last thing that you want during big market moves is somebody shouting or your message box being flooded with extreme views about markets. If this happens, your trading will suffer and you will not be able to take decisions.

How to Choose Stocks for Trading

Learn technical analysis thoroughly before you venture into trading. Once you become a technical analyst, you will easily be able to choose stocks for trading. However, it will greatly enhance your judgement if you learn to interpret certain financial data like income, earnings, debt, P/E ratio, etc., even if you are just a speculator. Understanding company fundamentals will support your analysis. For example, you can buy companies with good fundamentals if your technical analysis suggests that the index may rise, and sell companies with weak fundamentals if your technical analysis suggests that the index may fall. All these figures are available in financial newspapers, websites, special publications, etc. You do not need to be a fundamental analyst to check and analyse these figures. For instance, simple logic says that any company which is reducing its debt burden is a good buy.

The final aim of every investor is to buy stocks that are likely to give average to above average returns in the long run. Value investing is sometimes confused with buying low priced stocks. There is more to being a value investor than looking for low readings on price-to-earnings, price-to-book-value, and other value ratios. One must also assess if there has been a fundamental shift in the company's business or environment to determine if its troubles are temporary or permanent. Nevertheless, finding suitable stocks is not easy and most investors do not have the time or knowledge to study financial statements. The best approach for such investors and traders is to trade only in index stocks. Index stocks are, by default, some of the best companies from different sectors and so, for starters, it is a good approach to just stick to index stocks.

Even if you have been trading for a long time and know how to pick value stocks, stay away from illiquid, small-capitalization value stocks because if you go wrong and want to get out of the bad investment, there may not be any buyers for them.

Professor Joseph Piotroski of the Graduate School of Business, Chicago, came out with a simplified system of fundamental analysis based on financial statements of only the last two years that can be used by active investors for picking value stocks with a one- or two-year horizon.

There are nine steps or tests in the model. The stock gets a point for every step it passes and a zero for any step it fails. Buying stocks that score eight or nine points is recommended. Speculators can use this to short sell stocks that score low.

1. **Positive Net Income:** Net income, the bottom-line after-tax profits, is the simplest measure of profitability, and Piotroski favours profitable companies. Give one point if the latest year's net income is positive; otherwise, a zero.
2. **Positive Cash Flow:** Cash flow is considered a better measure of profitability than net income. Cash flow measures the money that actually moved into or out of a firm's bank accounts. Give one point if the latest year's operating cash flow is positive.
3. **Return on Assets (ROA):** Return on assets measures a company's earnings in relation to all of the resources it had at its disposal; i.e. the shareholders' capital plus short and long-term borrowed funds. Thus, it is the most stringent and strongest test of return to shareholders. Give one point if the current year's ROA exceeds prior-year ROA.
4. **Earnings Quality:** Many experts compare net income to operating cash flow to detect potential accounting manipulations. Cash flow normally exceeds net income because depreciation and other non-cash expenses reduce income, but not cash flow. Award one point if the latest year's operating cash flow exceeds the current year's net income.

5. **Decreasing Debt:** Piotroski rewards companies that are reducing their debt levels. Check if the full-year ratio of long-term debt to assets is down from the previous year. Award one point if the most recent annual figure is less than the value of the preceding year. The long-term debt / equity ratio is a reasonable substitute for debt / assets.
6. **Increasing Working Capital:** Working capital, the difference between current assets and current liabilities, measures the cash available to run the business. Current ratio, which is current assets divided by current liabilities, is the usual metric for measuring working capital. Award one point if the most recent annual figure exceeds the preceding year's number.
7. **Increase in Asset Turnover:** You can check this by comparing the full-year sales growth to asset growth. Give one point if the percentage increase in sales exceeds the percentage increase in total assets.
8. **Issuing Stock:** Piotroski penalizes companies that sell stock to raise cash. Give one point if the current number of shares outstanding is equal to, or less than, the year-ago figure.
9. **Gross Margin:** Increasing competition often forces companies to cut prices and, hence, profit margins to maintain sales. Conversely, rising profit margins signal an improving competitive position. Increasing gross margins (profit margin based on direct production costs) often signal that a company's competitive position is improving. Give one point if full-year gross margin exceeds the prior-year gross margin.

If the above process too seems complicated, use the following points by looking at the figure for the past five years:

1. Avoid companies with three down earning years in the past five.
2. Choose companies with a minimum average 20 per cent revenue and earnings growth.
3. Avoid any firm with return on average equity below 15 per cent.
4. Avoid firms with debt in excess of 35 per cent of total capital.

Investors usually buy stocks because they believe the company will continue to grow and the value of their shares will rise accordingly. Investors who acquire stock in a new company are taking more risk than those buying shares of well-established companies but the potential gain is much greater in the former case.

Glossary of Important Stock Market Terms

Annual Report: A publication including financial statements and a report on operations, issued by a company to its shareholders at the end of the fiscal year.

Arbitrage: The simultaneous purchase of a security on one exchange and sale of the same security on another exchange if the price difference is sufficient to give profits.

Ask or Offer: The lowest price at which someone is willing to sell the security. When combined with the bid price information, it forms the basis of a stock quote.

Assets: Everything a company owns, including cash, securities, equipment and real estate. Assets are listed on a company's balance sheet.

Averaging: Adding more positions without closing the previous ones. Negative averaging is when you add more positions while the previous position is still in loss. Positive averaging is adding more positions to an already profitable position.

Bear Market: A market in which stock prices are falling.

Beta: A measurement of the relationship between the price of a stock and the movement of the whole market.

Bid: The highest price a buyer is willing to pay for a stock. When combined with the ask price information, it forms the basis of a stock quote.

Block Trades: Large number of shares traded in a single deal, usually by big institutions.

Book Value: This is the value of a company if all its assets and common stock equity are added together and all liabilities are subtracted from it. Often there is little correlation between the book value and the market value but when the stock price is lower than the book value, it is considered a good buy.

Broker — Brokerage Firm: Brokers are the link between investors and the stock exchange.

Bull Market: A market in which stock prices are rising.

Business Day: Any days from Monday to Friday, excluding statutory holidays.

Capital Gain or Loss: Profit or loss resulting from the sale of certain assets classified under the income tax legislation as capital assets. This includes stocks and other investments such as property.

Commission: The fee charged by a broker for buying or selling securities as an agent on behalf of a client.

Delist: The removal of a security's listing on a stock exchange. This is done when the security no longer exists, the company is bankrupt, the public distribution of the security has dropped to an unacceptably low level, or the company has failed to comply with the terms of its listing agreement.

Demat: The move from physical certificates to electronic book keeping of securities. Physical stock certificates are slowly being removed and retired from circulation in exchange for electronic recording.

Delivery: The tender and receipt of the stock and exchange of payment in the settlement of a trade.

Diversification: Reducing investment risk by purchasing different types of securities from different companies representing different sectors of the economy.

Dividend: Distribution of a portion of a company's earnings among its shareholders, decided by the board of directors. Dividends may be in the form of cash or stock. Most secure and stable companies offer dividends to their stockholders.

Earnings per Share (EPS): The portion of a company's profit allocated to each outstanding share of common stock. EPS serves as an indicator of a company's profitability.

Equities: Common and preferred stocks which represent a share in the ownership of a company.

Exchange Traded Fund (ETF): A special type of financial trust that allows an investor to buy an entire basket of stocks through a single security, which tracks and matches the returns of a stock market index. ETFs are considered special types of index mutual funds, but they are listed on an exchange and are traded like any other security.

Inflation: Rate of increase in prices of goods and services.

IPO (Initial Public Offering): An issuer's first offering of its securities made to the public in accordance with a prospectus. The offering is often made in conjunction with an issuer's initial application for listing on an exchange.

Insider: All directors and senior officers of a company, and those who are presumed to have access to inside information concerning the company. An insider is also anyone owning more than 10% of the voting shares of a company.

Insider Trading: There are two types of insider trading. The first type occurs when insiders trade in the stock of their company and report these transactions to the appropriate securities commissions as required by the law. The other type of insider trading is when anyone trades securities based on material information that is not public knowledge and not disclosed to the securities board. This type of insider trading is illegal.

Issue: Sale of any of a company's securities or the act of distributing the securities. Issued shares refer to the portion of a company's shares that have been issued for sale. A company does not have to issue the total number of its authorized shares.

Liquidity: This refers to how easily shares can be bought or sold in the market. Liquidity is one of the most important characteristics of a good market. Liquidity also refers to how easily investors can convert their shares into cash.

Listed Stock: These are shares of an issuer that are traded on a stock exchange. Issuers pay fees to the exchange for their shares to be listed and must abide by the rules and regulations set out by the exchange to maintain listing privileges.

Long: A term that refers to buying of securities. For example, if you are long 100 shares of XYZ, it means that you have bought 100 shares of

XYZ Company. In trader's terminology, going long also means buying of a security purely for short term profits.

Margin Account: A brokerage account in which the broker lends the customer cash to trade securities.

Mutual Fund: A fund managed by an expert which invests in stocks, bonds, options, money market instruments or other securities. Mutual fund units can be purchased through brokers or directly from the mutual fund company.

Opening Price: The first traded price of a security.

Opening Time: The market opening time on each business day.

Portfolio: Holdings of securities by an individual or institution. A portfolio may include various types of securities representing different companies and industry sectors.

Price-Earnings (P/E) Ratio: A common stock's last closing market price per share divided by the latest reported 12-month earnings per share. In general, a high P/E suggests that investors are expecting higher earnings growth in the future compared to that from companies with a lower P/E.

Settlement: The process that follows a transaction when the seller delivers the shares to the buyer and the buyer pays the seller for the shares.

Settlement Date: The date when a stock buyer must pay for a purchase or a seller must deliver the shares sold. Settlement date may vary from two days to five days from the date of trade.

Share Certificate: A paper certificate that represents the number of shares an investor owns. Now shares are mostly kept in dematerialised form.

Short: A term that refers to selling of securities. For example, if you are short 100 shares of XYZ, this means that you have sold 100 shares of XYZ Company. In trading terminology, going short also means selling of a security purely for short term profits.

Short Selling: The selling of a security that the seller does not own, with the intention of buying equal amount back after the prices fall. This is known as naked or uncovered short. When the short selling is done after borrowing securities from someone else, it is known as covered short. Short selling is a trading strategy. Short sellers expect that they will be able to buy the stock later at a lower price, cover the outstanding short, and realize a profit from the difference.

Special Trading Session: A session during which trading in a listed security is limited to the execution of transactions at a single price.

Speculator: Someone prepared to accept calculated risks in the marketplace for attractive potential returns.

Stock Index Futures: Futures contracts which have a stock index as the underlying explained in Chapter 7.

Stock Split: A corporate action that increases the number of securities issued and outstanding, without the issuer receiving any consideration for the issue. Approval by security holders is required in many jurisdictions. For example, a two-for-one stock split involves the issuance of two new securities for every old security.

Trading Halt: A trading halt is imposed by the exchange, usually due to large price moves, when prices reach a set limit.

Trading Session: The period during which the exchange is open for trading.

Volume: The number of shares traded.

Yield: The measure of the return on an investment and is shown as a percentage. This is the percentage of a dividend paid against the stock price. For example, if you receive a $3 dividend on a $30 per share stock, your yield is 10%.

Chapter 3

The Bond Market

THE BOND MARKET, ALSO KNOWN AS DEBT MARKET or credit market, is a part of the fixed income market. Bonds are fixed income securities because your returns are fixed and you know exactly how much you are going to get if you hold the security for its full term. In spite of being the largest securities market in the world, most investors do not bother to learn or trade the bond market. Stock market is the first investment option for any investor. Stock markets are exciting, fast and extensively covered everywhere from newspapers to TV channels. The stock market is like a celebrity whom everyone wants to reach out to. When the stock market is in a bull move, more and more people get attracted to it, almost hypnotised by the returns being generated. Numerous stories of people getting rich overnight become a part of everyday discussion and people talk about their investments in euphoric tones. However, once the market starts falling, the euphoria dies and people see their profits and later investments vanish in thin air. It is during such times that everyone realises the value of money and look for avenues where they can get assured returns, no matter how small they are.

The bond market is one such avenue which, unfortunately, gets some importance only when the stock market is falling. Speculators and day traders can ignore the bond market but a long-term investor must be fully aware of the potential of bond market in safeguarding investments and as a hedging tool against inflation.

Let us first understand what a bond is. All of us go through a phase when we need to borrow money. We take loans from our family, friends, relatives, banks or from any other source that is possible. Just as we need money, corporate houses and governments also require funds for their needs. A company may need a loan to implement its expansion programme and a government may need loans to implement infrastructure project like roads, etc. The needs may differ but everyone requires money at some stage. Government and corporations need money in such huge amounts that it is almost impossible for a single entity to provide it and so they issue bonds. A bond is nothing more than a loan that you have given. It is a debt investment in which you as a lender loans money to a corporate or government entity. The duration of the loan can be 1 year, 5 years, 10 years, etc.

Now, the question is why would you give loan to somebody by investing in a bond? The answer is simple; because you would get something over and above the amount you have lent. You will earn interest on the amount that you have lent. Like a loan, a bond pays periodic interest, and repays the principal at a stated time.

Thus, a bond is a loan that the bond purchaser, or bondholder, makes to the bond issuer. The following are some important aspects of bonds:

- **Issuer:** Issuer is the entity that requires the funds and issues bonds. The most important factor while purchasing a bond is the issuer. The credibility and stability of the bond issuer decides how safe your investment will be. Low credibility of the issuers increases the default risk or the chance that the debt will not be paid back.
- **Maturity Date:** The date at which the issuer has to repay the borrowed or the principal amount to the investor. The maturity period can range from one to thirty years, with exceptions of longer duration. Normally, maturity period affects the interest rate. The longer the maturity period, higher the interest rate as longer term commitment means more risk to the bondholder, i.e. the person who has purchased the bond.
- **Face Value / Par Value:** The value of a bond as given on the bond certificate, or instrument and at which it will be redeemed at maturity. It is the amount that the bondholder will get back at the bond's maturity. Face value should not be confused with the price of a bond. Usually, a newly issued bond is sold at face value but as time passes, the price keeps on fluctuating depending on market conditions of interest rates, etc. While face value remains the same throughout the life span of the bond, its price will keep on changing. When a bond trades at a price higher than the face value, it is said to be selling at premium. And when a bond trades at price lower than the face value, it is said to be selling at discount.

- **Coupon:** The amount that a bondholder gets as interest payments is known as coupon. The term may be confusing but it is just the regular interest payment that a bondholder gets. In olden days, a bond certificate used to come with a bunch of papers known as coupons attached with it. When the interest was due, the holder would tear off one coupon and redeem it for the interest. Ever since, the interest payment on bonds is known as coupons.

  The coupon is typically indicated as a percentage of par value. Therefore, if a bond has a face value of ₹ 100 and the coupon is 10%, then the annual interest payment will be ₹ 10, i.e. 10% of ₹ 100. The interest payment can either remain a fixed percentage of the par value, or adjust according to market rates. The bond with fixed interest rates is known as "fixed rate bond" and a bond with adjusting interest rates is known as "floating rate bond". Prices of floating rate bonds remains relatively stable because capital gain or loss is adjusted as market interest rates go up or down.

Zero Coupon Bond

This is a type of bond that is issued at a discount to the par value and no coupon payments are made. At maturity, the bond holder gets an amount equal to the par value of the bond. For example, a government issues a zero-coupon bond with a ₹ 1,000 par value and 10-year maturity. When you buy this bond, you may just pay ₹ 600 for a bond that will be worth ₹ 1,000 in 10 years. You have bought the bond at highly discounted price because there will be no interest payments.

Yield and Price

Once you have bought a bond, it does not mean that you have to keep it until maturity. You can sell it in the secondary market at the prevailing market rate. It must be understood that just like stocks, bonds can also be bought and sold in secondary markets. This means that bond prices fluctuate, although not as much as those of stocks. Most investors are confused by the price and yield aspect of bonds. Let us take one factor that affects the price of a bond in a major way, the interest rate. A bond's price reflects the value of the income that it provides through its regular coupon interest payments. When prevailing interest rates fall, older bonds of all types become more valuable because they were sold, or price adjusted, in a higher interest rate environment and therefore have higher coupons. Investors holding older bonds can demand higher price, or charge a "premium", to sell them in the open market. On the other hand, if interest rates rise, older bonds may become less attractive because their coupons are low, adjusted to a lower interest rates situation, and therefore their prices fall — i.e., they trade at a discount. In a very simple way, the price of a fixed rate bond falls if interest rates rise. This process goes on and price keeps on fluctuating to adjust to the prevailing market interest rates.

The yield is the return that you get on a bond. As an investor, you really don't need to bother about calculating it so just an overview is given here. Simple yield is calculated by dividing the bond's annual interest rate by the current price of a bond. For example, a bond costing ₹ 100 that pays ₹ 10 a year in interest is 10 divided by 100, or a 10 per cent yield. If that same bond is priced at ₹ 50, its yield goes up to 20%. You are still getting the same ₹ 10 a year in interest, but you are paying less for the bond, therefore it is yielding more as a percentage. This assumes that you bought the bond at par value and held it until maturity.

The relationship of price and yield is inverse. This means that when a bonds price goes up, its yield goes down and when price goes down, the yield goes up. High yield and high prices can both be good depending on where your investment stands. If you are buying a bond, you would want higher yield but if you are already a bond holder and your interest rate is fixed, you would like to see the bond price go up.

Bond Issuers

Bonds are issued by different entities. The following is a broad classifications of bonds according to who issues them.

Government Bonds

Governments of different countries issue bonds to raise money for development projects, to finance fiscal deficit, and for other reasons. Governments have an obligation to purchasers to ensure that the issued bonds are liquid, marketable and of a size sufficient to ensure easy trading in secondary markets. Bonds issued by stable governments are more secure and find easy buyers. On the other hand, bonds issued by developing or underdeveloped countries are less in demand due to the inherent risk of investors not getting their money back. This is the reason why US bonds are the most accepted and widely traded bonds in the world as they are considered the safest investment.

Bonds issued by governments are known as treasury bonds. Bonds that mature in less than a year are called treasury bills, or T-bills in short. They are traded in money market. Bonds maturing in 2 to 10 years are called T-notes, and those that take more than 10 years to mature are treasury bonds. T-notes and T-bonds are traded in capital markets whereas T-bills are not. Investing in government bonds is the safest investment and it is almost certain that your interest and principal will be re-paid on time as the bonds are backed by the government itself. Due to this reason, interest rates on these bonds is lower than other debt instruments. In India, government bonds are issued through auctions carried out by RBI in the denomination of 10,000 and its multiple.

Corporate Bonds

Corporate bonds are issued by business houses to meet their credit needs. After the government sector, the next largest segment of the bond market comprises corporate bonds. Corporations borrow money in the bond market to expand their operations or fund new business ventures. Corporate bonds offer more variety to investors to choose from and they usually pay higher interest since they carry more risk than government bonds. Therefore, these bonds also require more caution while investing. Before investing in a corporate bond, you should look for the company's financials, like its debt, cash flow, earnings and all such factors that show a company's financial health. There are private credit rating agencies like Standard & Poor's, Moody's, Fitch, and in India, Credit Rating Information Services (CRISIL), Investment Information and Credit Rating Agency of India Ltd (ICRA) and Credit Analysis and Research Ltd (CARE), who do all the research and give a bond rating to the company. These ratings are expressed in letters like AA, BB+, etc., that indicate the strength of the company to honour its debt commitment. The broad classification is: AAA / AA+ (Prime and high grade), A- / BBB (Medium investment grade), BB, B, CCC, CC (non-investment grade, low quality, junk bonds), D (Bonds in default for non-payment with little chance of recovery). It is best to invest in bonds with AAA or AA+ ratings. You have the right to ask for credit rating of their bonds from the company before investing.

Municipal Bonds

These are the bonds issued by municipalities and local government agencies when such agencies fall short of money to implement local projects, like schools, office buildings, bridges, streets, etc. They are also rated by rating agencies.

Below are some more bond terms that you may come across while purchasing a bond:

- **Callability:** The company or agency that issues a bond has the right to call the bond back at a time of their choice. In other words, the company buys the bond back before it matures. A company might do this when interest rates are falling in order to issue new bonds at lower rates in order to save money. This is not always a bad deal for those who bought the bonds either, because there is an extra premium added to the face value of the bond.
- **Put Provision:** Just as callability allows the seller to call the bond back before it matures, some (but not too many) bonds have a put provision that gives the person who bought the bond a chance to sell it back at face value before it matures. This cannot be done at any time and the seller must schedule it ahead of time. People who own bonds sometimes put their bonds when interest rates are rising so they can invest their money where it will earn more.
- **Convertible Bonds:** Bonds which can be converted into stock in the company that issued them. At the time the convertible bonds are issued, it is also specified exactly when and at what price they can be converted to stocks. This type of bond usually offers lower interest rates initially, but it also offers the potential for higher earnings as a stock.
- **Secured Bonds:** Bonds that are backed by collateral are called secured bonds. This means that the company or agency that issue the bond

also has money or assets to cover the bond's value. Money or the assets would be given to the people who bought the bonds in the event that the company goes bankrupt.

- **Unsecured Bonds:** Also called debentures, unsecured bonds are not backed by collateral; they're simply backed by the creditworthiness of the company or agency issuing the bonds. Government bonds are unsecured because the governments are usually creditworthy.

Investing in Bonds

As an investor, you can access the bond market either through mutual funds or directly. You can buy a mutual fund that caters to fixed income securities or just buy the bonds directly from the government or corporations when they are issued. Bond issuers advertise in major publications at the time issue opens.

Chapter 4

The Commodity Market

COMMODITY TRADING is perhaps as old as human civilisation although many changes have occurred in the way commodities are traded during the course of time. The oldest form of commodity market, which still exists, is when a farmer brings his produce to a local market for sale to potential buyers. Wheat, potato, spices and other produce are still traded in such markets in huge volumes. These markets are mostly unregulated and sometimes unorganised, thereby making it easy for a few individuals to control them. This is neither good for farmers, nor for consumers. To bring in transparency, more and more countries have opened commodity exchanges that protect the interest of the producers as well as consumers. However, before we proceed any further, let us see what a commodity is.

Commodity

Commodity is a physical substance or a basic good used for consumption or production of other goods. In other words, commodities are things that you can touch, taste or smell, have some value, are of uniform quality and are produced and traded in large quantities. Some traditional examples of commodities are rice, wheat, gold, milk, etc. These goods are uniform across their producers with minor variations of quality and they hold a monetary value.

However, the definition of a commodity is now becoming more and more complex. Trading commodities is not limited to traditional goods like agriculture produce or metals, but also encompasses emission credits, electricity, weather derivatives, etc.

For a trader the simple definition of commodity is any product that you can trade on commodity exchange. Economist may not agree with this definition but that is all what a trader or an investor needs to understand without going into complicated definitions.

Commodity trading can be in two major ways. You can either physically buy a commodity at a lower price, store it and sell it later at higher price — but delivery, storage and shelf life may be problematic in most cases. The other way you can trade commodities is through futures exchanges. Markets for futures trading were developed initially to help manage the price risks faced by agricultural producers and consumers while harvesting, processing and marketing food crops each year. However, today it is a speculators' playground like any other financial market. Today, futures exist not only on agricultural products but also on a wide array of financial, stock and forex markets.

The concept of "futures" confuses many people. It simply means that someone is ready to buy or sell the commodity at some time in the future but at a price agreed upon today. Detailed explanation of futures is given in the chapter on derivatives (Chapter 7) and it would be advisable to go through that if you are new to this concept.

Commodity Futures Exchange

Many people, especially stock market investors believe that commodity markets are very complex and difficult to understand. The reason may be that commodities are mainly traded in the futures markets. There are certain basic aspects of futures market that one must understand before trading in commodities. I will give a brief explanation of the futures market here.

History

Although the first recorded instance of futures trading occurred with rice in 17th century Japan, there are strong grounds to believe that agriculture futures market existed in India thousands of years earlier. However, the birthplace of present day futures market can be traced to Chicago, USA, when agricultural futures contracts were first traded on the Chicago Board of Trade in 1865. Since then, commodity exchanges have grown exponentially across the world and now trade in ever expanding number of instruments, including metals, energy, financial instruments, foreign currencies, etc. Additionally, the industry introduced trading in options on futures contracts in 1982.

Just as the types of instruments traded on commodity futures exchanges have evolved, so has the method of trading those instruments. Until the 1990's, trading was conducted primarily on the floor of the exchanges. Traders crowded into trading "pits" or "rings", shouting and signalling bids and offers to each other. This type of trading, known as open outcry, resulted in competitive, organized price discovery. However, since 1990 virtually all of the commodity futures exchanges that have been created have opted for electronic trading systems. Many of the new contracts introduced on well-established open outcry exchanges are being traded only on electronic systems, not on the open outcry floor. Most of the recent initiatives for inter-exchange cooperation have been based on electronic linkages. NYMEX, the commodity exchange giant, had to abandon its plan to set up an open outcry trading floor in Britain in early 2007. Because of technological advancement, futures trading has truly become a 24 hours a day, seven-days a week financial marketplace.

A commodity futures market (or exchange) is a public marketplace where standard commodity contracts are bought and sold at an agreed price for delivery at a specific date in the future. These purchases and sales are made under specific terms and conditions through a broker who is a member of the organized exchange concerned.

Futures markets deal only in standardized contractual agreements, known as futures contracts. This is the main difference between a futures market and a market in which actual commodities are traded, whether for immediate or later delivery. The futures contracts provide for delivery of a specified amount of a particular commodity at a specified future date, but involve no immediate transfer of ownership of the commodity involved. This means that one can buy and sell commodities in a futures market without owning the particular commodity. In futures, buyers need not be concerned about taking delivery and sellers about giving delivery of the actual commodity, provided, of course, that positions are cleared before the expiry of the contract. At any time one can clear or cancel out a previous position by taking another equal offsetting position. So, if you have bought a commodity you can sell an equal amount — or *vice versa* — prior to the delivery date. This way the trades cancel out and there is no receipt or delivery of the commodity; only net settlement of profit /

loss is done. Although futures contracts were created for those with a commercial interest, like farmers or large flour mills, but, in reality, only a very small percentage, usually less than two per cent, of the total futures contracts that are entered into are ever settled through deliveries. For the most part, they are cancelled out prior to the delivery month because the players are financial market traders.

A trader must also remember that in the stock market there are both cash as well as futures markets whereas the commodity market is only a futures market. In addition, all the commodities are not necessarily traded on all the exchanges. Therefore, while gold is extensively traded on almost all global commodity exchanges, turmeric is only traded on Indian exchanges like MCX or NCDEX. London Metals Exchange (LME) trades only metals futures whereas Kansas City Board of Trade specialises in hard red winter wheat.

Participants and Functioning of Futures Exchange

The functioning of futures exchanges varies according to the local requirements, regulations, trade rules, etc. However, the basic functioning remains the same. Each futures exchange has its own clearing-house whose main function is managing the risk of exchange transactions and protecting the integrity of the marketplace. The clearing-house acts as a central counter party to all exchange trades — as the buyer to every seller and the seller to every buyer. The clearing-house becomes the "other party" for all futures trades between exchange members. This mechanism greatly simplifies futures trading. Considering the huge volume of individual transactions that are made, it would be virtually impossible to do business if the parties to each trade were obligated to settle directly with each other to complete their transactions.

The clearing-house is sufficiently well capitalized to cover any liability that arises. This minimizes the risk of counter party default. Clearing-houses are also typically responsible for administering the position monitoring and margining processes, regulating delivery of physical goods and reporting an exchange's trading data. When one establishes a position in a commodity future, either long or short, it is necessary to deposit with the broker a sufficient amount of money to protect the position and the broker against loss in the event the trade entered into is unprofitable.

This deposit is referred to as the margin. It should not be confused with the clearing-house margin required of an exchange member. The margin required of a customer by a broker is a different margin than that required of the broker by the clearing-house. Both margins serve the same purpose, they insure that obligations arising from commitments in commodity futures are fulfilled.

For example, if a member broker reports to the clearing-house at the end of the day total purchases of 150 units of November gold contract and total sales of 100 units of November gold contract (which may be for the broker, for customers, or both), then the broker would be net long 50 gold November contracts. Assuming that one contract is of 1 kg gold and margin requirement is 10% of the value, the broker will be long on 50 kg gold, this would mean that the broker would be required to have 10% of the value of 50 kg gold on that day as deposit with the clearing-house. Since all members are required to clear their trades through the clearing-house and must maintain sufficient funds with it to cover their debit balances, the clearing-house is placed in a position of being responsible to all members for the fulfilment of contracts.

How Commodities are Traded

As a trader, it is important for you to understand all the contract specifications, etc. of the exchange with which you are trading. This information is easily available with the broker or on the exchange website. Since each exchange has its own mechanism, and contract specifications keep on changing, it is advisable to check these on regular basis.

Types of Commodities

Traditionally, commodities have been classified in two broad ways — soft commodities and hard commodities.

Soft Commodities or "Softs"

Soft commodities are mostly agriculture commodities. Orange juice, corn, wheat, potato, lean hogs, coffee, turmeric, sugar and cocoa beans are all examples of soft commodities.

By their very nature, most soft commodities are subject to spoilage, which can create huge price volatility in the short term. The quality of soft commodities reduces as time passes. Weather plays a major role in the price volatility of soft commodity markets.

Hard Commodities

Hard commodities are those that are mined or derived from other natural resources, e.g. crude oil and metals. In many cases, initial products are refined into further commodities; crude oil is refined into gasoline or diesel.

Because hard commodities are an essential part of the industrial and manufacturing process and are easier to handle than softs, most investors focus on hard commodities, making their market very liquid. Most first-time traders also start with hard commodities — and rightly so. While, that is changing to an extent as former "softs" like corn and sugar are transformed into ethanol-based energy products, but, hard commodities still dominate the marketplace. For example, millions of dollars worth of oil and gold futures trade hands each day, which is far higher than the level of any soft commodity traded.

Some agricultural products such as cotton are also considered "hard" commodities because they do not get spoiled quickly and are raw industrial materials rather than foodstuffs.

Emerging Commodities

There are also "emerging commodities", like carbon credits, electricity, and ethanol, which are gaining more and more market share each day. Some other emerging commodities, like bandwidth and water are expected to develop into booming markets in the next 5 to 10 years. There are serious investors who believe that these function in a similar fashion to other commodities, and that they deserve a place in a commodities portfolio. For now, investors can only access these commodities by buying stock in companies that operate in these fields.

Commodity exchanges also trade different financial futures. Forex futures (only USD / INR, EUR / INR, GBP / INR and JPY / INR) can be traded on MCX. IMM, a division of the CME group, deals with the trading of currency and interest rate futures and options. It includes currencies such as the US dollar, the British pound, the Euro and the Canadian dollar. Along with currencies, the IMM trades futures of London Interbank Offer Rate, the 10-year Japanese bond and the US Consumer Price Index.

EUREX of Europe trades in derivatives of interest rate, equity, equity index, volatility index, exchange traded funds, credit, inflation, and carbon trading, sometimes referred to as emission trading.

Secondary Classification of Commodities

- Grains and Oilseeds — wheat, rice, barley, maize, canola, corn, oats, soybeans, soybean meal, soybean oil, flaxseed, RBD palmolin, castor (seed and oil), mustard (seed and oil), and groundnut oil, etc.
- Precious Metals — gold, silver, platinum, palladium.
- Base Metals — aluminium, copper, steel, lead, nickel, zink, tin.
- Livestock / Meat — pork bellies, feeder cattle, lean hogs, etc.
- Food — butter, cocoa, milk, sugar, dry whey, etc.
- Fibre — cotton, flaxseed, jute, etc.
- Energy — coal, crude oil, ethanol, gasoline, heating oil, natural gas, electricity, propane.
- Plantations — rubber, arecaunet, coffee, cashew, etc.
- Fertilizer — Diammonium Phosphate (DAP), urea, ammonium nitrate (UAN)
- Miscellaneous — wood (random length lumber), chemicals (benzene, mixed xylenes), weather, carbon credits, mentha (mint), gaur gum, etc.

Commodity Indices

Just like in the case of the stock market, commodities too have their indices. Two of the most common commodity indexes are the Goldman Sachs Commodities Index (GSCI) and the Dow Jones AIG Commodity Index (DJ-AIGCI).

The major distinction between the two indices is that the GSCI uses a strategy of overweighting the appropriate commodity sector (e.g., energy, metal or agriculture) based on economic demand. The DJ-AIGCI on the other hand, relies on both production and liquidity in determining weightings but has stricter guidelines on the maximum percentages allowed in one particular sector.

Major Commodity Exchanges of the World

CME Group, USA

CME Group is perhaps the largest and most diverse exchange in the world, handling over 1,000 trillion dollars worth of contracts a year. It was created on 12 July 2007 from the merger between the Chicago Mercantile Exchange (CME) and the Chicago Board of Trade (CBOT). On 22 August 2008, it formally acquired NYMEX Holdings Inc., parent company of the New York Mercantile Exchange. No wonder that today CME Group is the only exchange to offer access to all major asset classes from a single electronic trading platform. It has trading floors in Chicago and New York covering agricultural commodities, metals, foreign exchange, interest rates, equity indices, energy and alternative investment products such as weather and real estate.

London Metal Exchange (LME), London

The London Metal Exchange is the world's premier non-ferrous metals market, located in the heart of the city of London. It offers futures and options contracts for aluminium, copper, nickel, tin, zinc and lead plus two regional aluminium alloy contracts. In 2005, LME launched the world's first futures contracts for plastics, polypropylene and linear low-density polyethylene.

Intercontinental Exchange (ICE)

Intercontinental Exchange was established in May 2000. Since then, it has acquired International Petroleum Exchange (IPE), now known as ICE Futures Europe, New York Board of Trade (NYBOT), now known as ICE Futures U.S, Winnipeg Commodity Exchange, now known as ICE Futures Canada. ICE has also collaborated with the Chicago Climate Exchange (CCX) to host its electronic markets, and offers the leading

European emissions contract in its futures markets in conjunction with the European Climate Exchange (ECX). Its product line includes agriculture commodities, energy, foreign exchange and credit derivatives.

BM&FBovespa

BM&FBovespa Securities, Commodities and Futures Exchange was created in 2008 with the integration between the Brazilian Mercantile & Futures Exchange (BM&F) and the São Paulo Stock Exchange (Bovespa). Now it is one of the largest exchanges in terms of market value. Among its broad range of trading products, the exchange offers equities, financial assets, indices, interest rates, agricultural commodities, and foreign exchange futures and spot contracts.

Multi Commodity Exchange (MCX), India and National Commodity and Derivatives Exchange (NCDEX), India Established in 2003, MCX and NCDEX are among the fastest growing exchanges in the world. All trades are done electronically. Both these exchanges offers futures trading in a variety of commodities, such as agricultural, ferrous and non-ferrous metals, pulses, oils and oilseeds, bullion, energy, plantations, spices, etc.

Tokyo Commodity Exchange (TCI), Japan

Trades in precious metals, energy, rubber, etc. It is one of the most active exchanges in platinum contracts.

Dalian Commodity Exchange (DCE), China

Deals in agricultural commodities and Plastics.

Dubai Gold and Commodity Exchange (DGCX), Dubai

Deals in precious metals, energy, steel and currency. In 2007 the exchange launched the world's first Indian Rupee contract *versus* the US$.

Singapore Commodity Exchange (SICOM), Singapore

Deals in agricultural commodities and rubber.

How to Trade Commodities

The first thing to do is to find a reliable commodity broker and open an account. Do not start trading immediately but first learn the ropes of the market. Find out which commodities are traded and what the contract specifications are. Gain clear knowledge about the margins that are applicable and the investment you need to make. Once you decide to trade in a commodity of your choice, observe its trading pattern and understand what affects that commodity, and whether it is traded globally or locally.

Most important is to have a thorough understanding of technical analysis and all historical charts should be carefully studied.

Chapter 5

Foreign Exchange Market

THE FOREIGN EXCHANGE MARKET, also referred to as forex, FX or currency market, is the largest financial market in the world with a trading volume of over US$ 3 trillion a day. Even the combined volumes of the biggest stock exchanges and bond markets of the world look small when compared to the foreign exchange market. The forex market is global and trades 24 hours a day. It is open from Monday morning in New Zealand (when it is still Sunday night in the US) until Friday night in the US. No wonder it is the darling of traders and anyone who trades in the currency market even once, rarely leaves it.

For an Indian trader, there is a difference between domestic and global currency markets insofar as the legal aspect is considered. However, I have covered the currency market as a whole to give you complete knowledge about currency trading.

While you may come across many alternative avenues for trade currencies, before you actually start doing so, you must be clear on the legal aspects. Although Indians can now legally trade in currencies, they can only do so in rupee, and only on exchanges authorised by the RBI.

Not long ago, until the 1990's, the forex market was out of the individual trader's reach and was dominated by big players. You could only trade if you had millions of dollars. Then a series of events unfolded in the 1990's that made forex markets accessible to retail investors. One was deregulation of the brokerage system, which led many companies to form pools of liquidity where retail investors could take advantage of the huge speculative opportunity in forex. These intermediaries offered everything a retail trader could ask for — high leverage, low margins, and a new way to trade 24 hours a day. Speculators, big and small, make up more than 90% of the trades in the forex market making this market a sort of speculators' domain.

What is traded on the forex market? The answer is — money. The foreign exchange market is a place where currencies from different countries are valued and exchanged against one another. Since currencies have different values, there is a market in place to set those values. The forex market is the most active market among all financial markets as currencies of different countries are traded and transactions take place round the clock. Banks place deposits around the world, corporations hedge their exposure to currency risk in different countries, central banks change their monetary policy, big investment funds play the role of speculators, etc.

Just as you buy the shares of a company on the stock exchange if you believe their value will appreciate, in the forex market you similarly buy a currency whose value you believe is going to rise. In the stock market, you pay for the stock by money, but what happens when you are buying money itself? In that case, you sell another currency. The two currencies being traded are called a currency pair. Currency trading is done in pairs and involves simultaneously buying one currency and selling another. Therefore, if you intend to buy US dollar, you would need to decide against which other currency you would buy it. It could be the Japanese yen or the British pound, for example. That is why the quote is always in pairs, such as EUR / USD or USD / YEN where one currency of a pair is bought and the other sold. The first currency in the pair is known as the base currency and the second as the counter, or quote, currency.

When you buy a pair or go long on a pair, you are buying the base currency, and when you sell a pair or go short, you are selling the base currency. For example, when you buy the EUR / USD pair, you are buying euro and selling USD. And when you sell the EUR / USD pair, you are selling euro and buying USD. Other combinations of dozens of widely traded currency pairs are traded in the same way. So, remember, there is always a long (bought) and a short (sold) side to every currency trade, which means that you are speculating on one of the currencies rising in value in relation to the other. It may be a bit confusing for those of you who are new to forex trading, but things will get clear as you go through the rest of this chapter.

The word “market” usually invokes the idea of a central exchange, like the Bombay or London exchanges. This is not the case in the spot forex market. The forex market is unique in that unlike other financial markets, it is neither located physically at any one place, nor is it governed by a centralised exchange. The forex market is mostly an over-the-counter, or OTC market, where all trades are transacted directly between two traders — or a trader and a forex broker. This means that there could be several different exchange rates for the same currencies depending upon factors such as the location of the traders, and the brokers being used. However, this difference will be minor as any difference worth trading for is used by arbitrageurs. The market is run through a network of banks which also act as market makers by providing bid and ask prices. Trading of currencies between banks is known as the interbank market. Each of these banks trades with the other banks in the interbank market using dealing, or trading, desks. Each bank's dealing desk is in contact with the other banks' desks thus creating a virtual exchange floor. A number of transactions take place throughout the day which also helps in creating uniform pricing for interbank market participants. This is one major reason why volume data is not available for forex. It is also the reason why retail investors and small traders were left on the sidelines for long.

Forex derivatives, on the other hand, are traded on all major exchanges of the world and this constitutes the currency futures market. This means that they have centralized pricing and clearing, so the market price is the same regardless of the broker being used. Currency futures markets also trade globally throughout the day from Sunday night until Friday night in the US. The volume and liquidity in the currency futures market is negligible compared to the spot forex market.

The Indian Market

Globally, most retail currency trading is done in the spot forex market, but in India, there is no spot forex market and only derivative trading is allowed. This means that you can trade only in rupee futures and options on authorised exchanges through brokers. As an investor or a trader, this is a big advantage to you as the exchange ensures that all the contractual commitments are fulfilled.

At present, the following exchanges are allowed to carry on rupee trading:

1. National Stock Exchange (http://nseindia.com),
2. MCX Stock Exchange (http://www.mcx-sx.com),
3. United Stock Exchange (http://www.useindia.com).

The trading mechanism is the same as for stocks. To trade in the rupee, you would need to go to an authorised broker, open an account and trade. Some banks also provide a facility by which you can use your existing account to trade. Although it is your broker's responsibility to inform you about all the procedures and rules, etc., you too should be proactive in learning all that you can about forex trading.

Interbank Market

First, let us decipher the currency abbreviations. All currencies are assigned an International Standards Organization (ISO) code abbreviation. Forex currency symbols are always three letters, where the first two letters identify the name of the country and the third letter identifies the name of that country's currency. The most popular currencies along with their symbols are shown in Table 5.1 below:

Table 5.1

Popular currencies and their symbols*

Symbol	*Country*	*Currency*	*Nickname*
USD	United States	Dollar	Buck
EUR	Euro members	Euro	Euro
JPY	Japan	Yen	Yen
GBP	Great Britain	Pound	Cable
CHF	Switzerland	Franc	Swissy
CAD	Canada	Dollar	Loonie
AUD	Australia	Dollar	Aussie
NZD	New Zealand	Dollar	Kiwi

*The symbol for the Indian Rupee is INR.

In currency trading, these codes are often used to express which specific currencies make up a currency pair. For example, USD / INR refers to two currencies, the US dollar and the Indian rupee. The first currency, or the currency on the left side in the pair, is the base currency and the second, or the one on the right, is the quote or counter currency.

The quote currency is important because it is the currency in which the exchange rate is quoted. Therefore, in USD / INR, the US dollar is the base currency whereas in EUR / USD, the euro is the base currency. The base currency is the currency with the higher value at the start of the trading in a particular pair. It is important to know that the base currency is always equal to one monetary unit of exchange, in other words, how much one unit of base currency is equal to when converted into the counter currency. To illustrate: when the exchange rate between the US dollar and Indian rupee (USD / INR) is 45.25, it means that it costs 45.25 Indian rupees to purchase one US dollar. The same principle applies to the USD / CHF pair or any other currency pair. The Swiss franc is the quote currency in the USD / CHF pair. Therefore, when you say that the exchange rate between the US dollar and the Swiss franc is 1.2199, you are saying it costs 1.2199 CHF to purchase one USD.

An exchange rate is simply the ratio of one currency valued against another:

- When you buy, an exchange rate specifies how much you have to pay in the counter (quote) currency to obtain one unit of the base currency.
- When you sell, the exchange rate specifies how much you get in the counter (quote) currency when selling one unit of the base currency.

The following conventions are normally used to decide the base and counter currencies:

- EUR is always the base currency.
- GBP is always the base currency — except in case of the EUR / GBP pair.
- AUD, NZD are always the base currencies — except when paired with EUR and GBP.
- USD is always the base currency — except when paired with EUR, GBP, AUD and NZD.

The Indian rupee (INR) is traded against the US dollar (USD), the euro (EUR), the pound sterling (GBP) and the Japanese yen (JPY). Since the Indian rupee is lower in value than the dollar, the pound and the euro, the quotes are as follows:

1. Indian rupee and US dollar: USD / INR.
2. Indian rupee and euro: EUR / INR
3. Indian rupee and pound sterling: GBP / INR

However, the quoting of the Indian rupee against Japanese yen is an exception. Although the yen is lower in value, the quote is still JPY / INR. In this case, the quotation is for 100 yen. Therefore, when we talk of JPY / INR, it will be how many rupees you will get for 100 yen.

Major and Minor Currencies

Currently, there are seven currencies which are often viewed as major currencies. These currencies are the US dollar (USD), the euro (EUR), the British pound (GBP), the Swiss franc (CHF), the Japanese yen (JPY), the Australian dollar (AUD) and the Canadian dollar (CAD). Some people exclude the Canadian and Australian dollar from the list but they are also traded extensively.

Although the number of minor currencies fluctuates, some of the more frequently traded ones are the South African Rand (ZAR), the Singapore dollar (SGD), the New Zealand dollar (NZD), the Swedish kronor (SEK) and the Danish kroner (DKK). Generally, the minor currencies are less in demand in the spot and forward markets, have more volatility in value when compared to the major currencies, have an increased likelihood of artificial controls on their exchange rate, and tend to follow a major currency in value fluctuation.

The remaining currencies of the world are referred to as exotics. Most exotics are the currencies of countries that impose controls on currency conversion. The Chinese yuan is a highly restricted currency, which is not generally tradable. Earlier, the Indian rupee was also not traded due to restrictions, limited trading has now started in the Indian Rupee futures on the exchanges in which retail traders can participate.

Very few online foreign currency brokers offer trading in minor and exotic currencies.

Cross Currency

Almost 90% of trading in the foreign exchange market involves the US dollar. The dollar is either the base currency or the quote currency. A currency-cross is any currency pair in which the US dollar is neither the base nor the counter currency. For example, EUR / JPY, EUR / GBP, EUR / CAD, GBP / JPY and AUD / NZD are all considered currency crosses.

Quotes of Currency Values

Forex quotes are typically quoted to four decimal places, for example:

- EUR / USD = 1.2710
- USD / CHF = 1.2199
- GBP / USD = 1.4682

The exception to this rule, at least among the major currencies, is the Japanese yen (JPY). If the yen is being quoted, then the forex quotes are just to two decimal places, as in these examples:

- USD / JPY = 92.86
- EUR / JPY = 118.03

This is because the value of the Japanese yen is only about one hundredth of the value of one US dollar.

Indian rupee quotes are also to four decimal places. For example:

- USD / INR = 45.3650 (1 US dollar = 45.3650 Indian rupees,)
- EUR / INR = 64.6800 (1 euro = 64.6800 Indian rupee)
- GBP / INR = 73.8425 (1 pound sterling = 73.8425 Indian rupee)
- JPY / INR = 59.1000 (100 Japanese yen = 59.1000 Indian rupee)

Contract Size

As a forex trader, you are not buying and selling real money, but contracts (also referred to as lots); each transaction is of a standard unit size. Contract sizes may vary depending on the type of account you have. The three main contract sizes are as follows:

- Standard Contract Size: 100,000 in base currency.
- Mini Contract Size: 10,000 in base currency.
- Micro Contract Size: 1,000 in base currency.

You will choose a contract size to trade depending upon how much risk you can take or how well you understand the market. For a new trader, it is advisable that you trade in micro contracts first to understand the complete mechanism of the forex market.

In the Indian currency market, the contract size is referred to as unit of trading. The minimum you can trade in is one unit of the base currency. The value of one unit of the base currency is as follows:

- USD / INR: The base currency here is US dollar and one unit is equal to 1,000 US dollar. Therefore, if you buy one unit of USD / INR, you are buying 1,000 US dollars. If you wish to buy more, you can buy two, three or more units as per your investment capacity. Similarly, if you sell one unit, you are selling 1,000 US dollars.
- EUR / INR: The base currency here is EUR and one unit is equal to 1,000 euro. Therefore, if you buy one unit of EUR / INR, you are buying 1,000 euro.
- GBP / INR: The base currency here is GBP and one unit is equal to 1,000 GBP. Therefore, if you buy one unit of GBP / INR, you are buying 1,000 pounds.
- JPY / INR: The base currency here is JPY and one unit is equal to 100,000 yen. Therefore, if you buy one unit of JPY / INR, you are buying 100,000 yen.

PIP — Also Known as Tick or Point

A complete understanding of "pip" is very important for every forex trader. Pip is the smallest movement in the price of a currency and it is this movement that determines your profit or loss once you close your position. The smallest possible change in value can be a 1-unit change of last decimal place. For example, if EUR / USD is quoting at 1.2710, a smallest change that can happen is either 1.2709 if the value falls or 1.2711 if it rises. Therefore, when a last decimal value changes by one, it is the smallest value that a currency can change and is called a pip.

PIP Value

Pip value can be either fixed or variable depending on the currency pair. Whenever the US dollar is the quote currency, the pip value will always be $10 for a standard lot size of 100,000, $1 for mini-lots, and $0.10 for micro lots. So, if you are trading EUR / USD and the market moves in your favour by 5 pips, you will make a profit of $50 on a standard lot size. When the US dollar is not the quote currency, the pip value in USD terms will keep changing with the change in the exchange rate. You do not need to learn how to calculate pip value as this is readily available and will also be provided to you by your broker. What is important is that you should know what pip value is in order to keep a track of your open position.

If you trade one standard lot size and the market goes against you by 100 pips, you will lose 1,000 USD. If you trade one micro lot on the same day, you would only lose 10 USD.

In Indian currency trading, the minimum tick size is 0.0025 for all the pairs.

Bid / Ask Spread or Buy / Sell Spread

When we see a quote of EUR / USD as 1.2710, it means that the euro is the base currency and US dollar is the counter, or quote, currency and that 1 euro = 1.2710 USD. However, when it comes to currency trading, the market maker needs to add his profit when selling you a currency — or for buying currency from you. Therefore, the actual foreign currency exchange rate quotes are quoted at two somewhat different prices and would look like:

EUR / USD = 1.2710 / 1.2713 or EUR / USD = 1.2708 / 1.2712

This is commonly referred to as the bid / ask spread, or just the spread. On the left side is the bid price, and on the right side is the ask price. A market maker, who could be a broker or a bank, will bid to buy currency from you at the bid price. Therefore, when EUR / USD quote indicates 1.2710 / 1.2713, and you wish to sell one euro, you will get USD 1.2710. The currency's ask price is the price at which the market maker is willing to sell to you. So if you wish to buy, you will be quoted 1.2713. And just to remind you once again, it is the base currency which you would be buying or selling.

If you buy and sell at the same quote of 1.2710 / 1.2713, you are going to lose on the deal as you will buy at 1.2713 and sell at 1.2710. That means that you are going to lose the spread.

Taking an example of the Indian rupee, let's say USD / INR quote is 45.3650 / 45.3700. If you wish to sell one US dollar, you will get INR 45.3650, and if you wish to buy one US dollar, you will be quoted INR 45.3700.

If you buy and sell at the same quote of 45.3650 / 45.3700, you are going to lose on the deal as you will buy a dollar at INR 45.3700 and sell it at INR 45.3650. That means that you are going to lose to the extent of the spread.

Trading Example

Suppose you wish to buy US dollar against the Indian rupee — in other words, buy USD / INR pair, or go long on USD / INR — you will have to first decide how many units you want to buy. If you buy one unit at ₹ 45.3650, it means that you have bought 1,000 dollars for 45.3650 rupees. The total investment will be 1,000 × 45.3650 = ₹ 45,365. Suppose after some time, the price of USD / INR goes up to ₹ 45.3800. Your investment would then be worth 1,000 × 45.3800 = ₹ 45,380.

The total profit will be: ₹ 45,380 – ₹ 45,365 = ₹ 15

If you had bought 100 units, the profit will be ₹ 1,500 and so on.

Margin and Leverage

Margin and leverage are those essential concepts that every trader must completely understand, but in most cases, not much of a thought goes into these aspects. If you are a trader or about to start trading, remember that these two trading terms must be thoroughly incorporated into your trading plan. Margin and leverage are related terms in whichever market you are trading. However, they are not the same. Improper use of margin and leverage without understanding their repercussions is probably the most common reason for trading losses in the markets. Margin and leverage hold much more prominence in the forex market because unlike other markets, there is no governing mechanism in place to safeguard traders, leaving them on their own with huge risks.

Margin

When you take a position in the forex market with a lot size of your choice, you are not actually taking physical delivery of the currency and depositing it into your account. You have an arrangement with your broker that if you make a profit, the broker will pay you the amount of profit you made, and if you make a loss, you will pay the value of the loss to the broker.

Now since this is a business venture, the broker will ask for a margin from you. Margin is like a good faith deposit made by you to your broker against potential losses. It means that your broker will block some amount of money in your account per lot that you are trading. You cannot use that money for trading until you liquidate your open position. If you are in profit, good, but if you are in loss, then the broker will close your position once the loss goes above a certain percentage of your margin amount and leave you with whatever is left in the account.

This mechanism protects the broker who can be sure there is enough money available in your account to cover your losses. Your account may be so small that you may only buy one lot, or big enough to buy 100 lots.

Let us take an example, which is a real life trading experience of many traders:

Most brokers ask for a margin requirement of $1,000 for a standard lot of $100,000. Let's say that you have opened an account with one such broker with a balance of $5,000. When you take a position in one lot, $1,000 will be blocked from your account and will leave you with $4,000 available for other investments. The $1,000 of margin is not taken out of your account, but neither is it available for you to use until the position is cleared.

After taking a position, you start looking for some other trade because $4,000 is still available, and you believe that you have already covered for the open position. In the meantime, suppose the market starts going against you and you start making losses. Your broker will not automatically close your trade if your losses exceed $1,000. He will close your open position when your net balance (account deposits *minus* losses) is less than $1,000.

Therefore, if you leave a bad position open and losses accumulate to $4,001, the broker will close your position and you will be left with $999 on deposit.

Margin, therefore, is the minimum net amount you must have in your account to cover losses on your current positions. These types of trading accounts are also known as "margin accounts". If your account falls below the minimum margin account level, you will have your positions closed for you, whether you like it or not. That is the worst thing that can happen and a judicious trader never allows this to come about.

For Indian investors trading in INR, the margin is usually about 4% but this is subject to change. Your broker will inform you about the exact margin requirement when you are opening an account. Initially, it is better not to trade on minimum margin requirement. Trade in just one unit, with the maximum margin possible for you.

Leverage

Leverage is when you get more quantity than you pay for. Leverage lets you buy or sell a currency worth much more than what your investment is. The sum that you invest for getting leverage is called margin.

Therefore, if you have $1,000 and you buy currency worth $10,000 against it, it is a leveraged position and the $1,000 amount you have invested is the margin.

The leverage provided by brokers varies and can be in the ratio of 100:1, 50:1 or 10:1, etc. It can even go up to 400:1. This means that you require only 1 / 400 or 0.25% of the balance to open a position — plus, of course, the floating gains / losses. Most brokers offer 100:1, where every trader requires 1% of balance to open a position.

Let us take the example of a trader who wants to buy one lot in EUR / USD and he or she is using 100:1 leverage. Considering that the standard lot size in the forex market is 100,000 USD, to open such a position the trader requires 1% in balance, i.e. 1,000 USD. If the trader is using 200:1 leverage, the amount will be 500 USD and on a 50:1 leverage, the margin amount will be 2,000 USD.

Now, do not think that leverage is a big advantage. Brokers will want you to trade the highest leverage rates available because it increases the amount of lots you can, or will, trade. This is dangerous to you as a trader. The higher the leverage, the more likely you are to lose your entire investment if exchange rates go against your expectations. A leverage of 100:1 means that you will lose your margin when the currency loses or gains 1% of its value, and you will lose more than your security deposit if the currency loses or gains more than 1% of its value. If you want to keep the position open, you may have to deposit additional funds to maintain a 1% security deposit.

Let's say that you have a $10,000 account and you have entered with a position of 10 standard lots of USD / JPY. That means you would be using a $10,000 account to control $1,000,000 worth of currency or 100:1 leverage. Now what happens if the market moves 100 pips against you with 100:1 leverage? And what will the result be if you only used account leverage of 50:1 or 10:1? Table 5.2 shows the result.

Table 5.2

Leverage	*Lots*	*Margin*	*Loss*	*Exposure*
100:1	10	$1,000 / LOT	10,000	$1000,000
50:1	5	$2,000 / LOT	5,000	$1000,000
10:1	1	$10,000 / LOT	1,000	$1000,000

Therefore, the bottom line is that it does not matter what the maximum leverage that your broker is offering you. Your actual leverage will depend on many factors, primarily aimed at reducing your risk and using your balance in the best possible way at the same time. As you use more leverage, your account will become more volatile and the risk of losing your total amount increases.

Margin and leverage are under your control and your success will also depend on how you use them. It is better to keep your leverage at a maximum of 50:1, especially in the initial trading years.

How to Start Trading in the Forex Market

1. Check the law, rules and regulations of your country with respect to margin trading in forex.

2. Understand how the forex market operates.
3. Choose a broker. This is a very important step as a wrong choice of broker can be disastrous for your trading. There are many different options available to you. An Internet search will give you all the options. Make sure that the institution is a well-established, reputable one, preferably with ties to a bank or other financial institution. Presently some major banks have also started retail operations in the spot forex market.

   Another thing to look for in selecting a broker is which broker is providing the most comprehensive and wide range of research tools, such as real-time quotes, charts, and professionally written research reports. You should choose a brokerage house that makes available as much information as possible to its account holders.

   Choose a broker who offers lowest spread, as this difference in values represents the amount that the broker takes out of each trade; so the tighter the spread, the better it is for your trade outcome.

   Make sure that your broker offers all the major currency pairs and most of the minor currency pairs, even if you do not intend trading in those.

   Choose the broker that offers various leverage options like 100:1, 200:1, 50:1, etc. Leverage can make or break you. So more leverage choices means better trading opportunities according to prevailing market conditions.

   Instant execution of your trade is necessary while choosing a broker.

   Check which broker opens a trading account for a minimum amount. You should be able to open an account with $300 to $500.

   Check if the transaction costs and rollover charges are reasonable. Choose a broker that offers a demo trading account.
4. Once you have chosen a broker, do not jump into trading straight away. Open a demo account first before taking the plunge with real money. The demo account has a virtual balance that allows a new investor to get a general feel for currency trading, develop new skills and a trading strategy without the fear of losing money.
5. After you have practised with the demo account and are ready to invest real money, trade initially with a small amount. Small trades help

your account grow at the initial level. Also, do not use a lot of leverage in the first few months and stick to a leverage of 50:1 or less.

How Trading Works in the Spot Forex Market

Spot deal is a transaction at the current market rate with a settlement that takes place within two business days — except in a few cases such as the Canadian dollar, which settles the next day. This is normally known as T+2, i.e. today plus two working days. It means that delivery of what you buy or sell should be done within two working days and is referred to as the value date or delivery date. For example, a trade opened and closed on Monday has a value date of Wednesday. If, however, a position is opened on Monday and held overnight, the value date will then be Thursday.

A similar procedure applies to trades with a value date that coincides with a holiday. A trade executed on a Friday, when rolled over, would have a value date on Tuesday. Let us take the example of the EUR / USD pair quoting at 1.2710 in the spot forex market. Depending on your analysis, a position is opened by buying one currency and selling another at the same time on the lot size of your choice. Now you have an open position of a spot contract. If you close your position the same day, your account is debited, or credited, accordingly. However, what if you don't close your position and carry it overnight? In practice, nobody takes delivery of any currency in speculative forex trading; instead, one "rolls" one's positions forward on the delivery date. This facility is usually provided by the market-maker / broker and does not require retail traders to take any action. If the position is left open at the close of the business day, it will be automatically rolled over to the next transaction date to avoid delivery of the currency. The forex broker with whom the position is open will automatically keep on rolling over your spot contract for you indefinitely until it is closed.

Rollover / Overnight Interest / Cost of Carry

The spot forex market is dominated by the US dollar but a majority of spot forex is traded through London. Wherever the markets may be, most deals in forex are done as spot deals. A majority of the spot deals are due for settlement two business days later, referred to as the value date or delivery date. On that date, the counter parties theoretically take delivery of the currency they have traded.

In the spot forex market, the end of business day is 5 pm New York time. Any positions still open at this time on retail margin accounts are automatically rolled over to the next business day. This is necessary to avoid the actual delivery of the currency. As spot FX is predominantly speculative, traders never wish to actually take delivery of the currency. Nowadays, the brokers do this automatically unless you instruct that you actually want delivery of the currency as a routine procedure. Of course, most leveraged accounts are unable to actually deliver the currency, as there is no availability of respective currency funds to cover the transaction.

This procedure of rolling the currency pair over is known as tomorrow-next or tom next, which stands for tomorrow and the next day.

If you rollover your position, this exchange results in either interest being paid or earned by the trader. These charges are known as overnight interest or cost of carry. To simplify, if you bought a particular currency and that currency has a higher overnight interest rate, you will gain. If you sold the currency with a higher overnight interest rate, then you will lose the difference.

Let us take an example.

When you buy the EUR / USD pair, you are buying the Euro, and selling the US dollar to pay for it. If the Euro interest rate is 3.00%, and the US rate is 1.00%, you are buying the currency with the higher interest rate, and you will earn rollover, about 2.00% on an annual basis. If you sell the EUR / USD pair, you are selling the currency with higher interest rate, and you will pay rollover, about 2.00% on an annual basis, since you are paying the Euro interest rate and earning the US interest rate. You do not need to worry about this calculation as your broker will calculate all this and will charge / pay you.

Carry Trade

When the difference in interest rates is used as a trading tool to make money, it is called carry trade. It is a strategy in which an investor sells a particular currency with a low interest rate and uses the funds to purchase a different currency yielding a relatively higher interest rate. By applying this strategy, a trader is able to capture the difference between the interest rates. However, the uncertainty of exchange rates is a big risk in a carry trade as these transactions are generally done with a lot of leverage. Therefore, even a small movement in exchange rates can result in huge losses. Yen carry trades have traditionally been by far the biggest with estimates of several hundred billion dollars of positions. However, USD carry trade became prominent in 2009.

Why Trade Forex

1. 24-Hour Market

The forex market is open 24 hours a day. There is no waiting for the opening bell as the forex market never sleeps. This is positive for those who want to trade on a part-time basis because you can choose your trading time. As far as professional traders are concerned, this factor is a blessing as they have complete control over their open trade, unlike other markets, where the time from the closing of the market on one day to its opening the next day is long and uncertain.

In India, the futures forex market is only open during day time, 9 a.m. to 5 p.m., from Monday to Friday.

2. No One can Manipulate the Market

The foreign exchange market is so huge and has so many participants that no single entity — not even a central bank — can control the market price for an extended period.

3. High Liquidity

Because of its enormous size, the forex market is extremely liquid. Liquidity is a big advantage to any investor as it provides the freedom to enter or exit the market at any time. Under normal market conditions, you can trade any amount instantaneously with just the click of a mouse. You will never be stuck with your trade and can close it the moment you want to. Your limit orders and stop loss orders are always executed at the price at which you have set them.

4. No Commissions

Would it not be great if after taking the position, you need not pay any brokerage, clearing or exchange fees? The forex market offers all these advantages. So does that mean that you are getting a free service? No, the brokers are compensated for their services through the bid-ask spread.

5. High Leverage

In forex trading, a small margin deposit can control a much larger contract value. 100:1 leverage enables you to buy or sell $100,000 worth of currencies with a mere $1,000 margin deposit. That means you get to earn all of the profits on a $100,000 position while only risking a small amount of your own money.

Of course, the opposite reality is equally true. You get to bear all of the losses on a $100,000 position too. So be cautious about the leverage you are using, as it is a double-edged sword.

Factors Affecting the Forex Market

Currency prices usually fluctuate about 100 pips on a normal trading day. The forex market is most active during the period from Europe market open until US market close.

Currency prices are affected by a variety of economic and political conditions, the most important being interest rates. Other factors, like GDP, unemployment rate, inflation, political stability, etc. also affect the currency markets. Whenever the actual major economic data figures are significantly different from the forecast ones, the forex market will become volatile in reaction to the released data.

Governments, too, participate in the forex market — although rarely — to influence the value of their currencies, either by selling their domestic currency in an attempt to lower its value or, conversely, buying it in order to raise its value. This is known as central bank intervention.

However, even the central bank's intervention is not able to sustain prices for long if the levels are not justified. This shows the sheer enormity of the forex market where even central banks may fail to control prices.

Glossary

Appreciation: Describes a currency strengthening in response to market demand rather than by the central bank's action.

Ask: The price that a trader gets when he buys, or goes long, on a currency pair.

At or Better: An order to deal at a specific, or better, rate.

Authorized Broker: A financial institution or bank authorized to deal in foreign exchange.

Bank Rate: The rate at which a central bank is prepared to lend money to its domestic banking system.

Base currency: The currency that other currencies are quoted against, the first mentioned currency in a pair.

Bear market: A prolonged period of generally falling prices.

Bear: An investor who believes that prices are going to fall.

Bid: The price that a trader gets when he sells, or goes short, on a currency pair.

Big Figure: A phrase referring to the first few digits of an exchange rate. Since these digits rarely change in normal market conditions, they are omitted in broker quotes. For example, when USD / YEN rate is 95.30 / 95.35, it will be quoted verbally without the first two digits. Therefore, when you ask for a quote, you will be given "30 / 35". In case of EUR / USD, the rate may be 1.2710 / 1.2714 but you will be quoted "10 / 14".

Broker: An individual, or firm, which acts as an intermediary, bringing together buyers and sellers. Brokers do not take market positions.

Bull market: A prolonged period of generally rising prices.

Bull: An investor who believes that prices are going to rise.

Buying Rate: Rate at which a market maker is willing to buy the currency. Also called bid rate.

Cable: A term used in the foreign exchange market for the GBP / USD rate.

Cash Delivery: Same day settlement.

Central Bank: A government organisation of a country, responsible for development and implementation of monetary policy and printing the nation's currency. The Indian central bank is Reserve Bank of India and that of US is Federal Reserve.

Closed Position: A transaction which leaves the trader with a zero net commitment to the market.

Commission: The fee that a broker may charge clients for dealing on their behalf.

Convertible currency: A currency that can be freely exchanged for another currency without special authorization from the central bank.

Cost of Carry: The cost associated with borrowing money in order to maintain a position. It is based on the interest rate differential, which determines the forward price.

Cross rates: Rates between two currencies, neither of which is the US Dollar.

Currency: A country's unit of exchange issued by their government or central bank whose value is the basis for trade.

Day trader: Speculators who close trading positions in the same day.

Delivery date: The date of maturity of the contract when the exchange of the currencies takes place. This date is more commonly known as the value date in the FX or money markets.

Depreciation: A fall in the value of a currency due to market forces rather than due to central bank action.

Desk: Term referring to a group dealing with a specific currency or currencies.

Devaluation: Deliberate downward adjustment of a currency by the central bank against its fixed parities or bands, normally by formal announcement.

Economic Indicator: A statistic that indicates current economic growth rates and trends such as CPI and employment.

ECU: European currency unit.

EFT: Electronic fund transfer.

Euro: The currency of the European Monetary Union (EMU), which replaced the european currency unit (ECU).

Exchange Control: Rules used to preserve or protect the value of a country's currency.

Exchange rate risk: The risk of incurring losses resulting from an adverse change in exchange rates.

Exotic: A less broadly traded currency.

Fed Fund Rate: The interest rate on Fed funds. This is a closely watched short-term interest rate as it signals the Fed's view as to the state of the money supply.

Federal Reserve (Fed): The central bank of the United States.

Fixed Exchange Rate: Official rate set by monetary authorities. Often, the fixed exchange rate permits fluctuation within a band.

Flat (or Square): To be neither long nor short is the same as to be flat or square. One would have a flat book if one has no positions or if all the positions cancel each other out.

Flexible Exchange Rate: Exchange rates with a fixed parity against one or more currencies with frequent revaluations. A form of managed float.

Floating Exchange Rate: An exchange rate where the value is determined by market forces. Even floating currencies are subject to intervention by the monetary authorities. When such activity is frequent, the float is known as a dirty float.

FOMC: Federal Open Market Committee, the committee that sets the monetary policy of the US.

Foreign Exchange: The purchase or sale of a currency against the sale or purchase of another.

Forex or FX: Term commonly used when referring to the foreign exchange market.

G7: The seven leading industrial countries, namely US, Germany, Japan, France, UK, Canada, Italy.

G10: G7 plus Belgium, Netherlands and Sweden, a group associated with IMF discussions. Switzerland is sometimes peripherally involved.

Going Long: The purchase of a currency for investment or speculation.

Going Short: The selling of a currency or instrument not owned by the seller.

Good Until Cancelled: An instruction to a broker that unlike normal practice, the order does not expire at the end of the trading day, although it normally terminates at the end of the trading month.

Hard Currency: Any one of the major world currencies that is well traded and easily converted into other currencies.

IMF: International Monetary Fund, established in 1946 to provide international liquidity on a short and medium term, and encourage liberalization of exchange rates. The IMF supports countries with balance of payments problems with the provision of loans.

IMM: International Monetary Market, part of the Chicago Mercantile Exchange that lists a number of currency and financial futures.

Indicative Quote: A market-maker's price that is not firm.

Initial Margin: The margin required by a foreign exchange firm to initiate the buying or selling of a determined amount of currency.

Interbank rates: The foreign exchange rates at which large international banks quote other banks, which is the basis of the interbank market.

Intervention: Action by a central bank to affect the value of its currency by entering the market. Concerted intervention refers to action by a number of central banks to control exchange rates.

Kiwi: Slang for the New Zealand dollar.

LIBOR: Stands for London Interbank Offer Rate. It is the interest rate at which large international banks will lend to one another.

Limit Order: A request to deal as a buyer or seller for a foreign currency transaction at a specified price, or at a better price, if obtainable.

Liquidation: Any transaction that offsets or closes out a previously established position.

Liquidity: The ability of a market to accept large orders.

Maintenance Margin: The minimum margin that an investor must keep on deposit in a margin account at all times in respect of each open contract.

Make a Market: A broker is said to make a market when he or she quotes bid and offer prices at which he or she stands ready to buy and sell.

Managed Float: When the monetary authorities intervene regularly in the market to stabilize the rates or to aim the exchange rate in a required direction.

Margin: The amount of money that must be available in the account to ensure cover against losses on open positions. Initial margin is required on opening an account. Maintenance or variation margin must be added to the initial margin to maintain against losses on open positions.

Margin Call: A requirement from a broker for additional funds to bring the margin up to a required level to guarantee continuation of a position that has moved against the customer. Issued when an investor's account suffers adverse price movements.

Mark-to-Market or (End of day): Accounting for market positions is done in two ways — accrual or mark-to-market. An accrual system accounts only for cash flows when they occur, hence, it only shows a profit or loss when realized. The mark-to-market method values the trader`s book at the end of each working day using the closing market rates or revaluation rates. Any profit or loss is adjusted and the trader will start the next day with a net position.

Market Maker: A person or firm authorized to create and maintain a market in an instrument. A market maker provides the bid and ask prices.

Market order: An order to buy or sell a financial instrument at the present price.

Offer: The price at which a seller is willing to sell. The best offer is the lowest such price available.

Offset: The closing out, or liquidation, of a trading position.

Open Position / Net Position: A deal not yet reversed or settled and wherein the investor is subject to exchange rate movements.

Overnight: A trade that remains open until the next business day.

Overnight Limit: Net long or short position in one or more currencies that a broker can carry over into the next dealing day. Passing the trade to other bank dealing rooms in the next trading time zone reduces the need for brokers to maintain these unmonitored exposures.

Over the Counter (OTC): Used to describe any transaction that is not conducted over an exchange.

Pegging: A form of price stabilization; typically used to stabilize a country's currency by making it fixed *vis-a-vis* the exchange rate of another currency.

Pip (or Points): The term used in the currency market to represent the smallest incremental move an exchange rate can make. Depending on the context, pip is normally one basis point (0.0001) in the case of EUR / USD, GBP / USD, USD / CHF and .01 in the case of USD / JPY.

Profit Taking: The unwinding of a position to realize profits.

Quote: An indicative market price; shows the highest bid and lowest ask price available on a currency at any given time.

Rate: The price of one currency in terms of another.

Revaluation: Increase in the exchange rate of a currency because of official action.

Rollover: The settlement of a deal is rolled forward to another value date with the cost of this process based on the interest rate differential of the two currencies.

Same Day Transaction: A transaction that matures on the day the transaction takes place.

Scalping: A trading strategy that attempts to make multiple profits on small price changes resulting in a number of trades in a single session. Scalpers enter and exit the market quickly and frequently and are only interested in a number of small profits rather than waiting for a few big ones.

Selling Rate: Rate at which a bank is willing to sell foreign currency.

Settlement Date: The date upon which foreign exchange contracts are settled.

Short: To sell an instrument without actually owning it, and to hold a short position with expectations that the price will decline so it can be bought back in the future at a profit.

Short-term Interest Rates: Normally, the 90-day rate.

Spot: The most common foreign exchange transaction. A transaction that occurs immediately, but the funds will usually change hands within two days after the deal is struck.

Spot Price / Rate: The price at which the currency is currently trading in the spot market.

Spread: The difference between the bid and ask price of a currency. Narrower spreads usually signify high liquidity.

Square: Purchase and sales are in balance and thus the broker has no open position.

Squeeze: Action by a central bank to reduce supply in order to increase the value of money.

Stable Market: An active market, which can absorb large sales or purchases of currency without major moves.

Sterling: British pound, otherwise known as cable.

Swissy: Market slang for Swiss Franc.

Thin Market: A market in which the trading volume is low, and consequently bid and ask quotes are wide, and the liquidity of the instrument traded is low.

Tick: A minimum change in price, up or down.

Tomorrow Next (Tom next): A strategy used by traders to avoid actual delivery of a currency by closing positions at the daily close rate and opening a new position the following trading session.

Trade Date: The date on which a trade occurs.

Tradable Amount: Smallest transaction size acceptable.

Transaction Date: The date on which a trade occurs.

Transaction: The buying or selling of currencies resulting from the execution of an order.

Two-Way Quotation: When a broker quotes both buying and selling rates for foreign exchange transactions.

Uncovered: Another term for an open position.

US Prime Rate: The interest rate at which US banks will lend to their prime corporate customers.

Value Date: The date that both parties of a transaction agree to exchange payments on.

Whipsaw: A term used to describe a condition in a highly volatile market where a sharp price movement is quickly followed by a sharp reversal.

Chapter 6

The Money Market

THE MONEY MARKET PROVIDES SHORT TERM LIQUIDITY FUNDING for the financial system where governments, banks, corporations and securities dealers borrow and lend money for short periods. This contrasts with the capital market for longer term funding, which is supplied by bonds. Money market loans may be due in a few days, a few weeks or a few months, but never more than a year. The short term financial instruments traded in money markets are commonly called "paper". Money market instruments are usually issued at a discount to the par value and are redeemed at par to the holder at maturity.

The money market is a part of the fixed income market which includes bonds. However, unlike bonds that are longer-term fixed income securities, the money market specializes in very short-term debt securities. Banks are the most active players in the money market. They need to borrow and lend money on a regular basis depending on their cash situation. Banks need to take loan or borrow money when they fall short of cash due to increased withdrawals by customers or when they fall short of statutory reserve requirements due to some reasons or maybe when they can lend the money at better rates. On the other hand, when the banks have surplus funds, they prefer to lend them rather than keeping them idle.

Money markets are not like the stock, commodity or forex markets where an individual investor can trade directly. The reason is that most money market securities (except T-bills) trade in very high denominations and so individual investors have limited access to them. The money market is primarily a place for large institutions and government to manage their short term cash needs. However, for the benefit of individual investors, money market instruments are repackaged into money market funds. A money market fund is an investment fund that invests in money market instruments. It is like a mutual fund, except that mutual funds cater to capital market while money market funds cater to the money market. Investors who have excess cash but are not able to find good stocks can use money markets to temporarily park some cash until good opportunities are found. These markets can also be used when the stock market seems overbought and indicating a fall. At such times, money can be withdrawn from stocks and placed in money market funds.

Types of Money Market Instruments

Treasury Bills (T-Bills)

These are the safest and most traded money market security. They are short term borrowing instruments of a country's government and are issued through the country's central bank, like the Fed in USA or RBI in India. The returns are not attractive as they are zero risk instruments. T-bills are available both in the primary market as well as the secondary market. T-bills are popular because they are one of the few money market instruments that are affordable for the individual investors. T-bills are usually issued in denominations of as low as $1,000 in US or ₹ 25,000 — (and in its multiples) — in India. T-bills (and all Treasuries) are supposed to be the safest, risk free investments in the world because of the backing of central governments. The Government of India issues three types of treasury bills through auctions, namely, 91-day, 182-day and 364-day.

Repos

Repo is the short form used for repurchase agreement. These are short-term loans in which two parties who deal in government securities agree to sell and repurchase a money market security (usually T-bills) at an agreed future date and price. Repos are very short-term transactions, from overnight to 30-days. In repurchase agreement, the seller sells specified securities with an agreement to repurchase the same at a mutually decided future date and price. Similarly, the buyer purchases the securities with an agreement to resell the same to the seller at a mutually decided future date and price. Although this is just one transaction but it is usually described by two terms, repo and reverse repo. When viewed from the seller's perspective, it is called repo and when viewed from buyer's perspective, it is known as reverse repo. Repos are popular and have great importance as they help in eliminating immediate credit problems faced by institutions.

Certificate of Deposit or CD

CD is a promissory note generally issued by a commercial bank in a form of a certificate. CDs have specific maturity, a specified interest rate, and, like bonds, they can be issued in any denomination. CDs usually offer higher yield or returns than T-bills as they carry a slight default risk from a bank in case the bank fails. The important thing to watch out for while buying a CD is the method of return, which can be based on annual percentage yield (APY) and annual percentage rate (APR). APY is the total amount of interest you earn in one year, considering compound interest. APR is simply the stated interest you earn in one year, without taking compounding into account. If the interest is paid annually, equal return is generated by both APY and APR methods. However, if interest is paid more than once in a year, it is better to go for APY over APR.

Commercial Paper (CP's)

Commercial papers are unsecured short-term debt securities issued by big corporates for financing their accounts receivables, inventories and meeting short-term liabilities. They are issued at a discount in the form of promissory notes, redeemable at par to the holder at maturity. It helps corporates raise short term finance whenever required without going to the bank for short-term loan that sometimes becomes difficult. Since commercial paper is not backed by any collateral, only firms with high credit ratings are able to sell CP's without offering any substantial discounts. In India, as per RBI rules only corporate with investment grade rating can issue CP's.

Bankers Acceptance (BA)

A banker's acceptance is a short-term discount instrument created by a non-financial firm, that usually arises in the course of international trade and are guaranteed by a bank. For example, an importer plans to purchase some goods from an exporter but does not have enough credit. Since the exporter will not grant credit, the importer turns to its bank. They execute an acceptance agreement, under which the bank will accept drafts from the importer. A draft is a legally binding order by one party, the drawer (in this case the importer) to a second party, the drawee (in this case the bank) to make payment to a third party, the payee, (in this case the exporter). A simple example of a draft is a bank cheque, which is a signed draft. Usually in international trade, time drafts are used, known as bills of exchange. In this way, the bank extends credit to the importer who agrees to pay the bank the face value of all drafts prior to their maturity. The importer draws a time draft, listing itself as the payee. The bank accepts the draft and discounts it — paying the importer the discounted value of the draft. The importer uses the proceeds to pay the exporter. The bank can then either hold the banker's acceptance in its own portfolio or it can sell it at discounted value in the money market. For business firms, a BA is especially useful when the creditworthiness of a foreign trade partner is not known.

Eurodollars

Eurodollars are US dollar that have been deposited in banks outside the United States. Eurodollars are named so because this practice started from Europe. The dollar deposits could be in Dubai or Singapore but will still be called Eurodollars as long as they are outside the US. Eurodollar deposits usually mature in six months and the market is only for the biggest institutions as the average Eurodollar deposit runs into millions. Eurocurrency is the general term for any currency deposited in bank branches outside countries where it is the national currency. So, now, there are Euroyen, Eurosterling and Euroeuro.

Conclusion

- Only debt securities that mature in less than one year are traded in the money market.
- Money market securities offer a lower return than other market securities as they are among the safest and most liquid securities.
- Individuals can access the money market through a money market mutual fund.

Chapter 7

Derivatives

NEW IDEAS ARE CONSTANTLY TRIED AND TESTED IN ALL AREAS of human activity. Financial markets, too, have their share of new ideas and innovative products, and a derivative is one such invention in the financial world that has thrown up immense trading opportunities. However, even most seasoned investors find it difficult to fully understand derivatives. The reason is not so much that the derivative is some very complex concept, but rather that far too much of analytical explanation is used while describing derivatives. Here, I have explained derivatives from the point of view of a trader and investor in a simple language. Once you are finished with this chapter, you would be able to use derivatives with ease while trading. You can later venture into further study of derivatives if you wish, but my personal view is that derivatives are best used with simple strategies. Complex derivative strategies are time consuming to learn and use, and do not offer much to a trader.

Short Selling

Before venturing into derivatives, let me explain the concept of short selling for those of you who are not familiar with it. This is because it is essential for you to be clear on what short selling is in order to utilise the full potential of derivatives.

The markets move up and they move down. Many people think that the only way to make profit is to buy stocks, wait for the prices to go up, and then sell them. However, one can also make profit when the prices are falling and the markets are crashing. Once you have analysed the market, you may buy a stock if your analysis says that the stock will rise or you may sell a stock in your portfolio which, according to you, may fall. However, what if you have no stock holdings but would still want to profit from the anticipated fall in stock prices? You can do this by short selling. Short selling is the selling of a stock that the seller does not own. Later, once the prices have dropped, the seller buys an equal amount of stock and clears the trade. Short sales are of two types, covered and naked. Covered short sales are those in which the seller borrows the stocks and arranges for the delivery of shares he has sold. Naked short sales are those in which the seller does not borrow and does not intend to give delivery of shares he has sold.

Gold is a commodity traded by investors throughout the world. In India, too, almost every household has invested in gold in some form or the other. Suppose there is a marriage in your family after three months and you want to gift a gold bar. You have three months to buy the gold bar. The present price of gold is say, $800 an ounce. You prefer to buy gold immediately as you feel that it is better to buy it now rather than wait for some more time. You go to a shop, buy the gold bar, pay the money and come back home with the gold bar. What you have done is made a cash transaction and taken ownership of the gold bar by paying the equivalent amount in cash. Now you have the possession of a gold bar and you are its owner. To you, it may just be a simple transaction but it is important to understand here that by buying gold you have also become a factor in fixing the price of gold at $800. The amount may be small but you have played your part in fixing the gold price by increasing the demand. If more buyers enter the scene, the price will keep on rising; if more sellers come in, then the price will keep on falling. This is the cash market price, decided by the numbers of actual buyers and sellers in the market across the world and every trade is executed only on the prevailing cash market price.

Now let us come to a situation where you do not want to block your funds right now. At the same time, you don't want to take risk of paying higher prices after three months. You also want to make sure that you will have the gold bar at the time of marriage. So, what do you do? You go to the shop from where you intend buying the gold bar and tell the owner that you will buy a gold bar from him after three months. The owner agrees. You have committed to take delivery and the owner has committed to give delivery after three months. However, what about the price? The owner says that the present price is $800, but he will charge the extra $5 and the delivery will be made at $805. You agree to the price since now you are sure that you will have a gold bar costing a fixed amount. You and the owner are now in a contract (whether verbal or written) for delivery of a gold bar of mutually decided price, weight and purity at a future date. This is the simplest form of derivative contract called a forward that is explained in detail later. Just keep in mind two points. First, that the price that you arrived was based on the cash price of gold and, second that this contract does not constitute ownership; it only promises to transfer ownership at a future date.

It is clear that trust is very important in a forward contract. Let us see what may happen after three months when the date of delivery arrives. The gold price may be around the same levels. You pay the money and take the delivery of gold bar. However, what if gold prices have moved drastically to either $600 or $1,000? If the gold price is $600 then you will be in a big loss because you have committed to pay $805. However, if the gold price is $1,000- then the shop owner will be in a big loss because he has committed to give you the gold bar at $805. If you are in a loss, you may break the contract by refusing to complete the deal and if the shop owner is in a loss then he may break the contract by refusing to give delivery. This is the biggest disadvantage of a forward contract as there is always a chance of one party defaulting and there may not be any relief for the aggrieved side due to the basic nature of the contract.

If the forward contract is so doubtful then you may not like this concept at all. However, your basic need remains the same. You do not want to block the funds early but still want surety of delivery after three months and avoid the risk of higher prices. Is there a way out? Yes, the way out is a futures contract. Futures are the second type of a derivative, which is just like a forward contract but made on an exchange. You can go to a commodity exchange and enter into a futures contract. A futures exchange is like an intermediary, which guarantees that all the contracts are honoured and there is no default. Thousands of buyers and sellers come to an exchange and enter into futures contracts. In a forward contract, two parties are involved making it possible to enter into a negotiated contract but on an exchange there are huge numbers of people wanting to enter into a contract, so the contracts are standardised. Forward contracts are custom-tailored according to the needs of the two parties and are over-the-counter agreements, whereas futures are standardized contracts that are traded on the exchanges, and between parties who most of the time, never even know or meet each other. The terms of the contract, such as the exact quantity, quality, and place of delivery can be negotiated in a forward contract but in a futures contract the terms are fixed by the exchange. Therefore, in a forward contract, you can decide on time, purity of gold, the weight of gold bar, the place of delivery, etc. but if you go to an exchange, you will have fixed parameters to choose from. However, there are two points to keep note of; the first is that the price of a futures contract was based on the cash price of gold and the second that this contract does not constitute ownership; it only promises to transfer ownership at a future date.

In both the above situations of forward and futures, your basic demands were fulfilled. Your funds were not blocked immediately, you had the surety of getting gold in three months time and the prices were fixed based on gold's present price, which took away the risk of you paying a higher price if the gold prices increased in three months.

However, there is a downside to all this. What if the gold price fell after three months? Naturally, you would not like to pay $805 for gold that now costs $600. Since you are bound by the contract, you will have to take the delivery at higher price. You may not like to enter into such a contract where you must pay higher price of gold even while the market price is much lower. However, your basic need remains the same. You do not want to block the funds early but still want surety of delivery after three months and avoid the risk of higher prices. Is there a way out? Yes, the way out is an option contract.

Welcome to the third and the most interesting type of derivatives, namely options. Like futures, option contracts are mostly exchange-traded making them secure and with no chance of default. Of course, there is much more to options and this example is just a concept at a very basic level. Detailed explanation of options is given in Chapter 10.

The example of considering you as a buyer of gold bar was to introduce the concept of derivatives. Now we are ready to understand derivatives in detail, starting with the commonly used definition of a derivative:

> "Derivative is a financial contract that has its price derived from the price of an underlying cash product."
>
> OR

"A derivative is a financial instrument that derives its value from some other asset."

These definitions make two things clear:

1. By themselves derivatives have no value.
2. They derive their value from some other asset, known as the underlying. This underlying asset could be a stock, a commodity, a bond, a currency, or an intangible asset like a stock index.

In our example, the underlying asset was gold and the forward, futures and option all derived their value from the cash price of gold.

The various types of derivatives are:

1. Forwards;
2. Futures;
3. Options;
4. Swaps.

Chapter 8

Forwards

A FORWARD CONTRACT IS THE SIMPLEST FORM of a derivative. A forward is contract between two parties to enter into a trade where one person agrees to buy and the other person agrees to sell a certain quantity of a financial instrument or commodity at a pre-determined price — but for delivery at an agreed future date. Forward is an over the counter, or OTC derivative, and is not traded on an exchange.

A forward contract has four major variables:

1. **The Underlying Asset.** The underlying asset could be a commodity, like gold, wheat, rice, crude oil, etc. or a financial instrument, like a stock, bond, etc.
2. **Quantity of Underlying Asset.** This is the quantity of underlying asset for which the contract has been made and which is agreed to be delivered at the time of delivery.
3. **Delivery Price.** This is the price at which the delivery is to be made at an agreed future date and is also known as forward price, which is decided at the time of contract based on spot or cash rates of the underlying asset. Factors such as the time value of money, short term supply and demand, market expectations of future spot prices and cash-and-carry arbitrage are considered while finalising the delivery price.
4. **Settlement Date.** Date when the underlying asset will be delivered and the payment made for the same.

All the above variables are negotiable and are finalised according to the need of the trade.

Chapter 9

Futures

FUTURES ORIGINATED FROM FORWARDS and so the basic concept is same. Futures trade on a variety of underlying commodities and financial instruments and represent agreements to buy or sell some underlying asset in the future for a specified price. Like forwards, futures eliminate the need to immediately pay for, take delivery of, or hold the underlying asset for small initial cash payment.

However, forward contracts have many disadvantages and futures are designed to reduce the risks of forward agreements and make them more secure. Futures are traded on an exchange and the terms of futures contracts are standardised. Anybody wanting to enter into a futures contract has to accept the terms for such contracts specified by the exchange concerned. Due to such standardisation, futures are very liquid. The standardisation specifies the following:

- **The Underlying Asset or Instrument:** This may be anything from a broad range of individual stocks, commodities, indices, foreign exchange, bond and money market instruments, etc.
- **Quantity of Asset:** The quantity of the underlying is specified; e.g. one contract of a stock futures may consist of 500 shares, or one contract of crude oil may be of 100 barrels depending on the exchange and contract specifications.
- **The Quality of Underlying Asset:** The quality is specified and is particularly applicable in the case of commodity futures. For example, gold futures may specify gold with 99.9% purity or wheat futures may specify the 1% limit for foreign matter, 2% limit of broken grain, 10% moisture content, etc.
- **The Delivery Month:** This is the month in which the contract expires and the seller must make delivery and the buyer must accept, and pay for,

the underlying asset. The date is decided by individual exchanges and vary considerably so one must check with the broker or the exchange concerned. The delivery months may be consecutive months or with a gap. Usually trading in the immediate month is the most active and liquidity goes down if one decides to trade on far-dated delivery months.

- **Type of Settlement:** Settlement can be either cash settlement or physical settlement. Some underlyings, such as indices, are always cash settled.
- **Location of Delivery:** Exchanges decide beforehand about the location where the delivery will be made.
- **The Quote Currency:** It is usually the national currency of the country in which the exchange is present.

Apart from these, many other minor aspects such as the range of price fluctuation, tick value, margins for individual contracts, etc., are also specified.

The following are some more distinctions between forwards and futures:

1. Forwards are directly traded over the counter between the buyer and the seller. Futures contracts, on the other hand, are traded on organized exchanges.
2. Forward contracts are usually meant for delivery. For parties entering into a forward contract, it's a business decision. On the other hand, futures contracts are not used for actual delivery of an asset and are cash settled in most cases. In fact, only about 3 % of futures contracts are finally settled by delivery; the rest are all cash settled.
3. Forward contracts are settled at the expiration of the contract. Futures are marked to market. This means that the daily changes in the price of the futures contracts are settled daily until the contract expires.
4. Forwards have inherent credit risk. Since either party of a forward contract can default on their respective obligation of delivery and payment, forwards are riskier than futures. With futures, there is no credit risk as the contracts are guaranteed by the exchange and backed by the clearing-house.

Futures Trading Mechanism

Futures trading is no different from cash trading. The point to remember is that in the cash market, you can trade in even a single share but in futures you have to trade in a standard contract that may have 100, 500 or any other number of shares, depending on a particular underlying or exchange. This increases the profitability but has equal associated risk. So you have to first look at the futures contract and judge whether you can afford to trade in that particular contract or not. An advantage of futures trading over cash market trading is that you can keep the position for the duration of the futures contract by just paying the margin whereas you have to block the whole amount if you take delivery of a stock.

Once you decide to trade in futures, you will need a broker who is member of the exchange concerned. Before you can trade a futures contract, the broker collects a deposit from you which is called the initial margin. This is mostly in the form of cash but in some cases acceptable securities are also used as margins. The amount of initial margin is determined according to the norms of the exchange. For a single futures contract, it will be a small fraction of the market value of the underlying. Usually, initial margin represents the maximum one-day net loss you may incur on an open position. You should ask the broker about all the exchange specification and also get the list of months for which the futures are available. As futures contracts are traded in lots, so you cannot go and buy futures of a single share or one ounce of gold. Each futures contract has a standard size that is set by the futures exchange it trades on. For example, if the contract size for gold futures is 100 ounces, it implies that when you are buying one contract of gold, you are actually trading in 100 ounces of gold. If the price of gold moves $1 higher, that will affect the position by $100 ($1 × 100 ounces). In the case of stocks, if the value of a single share is $10 and one stock futures contract is of 100 shares, your actual position would be of $1,000 ($10 × 100). Therefore, it is important to check each futures contract as they differ in underlying and exchange.

After you take a position, the profit or loss on your futures position is calculated on a daily closing basis known as the daily margining process. If your position is in loss, your broker transfers that amount from your margin account to the exchange. If the position is in profit, the exchange transfers that amount to your broker who then deposits it into your margin account. Unlike a forward, where all contract obligations are satisfied at maturity, obligations under a futures contract are adjusted every day on an ongoing basis as mark-to-market profits or losses are realized. This eliminates credit risk in the case of futures.

The margins are calculated on settlement prices. These are official prices calculated by the exchange at the close of trading for the purpose of making margin calculations and are calculated by different methods, the most common being the average prices of last half-hour trading.

You can close your futures position in the following ways:

1. By going for an equal but opposite position known as offsetting. If you are long or have bought one contract of July gold futures, you can close the position by taking an offsetting short position of one contract of July gold futures. If, for example, you had sold one contract of July gold futures, you could close your position by buying one contract of July gold futures.
2. In the case of cash settled futures like stock index futures, you can simply hold the futures until expiration. At that time there is a final margin payment, and the contract then expires.
3. In the case of physically settled futures like commodities, you can hold a futures contract until it is physically settled according to exchange rules. Speculators and traders have to be careful in this case and need to close their position before the contract expires.

The majority of futures contracts are traded by speculators who have no interest in either taking or giving delivery of the underlying asset, so most futures are closed out by offset.

Chapter 10

Options

OPTIONS ARE THE MOST INNOVATIVE INVESTMENT TOOL available to an investor. The advantage of options is the flexibility and versatility they offer. You can use options in any market condition both for protecting your position and reducing risk, and as a complete speculative tool. Understanding options is therefore necessary for every speculator, trader or investor.

Options are the third type of derivatives after forwards and futures. As we saw in chapter 9, Futures are derivative instruments where one takes a position for giving or taking delivery of an asset at a future date. It is a contract that has to be honoured as the seller has to make delivery and the buyer has to take delivery. In other words, there is an obligation on both parties to fulfil the contract. Option, as the name suggests, however, is a choice and not an obligation. In our example of the gold bar, if you had bought gold futures, you would have to take a delivery at the agreed price, no matter how much the gold prices may have fallen in three months. However, if you had bought an option and the gold price falls, you have no obligation to take delivery. You can instead buy gold at whatever its prevailing price is after three months.

Therefore, an option is a contract between two parties, the buyer and the seller, that gives the buyer the right, but not the obligation, to buy or sell an underlying asset at a specific price on or before a certain date. It must be clearly understood that the option is given to only one party in the transaction, namely the buyer of an option. The other party (the seller of an option) has an obligation to take or make delivery. The example of an airline ticket will make it clearer. When you buy an air ticket, it is like an option. As a buyer of the ticket, you have the option to travel. However, if you decide not to travel, the airline cannot compel you and put you on the plane. On the other hand, the airlines are obliged to take you to a destination for which the ticket is made. They have no right to say no to you once you have bought the ticket and will have to honour the ticket.

Coming back to our example of the gold bar, if you are a buyer of an option to buy gold at $800, you have a choice whether to actually take the delivery or not. If the gold prices fall to $600, you would not want to take the delivery at price of $800 and you have the choice not to do so. But the other party that has sold you this option has no choice and is obliged to give you delivery should you want it. That means that even if the gold prices were to rise to $1,000, the seller of the option has to give you delivery at $800, he does not have an option. To repeat: it is only the buyer of an option who has the right, but no obligation to buy or sell something, whereas the seller of the option has the obligation to make, or take, the delivery as the case may be.

Isn't this too good to be true, you might say. As a buyer of an option, you have no risk, you have full right over the contract but, if you feel, you can forget about the whole contract and nobody can compel you otherwise.

What about the seller of the contract, who is taking all the risk? Why would any intelligent person ever become a seller of an option? The answer is simple; the seller receives some amount of cash for the risk he is taking. This amount is known as premium and is paid by the buyer of the option. Coming back again to our example of the gold bar, let us suppose the present price of gold is $800. You buy an option of buying gold at $800. If the gold prices go above $800, you will take delivery because you are still getting the gold bar at $800. However, if gold prices are below $800, you have the option of not taking the delivery at $800 as you can get the gold bar at a lower price in the market. Nevertheless, the other party has taken the risk and so he will charge you a premium. You have to give this premium payment if you buy an option. Suppose the premium you paid is $50. Now your actual profit will start after $850 ($800 + $50 premium). Therefore, until the price of gold is below $850, you are in a loss. On the other hand, the actual price for the seller is also now $850. He will be in a profit so long as the gold prices are below $850. It is clear that $850 is the price from where your profit and the seller's loss starts. As a buyer, your profit is unlimited as the gold price can rise to any level but your loss is limited to only $50, the premium you have paid to the seller. Whereas for the seller on the other hand, the profit is limited to $50, the premium that he has received, but the loss is unlimited.

Thus, instead of buying gold, you have just bought an option to buy gold at a certain price. However, what if you feel that gold prices may go down and you want to speculate on that? In our example of the gold bar, you wanted the delivery of the gold and did not want to wait and take the risk of higher gold prices. But as a trader, let's suppose you analyse that gold price will be $600 in three months and that you would like to speculate on the falling gold prices. In futures, you can do this by short selling, i.e. you sell gold futures and cover it when the gold prices fall. But how do you make profit in options when you expect the gold prices to fall? Here, too, you will buy an option, but instead of buying an option to buy gold, you will buy an option to sell gold.

In our example of the gold bar, when you bought an option to buy gold at $800, you protected yourself from any rise in gold prices. However, if you think that gold prices may fall, you will either do nothing, wait for the prices to come down and buy then, or, you may want to profit from the falling gold prices. When you wish to profit from falling prices, you can short sell gold futures or buy an option to sell gold. When you buy an option to sell gold, it works in the same way as when you buy an option to buy gold but the position is reversed. Once you buy an option to sell gold at $800 by paying a premium of $50, your actual price will be $750 ($800 -$50 premium). Your profit will start when gold falls below $750. If the gold prices rise, the maximum loss that you will suffer is the premium you have paid i.e. $50. For the seller of this option, on the other hand, the maximum profit is limited to the premium he has got ($50 in this case) but the maximum loss is unlimited till gold comes to $0.

Now that we are through with the concepts, let us understand options and their associated terms. Options are divided into two categories: call option, or calls, and put option, or puts.

Call Option

A call option gives the buyer the right to buy an asset or a security at a certain price within a specific period. Buyers of a call option anticipate that the price of the underlying security will rise before the expiry of the contract. Buying a call option is akin to going long on a security. The value of a call option increases when the price of the underlying security is going up, and decreases when the price of the underlying security declines.

Put Option

A put option gives its buyer the right to sell an asset at a certain price within a specific period. Buyers of put option anticipate that the price of a security will fall before the contract expires. Buying a put option is thus just like going short on a security. The value of a put option increases when the price of the underlying security is going down and decreases when the price of the underlying security is going up.

So depending on what you anticipate happening in the market, you can buy a call or a put and profit from the price movement. The important thing to understand is the right each type of option gives you once you have purchased it, and why the values of calls and puts fluctuate when the market moves up and down.

A call option gives you the right to buy an asset from the person who sold you the call option at a specific price on or before a specified date. For instance, if you bought a call option on gold at $800 (the strike price), the option gives you the right to buy gold for $800 any time before the expiration date. What this means is, that if gold rises anywhere above $800 before the expiry, you can buy gold for less than its market value. And if you don't want to buy the gold yourself, or exercise the option, you can sell your option to someone else for a profit. In that case, you will get the difference between your buy premium and sell premium in the form of cash deposited in your account.

However, what if gold never rises above $800? Your option will then be worthless because nobody would want to buy an option that allows them to buy gold at a higher price than what they can get the gold in the open market.

A put option gives you the right to sell a security, to the person who sold you the put option, at a specific price, on or before a specified date. For instance, if you buy a put option on gold at $800 (the strike price), the option gives you the right to sell gold for $800 any time before the expiration date. What this means is that should gold fall anywhere below $800 before the option's expiry, you can sell the gold for more than its market value. And if you don't want to sell the gold yourself, you can sell your option to someone else for a profit.

There are four ways in which you can participate in an options market. You can be any one of the following depending on your position:

1. Buyer of a call (long on call).
2. Seller of a call (short on call).
3. Buyer of a put (long on put).
4. Seller of a put (short on put).

A buyer of an option is called the "holder", whereas the seller of an option is known as the "writer". By now, it must be clear that the call and put buyers (holders) are not obliged to buy, or sell, the asset. They have the choice to exercise their right that they have as buyers, if they feel so. On the other hand, call and put sellers (writers) are obligated to buy or sell the asset. They have no choice and are bound to give or take delivery of an asset if the buyers choose to exercise their option.

Strike Price

This is also known as exercise price. It is a pre-determined price at which you can buy, or sell, the asset. This cannot be changed during the life of the option contract. Therefore, if you buy a call option on gold with strike price of $800, this will be the price at which you can buy gold throughout the life of the call option contract. If at any time the price is above $800, you are making a profit. If you buy a put option on gold at $800 strike price, this will be the price at which you can sell gold any time before the contract expires. If the prices are below $800 at any time during the option period, you will be in profit.

For call options, the higher the strike price, when compared with the security's cash or spot price, the cheaper will be the option while the lower the strike price, the more expensive will be the option.

For put options, the lower the strike price, the cheaper will be the option and higher the strike price, the more expensive it will be.

Therefore, if the cash price of gold is $800, the higher the strike prices you opt for lower the premium you have to pay for a call option and higher the premium for a put option. Similarly, the lower the strike price you go in for, the higher the premium you have to pay for a call option and lower the premium for a put option.

Expiration Date

This is the date at which the option contract must be settled and after which the contract ceases to exist. This too cannot be changed during the life of the option. The expiration date on Indian NSE is the last Thursday of the month.

Exercise

Exercise means to invoke the rights granted to the owner of an option contract, after which the option contract cease to exist. In the case of a call option, the holder of the option purchases the underlying security at the strike price from the option seller. In the case of a put option, the owner of the option sells the underlying security to the option seller at the strike price.

Option Moneyness

Option moneyness is the price of the option's underlying security relative to the strike price of a specific option on that security. The option may be "in-the-money", "at-the-money", or "out-of-the-money".

In-the-Money (ITM)

If the spot gold price is higher than the call option strike price, then the call option will be in-the-money. For example, if the cash, i.e. spot price of gold is $800, then all the call options with a strike price below $800, i.e. $750, $600, etc. will be known as in-the-money call options.

If the gold price is lower than strike price of the put option, then the put option will be in-the-money. For example, if the cash or spot price of gold is $800, then all the put options with a strike price above $800, like $850, $1,000, etc. will be known as in-the-money put options.

Out-of-the-Money (OTM)

If the spot gold price is lower than the call option strike price, then the call option will be out-of-the-money. If the gold price is higher than the put option strike price, then the put option will be out-of-the-money. Therefore, if gold price is $800, any strike price of the call option above $800, will make that option out-of-the-money whereas any strike price of put option below $800 will make that option out-of-the-money.

At-the-Money (ATM)

In our example of gold, an option, whether call or put, is at-the-money if its strike price is the same as the spot price of gold. thus, a strike price of $800 will make the option at-the-money if the spot price is also $800.

Premium

Premium is the amount one has to pay for buying an option contract. Conversely, it is the amount one receives for selling an option. Each security has a given list of strike prices for trading. The amount one has to pay as premium depends on where the strike price is in relation to the security's current price.

Let's take a situation when the present market price of gold is $800. In the case of a call option, the higher the strike price you go in for, the lower will be the premium while in the case of a put option, the lower the strike price you go in for, the lower will be the premium. At a current market price of $800, a call option with $1,000 strike price will have lower premium than the option with $900 strike price. Similarly, in the case of a put option, the option with strike price of $600 will have lower premium than an option with $700 strike price.

The option premium has two parts, an intrinsic value and a time value.

Intrinsic Value

This is the value of the option if the option is in-the-money. Therefore, if the price of gold is $800 and you have a call option of $700, the intrinsic value of your call option will be $100; whereas if the gold price is $800 and you have a put option of $850, the intrinsic value of your put option will be $50.

An out-of-the-money option has no intrinsic value.

Options almost always trade above intrinsic value.

Time Value

A portion of an option's value depends on the time remaining until the expiration of the contract. The more time there is for expiration, the higher the time value the option will carry.

The time value of an option will always be positive and will decline as time passes. Therefore, when you buy the gold option, you also pay for the time value that will only diminish, no matter where the gold prices go.

An option may or may not have an intrinsic value but it will always have some time value. Therefore, if your option is in-the-money, your premium will be the sum of intrinsic value and time value and if your option is out-of-the-money, the premium will only be the time value as the intrinsic value will be zero. Because time value declines continuously until expiration, options are considered wasting assets.

For any given time until expiration, time value is the greatest when an option is at-the-money, and diminishes as it moves farther either out-of-the-money or in-the-money.

Volatility also plays an important part in the time value. Higher volatility of the underlying increases the premium value as the chance of an option going in-the-money increases.

The most important factor that determines the premium of an option is the relationship of the strike price to the current price of the underlying security. As the option goes in-the-money, the premium will increase by at least $1 for every $1 increase in the intrinsic value of the option. For a call, the premium increases by at least $1 for every $1 increase in the underlying security price. For a put option, the premium increases by at least $1 for every $1 fall in the underlying security price. When the option is in-the-money, there is still some time value but it decreases as the intrinsic value increases.

At this point, let me advise you to go and check out option trading practically with your broker — or if you are trading online, pick any one security and see how all its available options are trading. This will give you practical insight into options and your doubts, if any, will be removed. Also, do remember that, like futures, options contracts are also quoted in per share prices in case of stocks or per ounce cost of gold, but are traded only in lots. For example, when you buy one gold option contract, it might be quoted at $800 but your account will be calculated on $80,000 for one contract because the contract is of 100 ounces.

Let us now review the concept of options using the terms we have learnt.

Suppose, the current month is November, you will have options for November, December, January or any later months depending on the exchange. The price of gold can rise, fall or remain the same. If you foresee that gold prices will remain the same you probably would not do anything but in the cases of rising and falling prices, you may want to enter into a trade depending on your analysis.

Let's say that on 1 November, the gold price is $800. You wish to buy January 900 call. This means that the strike price is $900 and the contract expires in January. The premium cost for a January 900 call is $20. Assuming that the contract is of 100 troy ounce, the total price of the contract will be $20 × 100 = $2,000. I have ignored the commissions but you would have to take them into account while trading.

The strike price of $900 means that the gold price must rise above $900 before the call option is of some value. A gold option contract is the option to buy 100 ounce of gold, that's why you must multiply the contract by 100 to get the total price. And since you have paid the premium of $20, the actual price of gold from where your profit will start will be $920.

If gold price stays below $900 until the expiry, you will lose the premium. However, if gold prices rise above $920 — your breakeven price, — you will make a profit.

In the above example, you were the option holder or buyer. If you are the option writer or seller, you will receive the premium, which will be your profit. If gold prices remain below $900 until expiry, the premium amount will be your profit. However, if gold prices rise above $920, you will be in loss and the higher gold prices go, the more loss you will incur. Therefore, as a writer of the option, your profit is limited but your loss is unlimited.

Exercising *versus* Closing Out

Until now we have seen that the option holder has the right to exercise. That means the holder has the right to give, or take, the delivery of the underlying asset at any point of time

When gold price goes to $1,000 and you have a call option of $900, you could make money by exercising the $900 call and then selling the gold back in the market at $1,000 for a profit of $100 an ounce. Alternatively, you may also choose to keep gold until you are ready to sell it. Exercising options in the case of stocks is not much of a problem as shares are either paper certificates or in demat form but it would be really difficult to manage 100 ounces of gold or 100 barrels of crude oil! Whatever be the underlying asset, in reality, a majority of options are not actually exercised.

Most of the time holders choose to take the profits by closing their position. This means that holders sell their options in the market, and writers buy their positions back to close.

In the example above, you can also close out your position. If you are a buyer of gold option, you can sell the option and if you are a writer of the option, you can buy it back.

After few weeks, if gold is still at $800 and if you had bought the out-of-the-money call option, the premium you had paid was time value and it would come down. Therefore, if you decide to sell your option, you will get much less than $20 as premium due to the reduced time value.

Types of Options

Option trading is much more complicated than trading in simple cash or futures and option traders have to look at many factors. Options are divided into two main types, or styles, American style options and European style options.

Both these option styles are almost similar except for one major difference relating to when they can be exercised.

American Style Options

American style options are the most common ones. Almost all stock and commodity options are American style. You can exercise American-style options any time you want to before expiration. For example, if you buy an American style call option on gold today and it expires in one month, you can exercise it on any trading day until the option expires. Therefore, you can demand the delivery of gold at any time during the life of the option.

European Style Options

European style options are much less common and you can only exercise European style options at expiration. Options on stocks indices, like the Nifty, S&P 500 and the Nasdaq are European style options. Currency pairs like EUR / USD also trade in European style options.

The right to exercise your option at any time, rather than just at expiration, increases the price of the option. American style options are usually more expensive than European style options because the seller of an American style option is assuming greater risk. European style option sellers know that such an option cannot be exercised until expiry, making it less risky and lowering the price of the option.

- **Long-term Options:** Options are not only available for short term but also for longer terms like one year or more. For an investor, longer-term options make an excellent investment opportunity. However, remember that longer term options will be expensive due to the huge time value that will only come down as time passes.
- **Exotic Options:** What we have discussed so far are plain vanilla options and no matter how confusing they might be, they are still the easiest to understand and trade. Exotic options are advanced variants of plain vanilla options. As a trader, you don't need to go into exotic options and what you have learnt till now is sufficient.

Option Strategies

Options give you a vast opportunity to use your trading skills. You will hear many terms, like straddle, strangle, and butterfly spread, etc., when somebody discusses options. There are graphical pictures that will tell you what a strategy will do. However, if you have understood options, you do not require learning these terms and making an extra effort of drawing graphs.

The reason I have not given detailed explanations with graphs is quite simple; first, it just creates more confusion and, second, it is not required for trading options. If you have understood that the buyer of the option has limited loss but unlimited profits, you do not need to understand how to show it graphically.

The important thing for you to understand is that most of the advanced derivative strategies, which include options, are better avoided because not only do they increase the margin requirement in case of writing, but also because they take too much time for nothing. As a trader and speculator, you are neither hedging nor arbitraging. You are taking risk and want corresponding profit. You should approach options logically, think as to what all the tools you have and what can be done once you have analysed the market and you will come up with an option strategy, even though you may not know its term.

Throughout the second part of this book which deals with technical analysis, I have mentioned where and how a derivative strategy can be applied. Once you understand that, you will be comfortable in using any derivative strategy and be able to devise your own method depending on the situation.

Wait for the right opportunity to go for an option trade. Options are not like futures that you can trade whenever you wish. There is a time for option trading and you must be patient enough to let that opportunity present itself.

Do remember that there is no substitute for practical trading and that goes for options too. Actual trading will give you a clear insight into options, which no theoretical knowledge can provide.

Bullish Strategies

If your analysis indicates a bullish market ahead, you can go for an option strategy that will help you profit from the rise in prices. Here are the important ones:

Buying Call

Buying a call option, also known as long call option or simply long call, is the most widely used option strategy across the world. It is the simplest yet the most powerful bullish option strategy in the hands of traders. Beginners should start with this and, once adept, can slowly move to a combination of long call, futures and cash positions. It should be used when you feel the market will make a significant up move. You can use this strategy in place of owning an underlying. If you anticipate a very strong rise in prices, then you can go for more out-of-the money options which will be cheaper but give you good leverage.

Remember that you may be tempted to buy deep in-the-money options due to the lower time value they hold, but this would put you at the risk of a big loss in a short span of time if the market moves against you. This is so because the intrinsic value will erode at a faster pace the deeper in-the-money an option is.

Price is the key to success in the options market and you can go for in-the-money or out-of-the-money option depending on your personal preference. However, buying out-of-the-money options is always advisable because when you pay too much for an option the odds against you increase. If your analysis is correct, an out-of-the-money option will become in-the-money before it expires, giving you much better returns on your investment. However, if your analysis is wrong then it is easier to book a loss of, say, $10 which you might have paid for out-of-the-money option rather than taking a $100 loss for buying an in-the-money option.

Bull Call Spread

A bull call spread involves the purchase of a call option on a particular underlying, while simultaneously writing a call option on the same underlying with the same expiration month, at a higher strike price.

For example, a bull call spread in gold can be established by buying a December 900 call and simultaneously selling a December 1,000 call.

You actually have two positions as both the buy and the sell sides of this spread are opening transactions, and both will always have equal number of contracts. You pay a premium on your long call position and at the same time will receive a premium on the call you have sold, or written. You can decide on the strike prices of both the positions but, usually, the purchased call is at-the-money or in-the-money and the written call is out-of-the-money.

This strategy is useful if you anticipate a moderate rise in prices because if you anticipate a significant rise in prices then you would go for a single long call position.

This type of spread is sometimes also called vertical spread as it involves options of the same underlying, the same expiration month, but different strike prices.

The bull call spread can be considered a double safety measure taken by a trader who is not willing to risk even the premium paid for buying a call. The price paid for the call with the lower strike price is partially offset by the premium received from writing the call with a higher strike price. Thus, the investor's investment in the long call, and the risk of losing the entire premium paid for it, is reduced.

The financial risk of the written call with the higher strike price is hedged by the long call with the lower strike price. If the investor is assigned an exercise notice on the written call, he is safe as he too has the option to exercise the purchased call with the lower strike price.

The profit potential is limited in bull call spread and is maximum if both options expire in-the-money

Selling Put or Writing Put

This is also known as naked put since you have a position without being short on the underlying. If you are bullish about the market, you might want to earn the premium received by writing a put. Remember, though that this is a risky position and should be used carefully as your profit is limited to the premium but your loss is unlimited. Traders who are risk takers usually go for this option strategy.

Strategies, such as the naked put write have their own advantage. This position offers profit even if the underlying security stays at the same price, or falls slightly instead of rising. This is because short option positions give you the advantage of profiting from time decay, the more the time value of the options you've sold reduces, the more profit you make.

If you short an equivalent amount in the underlying security while writing or selling a put, it is called as covered put.

Married Put

A married put position is a hedging strategy and is used by investors who want to save themselves from falling underlying prices but at the same time want all the benefits of underlying ownership. In this strategy, an investor purchases a put and at the same time purchases and takes delivery of an equivalent amount of the underlying security from the cash market. For example, an investor may wish to buy a particular stock in the cash market but fears that the price may fall. To avoid the unforeseen event of stock prices falling, the investor buys the equivalent number of put options contract. This strategy allows the investor employing the married put strategy to enjoy the benefits of stock ownership (dividends, voting rights, etc.) and, at the same time dealing with his concerns about unknown, near-term, downside market risks.

This strategy limits the loss potential but offers unlimited maximum profit. It is like an insurance policy on your underlying.

Bearish Strategies

Buying Put

Buying put options, also known as long put options or simply long put, is the simplest bearish option strategy. If your analysis indicates a significant fall in prices ahead, you can buy put options of that particular security. Traders wanting to profit from a price drop in the underlying security can either sell futures or buy put options. Futures have associated risks like unlimited loss potential and margin requirements. Buying put options allows an option trader to profit from a down move without all the margin and credit requirements of shorting the security or its futures.

In this strategy, your loss is limited to the premium you pay while the profit is unlimited. Of course, the profit cannot go beyond the point where the security price comes to zero.

Price is the key to success in the options market and you can go for in-the-money or out-of-the-money options depending on your personal preference. However, buying out-of-the-money options is always advisable because when you pay too much for an option the odds against you increase. If your analysis is correct, an out-of-the-money option will become in-the-money before the option expires giving you much better returns on investment. However, if your analysis is wrong then it is easier to book a loss of, say, $10 which you might have paid for the out-of-the-money option rather than taking a $100 loss for buying an in-the-money option.

Bear Put Spread

A bear put spread is the reverse of a bull call spread and works the same way but in the opposite direction. Establishing a bear put spread involves the purchase of a put option on a particular underlying, while simultaneously writing a put option on the same underlying with the same expiration month, but with a lower strike price. For example, a bear put spread in gold can be established by buying a December 700 put and selling a December 600 put. You can decide on the strike prices of both the positions but usually the purchased put is at-the-money or in-the-money and the sold put is out-of-the-money.

Selling Call or Writing Call

When you sell a call without owning the underlying, it is known as call write or, more specifically, naked call write. Call write is a bear strategy to capitalize on a quick drop in the price of the underlying. Selling an option, whether call or put is a profitable position even if the underlying stays stagnant due to an erosion in its time value. The profit in this strategy is limited to the option premium whereas the potential loss is unlimited.

When an investor writes a call option contract while at the same time owning an equivalent quantity of the underlying, it is known as covered call. Covered call writing is a very important strategy for those investors who actually own the underlying and is used when the investor, while bullish on the underlying, predicts that its market value will not change much over the lifetime of the call contract. This strategy gives an additional income in the form of the premium and in the case of stocks, the dividends, etc. add to the income (Of course, if the investor is assigned an exercise notice on the written call then he is obligated to sell his shares). Just remember that if the stock prices rise too high then the investor will not be able to earn that much profit because he has written a call.

Neutral Strategies

Sometimes it may so happen that you are not able to decide whether the market is bullish or bearish. This confusion arises especially in volatile market conditions when the direction the market will finally take is difficult to judge. In such circumstances, the following option strategies are used.

Long Straddle

Long straddle or, simply, straddle is the simultaneous buying of a call and a put on the same underlying security, with both options having the same expiration and the same strike price. For example, a straddle in gold can be initiated by simultaneously buying a December 800 call and December 800 put. An at-the-money strike price is best suited for this strategy.

In using this strategy it should be understood that some major move up or down is expected. You have paid a premium on both the positions and if the market remains in the same place then you will lose the premium amounts on both positions. Therefore, use this strategy only when you are sure that the market is not in a trading range and some large directional move is inevitable.

You can also use this strategy if some important news, like revenue figures, is about to come which may provide huge price moves.

Long Strangle

The long strangle or, simply, strangle is the simultaneous purchase of a call and a put on the same underlying security with both options having the same expiration but where the put strike price is lower than the call strike price. For example, a strangle on gold can be initiated by simultaneously buying a December 800 call and December 700 put. The best strike price would be when both call and put are out-of-the-money as it costs less to purchase out-of-the-money options but returns are big if the market makes a major move in any one direction.

The long strangle is similar to the long straddle. The only difference is the different strike prices of call and put. While the straddle uses the same strike price for the call and the put, the strangle uses different strike prices in which the put strike is below the call strike.

This strategy should only be used if you are unsure of the direction but anticipate extremely large price move in either direction.

Options Glossary

American-Style Option: An option contract that may be exercised at any time between the date of purchase and the expiration date.

Assign: Notice to an option writer that an option holder has exercised the option and that the writer will now be required to deliver or receive the underlying security under the terms of the contract.

At-the-Money: Option whose exercise price is the same as the market price of the underlying asset.

Call: An option contract granting the purchaser the right to buy the underlying instruments at the agreed strike price. A call obliges the seller to sell the underlying instrument at the agreed strike price, if the option is assigned to him.

Cash Settlement: Settlement of a contract by payment or receipt of a settlement amount instead of the physical delivery of the underlying asset.

Clearing House: An agency associated with an exchange, which settles trades and regulates delivery.

Closing: A transaction, which offsets the original trade and liquidates an existing position.

Contract Size: The quantity of an underlying security that the holder of an option has the right to buy or sell.

Customer Margin: Margin required from both buyers and sellers of futures contracts and sellers of options contracts to ensure fulfilling of contract obligations.

Daily Trading Limit: The maximum price range set by the exchange for intraday movement.

European-Style Options: An option that can be exercised by the buyer only on the contract expiration date.

Exercise: A decision by the option holder to execute the contract and implement the rights of an option, by purchasing (in the case of call options) or selling (in the case of put options) the underlying asset.

Expiration Cycle: An expiration cycle relates to the dates on which options on a particular underlying security expire.

Expiration Date: The date on which the option contract expires.

Expiration Time: The time of day by which all exercise notices must be received on the expiration date.

Hedge: A conservative strategy used to limit investment loss by effecting a transaction, which offsets an existing position.

Holder: The party who purchased an option.

In-the-Money: A call is said to be "in-the-money" when the value of the underlying instrument is greater than the option strike price. A put is "in-the-money" when its strike price is greater than the value of the underlying instrument.

Intrinsic Value: The intrinsic value of an option is the difference between the actual price of the underlying security and the strike price of the option. The intrinsic value of an option reflects the effective financial advantage that would result from the immediate exercise of that option.

Lots: Number of contracts you want to buy or sell.

Maintenance: A set minimum margin that a customer must maintain in his margin account.

Mark-to-Market: Valuation of a financial instrument according to the current trading value (price) on the exchange.

Maximum Price Fluctuation (Futures): The maximum amount the contract price can change, up or down, during one trading session, as stipulated by Exchange rules.

Open interest: The number of outstanding option contracts in the Exchange market or in a particular class or series. The total number of futures contracts or option contracts that have yet to be exercised, expired, or fulfilled by delivery.

Option: A contract that conveys the right, but not the obligation, to buy or sell a particular item at a certain price for a limited time. Only the seller of the option is obligated to perform.

Original Margin: The amount a futures market participant must deposit into his margin account at the time he places an order to buy or sell a futures contract. Also referred to as initial margin.

Out-of-the-Money: A call is "out-of-the-money" when the value of the underlying instrument is less than the option strike price. A put is "out-of-the-money" when its strike price is less than the value of the underlying instrument.

Position Limit: Limitation of the maximum size of a position in futures or options, which may be held by an individual or a group.

Premium: The price of an option — the sum of money that the option buyer pays and the option seller receives for the rights granted by the option.

Put: An option contract granting the purchaser the right to sell the underlying instruments at the agreed strike price. A put obliges the seller to purchase the underlying instrument at the agreed strike price, if the option is assigned to him.

Spot or Cash Price: Refers to the underlying market price.

Strike Price or Exercise Price: The price at which the option holder may purchase (in case of call) or sell (in case of put) the underlying instrument.

Tick: Smallest increment of price movement possible in trading a given contract.

Time Value: It is determined by the remaining lifespan of the option, the volatility and the cost of refinancing the underlying asset (interest rates).

Time Value = Option Price – Intrinsic Value.

Underlying Asset/ Instrument: The instrument (commodity, share, bond, etc.) that can be purchased (in case of call) or sold (in case of a put) by a buyer who exercises his option.

Volatility: It is a measure for the fluctuation range of the underlying price. The greater the volatility, the higher the option price will be.

The historic volatility is based on past data. It is often expressed as a percentage and computed as the annualized standard deviation of the percentage change in daily price.

The implied volatility corresponds with the expectation of the market participants about the future volatility of the underlying, which is reflected in the current option price.

Writer: The seller of an option contract.

Chapter 11

Swaps

THE SWAP MARKET IS NOT AN ARENA FOR TRADERS, so I have avoided any detailed explanation of swaps and just focused on explaining the concept of swaps.

Every business has a basic characteristic and that is the flow of cash. Cash may either be receivable (asset) or it needs to be paid (liability). In either case, sometimes the party may wish to change the basic nature of cash flows without liquidating that asset or liability. If there is another party which is ready to accept the cash flow structure of the first party and provide for another structure as required, they can enter into a swap. Therefore, a swap is an agreement between two parties to exchange two streams of cash flows for a set period.

Swaps are over the counter agreements unlike futures or options, which are standardised and exchange traded. Because swaps occur on the OTC market, there is always the risk of a counterparty defaulting on the swap. Financial institutions and big firms dominate the swap market with hardly any individual presence.

The most commonly traded swaps are interest rate swaps and currency swaps.

Interest Rate Swaps

This is an agreement between two parties based on a specified principal amount where one stream of future interest payments is exchanged for another. The most popular interest rate swaps are fixed-for-floating swaps under which cash flows of a fixed rate loan are exchanged for those of a floating rate loan.

For example, suppose Company A has borrowed money at a floating rate of interest from the lender but later prefers a fixed rate. It can do so by entering into a swap with another party and exchange its floating rate payments into fixed rate payments. The original lender has no part in this transaction and he will be getting payments as per the agreement. The swap is another contract between the company and a third party. Of course, both the parties are benefited in some way by this swap contract.

In an interest rate swap, the principal amount is not actually exchanged. Only the fixed interest payment is exchanged for a floating interest payment that is usually linked to LIBOR.

Currency Swap

The currency swap involves exchanging of both the principal and fixed interest payments on a loan in one currency for principal and fixed interest payments on a similar loan in another currency. Unlike an interest rate swap, the parties to a currency swap will exchange principal amounts at the beginning and end of the swap because the cash flows are in different currencies and, therefore, cannot be netted.

For example, an Indian firm may wish to obtain a loan in euro and a European firm might need the same amount in Indian rupee. The two firms will take loans in their respective countries as it would be easier and then enter into a currency swap to exchange cash flows. All transactions like the initial exchange of principal, payment / receipt of interest (in the same currency) on that loan and final exchange of the principal at the end of the loan are part of the currency swap.

In general, both interest rate swaps and currency swaps are derivatives that help to limit or manage exposure to fluctuations in interest rates or to acquire a lower interest rate than a company would otherwise be able to obtain. These derivatives allow companies to take advantage of the global markets more efficiently and are often used because a domestic firm may receive better rates than a foreign firm can. Swaps are used as a hedging mechanism by firms against interest rate exposure that helps in identifying the future cash flows.

Chapter 12

Structured Products

THE CONCEPT OF STRUCTURED PRODUCTS IS RELATIVELY NEW for retail investors. These are customised products based on a combination of some, or many financial market instruments that we have discussed, such as derivatives, bonds, stocks, forex, indices, etc. A combination of these instruments and strategies is clubbed into one investment product and called as structured product.

Suppose, you have $100 to invest. You can simply invest the amount in equity, bonds, options, etc. according to your analysis, or you can create a structured product on your own with a combination of the available investment instruments. Let us see one example of how a structured product is created.

Out of the total available investment of $100, you invest $80 in a zero coupon bond with face value of $100 and maturing in 5 years. The balance $20 you invest in a stock. After 5 years, you are sure to get back $100 from the bond, which ensures that your principal of $100 is intact. The $20 invested in stock will give you returns according to the performance of the stock. Assuming that an average return of 20% can be expected from investment in equity, your investment will double in five years. The $20 that you had invested will be $40 in five years time and your overall return on $100 will be $140. This is a very good return considering that your principal amount of $100 was absolutely safe. Instead of investing in equity, you could also buy long term call option on a particular stock or index that will significantly increase the amount of profit you can earn.

The above example is one of the simplest forms of structured products and belongs to the capital protection category. This means that no matter what the market conditions are, your initial capital of $100 is protected.

Of course, you have to be careful about the credentials of the bond issuer. There are structured products ranging from low risk to high-risk category and you can choose any type depending on your risk outlook.

Banks and big brokerage houses offer structured products to retail investors. Initially, only high net worth individuals (HNI's) had access to structured products but now these are available to everyone, primarily through the mutual fund route.

Fund houses usually give fancy terms to structured products like equity-linked debentures, etc. as a marketing tool to attract retail investors. If you are going to invest in structured products of any fund house, the first thing that you must do is to look into all the components of that particular structured product and understand its objective, the risks involved and the projected returns.

PART 2

Technical Analysis

Chapter 13

What is Technical Analysis?

TECHNICAL ANALYSIS IS THE STUDY OF PAST PRICE DATA in order to understand how the price may move in future. Volume data is used as a supporting study to price data.

Price

Everything that you buy or sell has a price and this price keeps on fluctuating. You might be a trader in the stock market, the commodity market or the currency market but the only reason that you would trade in any of these markets is because the price keeps on changing. Therefore, no market would exist without price movements. Technical analysis uses the available data of past price movements to analyse the likely future price movements.

Volume

A price change occurs each time a certain quantity changes hands from a seller to a buyer. For example, if gold rises from $800 to $801, it happens because someone has bought a certain quantity of gold from the seller at $801. This is known as volume.

It is price data that is primarily used in technical analysis, and volume data is used as a secondary tool to confirm price analysis.

Time Frame

In technical analysis, we study the past price data. The price data can be analysed for various time-frames, ranging from years to seconds. You could use any period, such as a year, month, day, hour, etc. in your study of price. Whatever be the period, the price will have four variables.

Price Variables

- Open: This is the first traded price at which the security has opened.
- High: This is the highest price that the security has attained.
- Low: This is the lowest price that the security has fallen to.
- Close: This is the last traded price at which the security has closed.

The security, as noted earlier, could be anything, such as a stock, gold, oil, currency, index, etc. Let us take an example of the stock of Google. When the market opens for trading, the first price on which the trading happens will be the open price for Google. During the full day's trading session, the highest price that Google stock reaches is called the high, and the lowest that the stock falls to during the trading day is called the low. Finally, the last price traded before the markets close for the day is called the closing price, or simply close. This is the daily price data of Google. Instead of a day, if we consider a 1-hour period then it will be the hourly price data of Google. Therefore, when the market opens, the first traded price of Google will be the open for first hour. The highest price that Google will reach in one hour will be the high and the lowest price that Google will fall to will be the low. The last price traded in one hour will be the close price of that hour. When the next hour starts, the first price traded will become the open price for that (next) hour. Like this, you can choose any period, whether it be a year, a month, or even a minute.

Close price is considered the most important because it is the final price where markets closed for a particular period. Open, high and low prices hold less importance than close because no matter how the market has moved during a period, it is the closing price which indicates what the final market sentiment is.

The open, high, low and close form the basis of technical analysis. These prices are plotted on a chart and analysed.

Chapter 14

Charts

IN TECHNICAL ANALYSIS, THE PAST PRICE DATA IS STUDIED after it has been plotted on a chart. The chart shows the movement of price with time and is a pictorial representation of any security's trading history over a period of an hour, a day, a week, a month, or several years.

A chart has an x-axis (horizontal) and a y-axis (vertical). Time is plotted on x-axis and price on y-axis (*see* Figure 14.1).

Volume can be plotted in the same way for any chosen period of time.

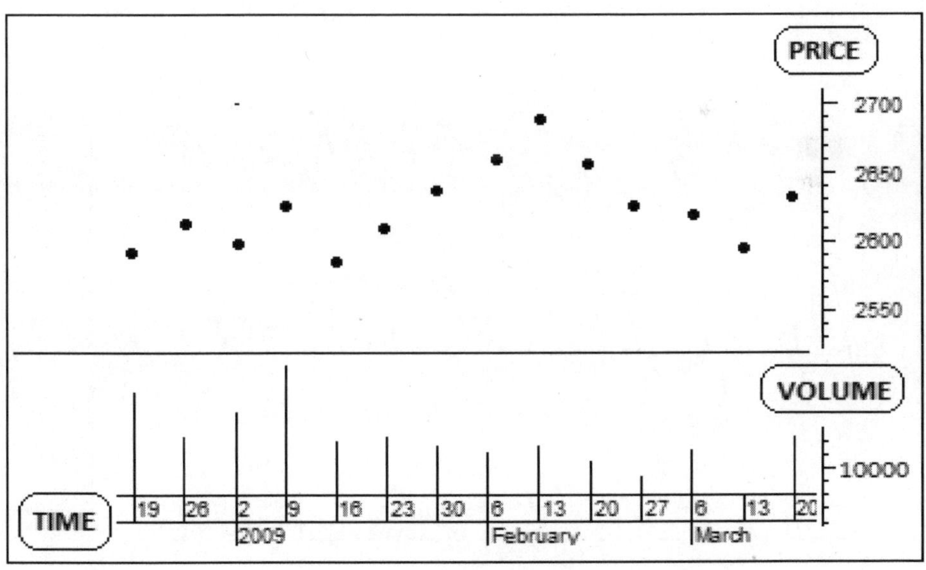

Figure 14.1: **Chart showing x-axis (horizontal) and y-axis (vertical)**

Charts can depict prices in a variety of ways. You can use just the closing prices or make use of the open, high, low, and closing prices in different ways for any time-frame, such as an hour, a day or a week.

You do not need to collect the data and draw the chart yourself. All this is done through several charting software which are easily available, such as Metastock, and the only thing required is to learn how to interpret the charts.

Types of Charts

Line Chart

This is the most basic type of chart and uses only the closing prices. On a line chart, a dot is placed for each closing price and the various dots are then connected by a line (*see* Figure 14.2). So, if we have to draw a 10-period daily line chart of any security, we will first take the closing prices of the last ten days, put them on a chart and connect them by a line. If you wish to draw a weekly line chart, you will use the weekly

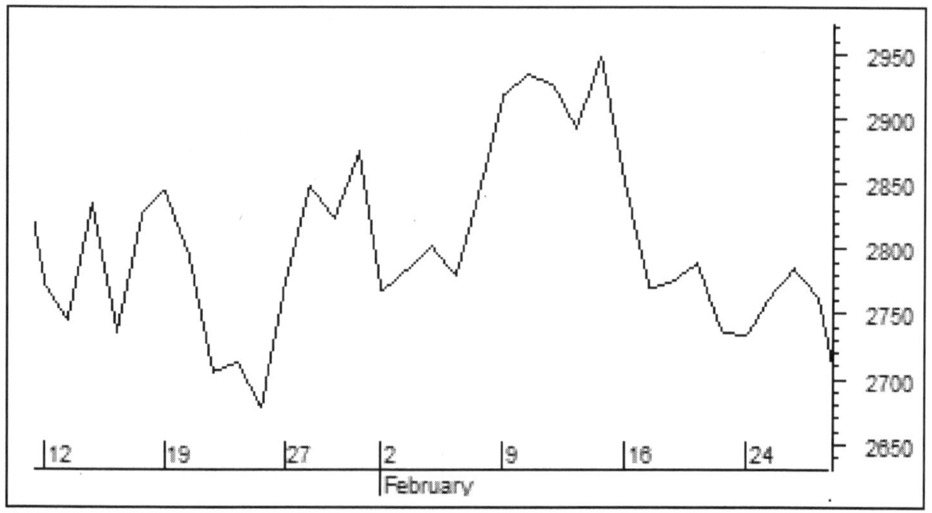

Figure 14.2: **Line chart**

closing prices of the security; for an hourly chart you will use the hourly close — and likewise for other time frames. A line chart gives a clear view of how the prices have moved in the past.

Bar Chart

A bar chart depicts all four price variables, namely open, high, low and close (*see* Figure 14.3), and thus provides more information about the movement of the price than does a simple line chart which only uses the closing prices. In a line chart, a dot is placed for each period's closing price, whereas in a bar chart a bar is placed for each period that shows all four price variables.

The high and low for each period are used to draw a bar. The top of the bar is the highest price that the security has reached in that period (hour, day, 10 minutes, etc.) and the bottom of the bar is the lowest price

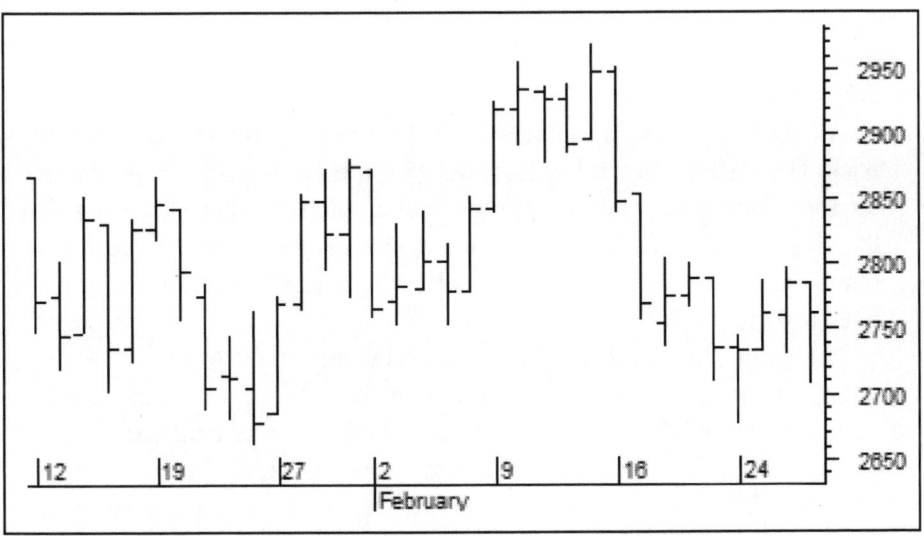

Figure 14.3: **An example of a bar chart, as it is plotted using bars**

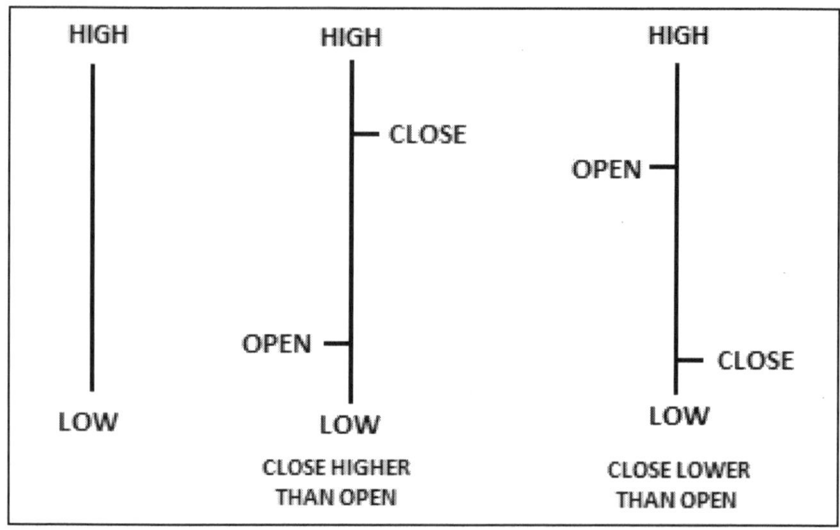

Figure 14.4: **Bars showing open, high, low and closing prices**

for the same period. Open price is shown by a tick on the left side of the bar and the close is shown by a tick on the right side of the bar (*see* Figure 14.4).

All charting software provide the option of using coloured bars if you wish. Generally, a green bar indicates that the closing price was higher than the open price, thus signifying a bull move. A red bar indicates that the closing price was lower than the open, signifying a bear move. Coloured bars make it easier to get a feel of the market without looking for open and close ticks.

A bar can take any shape depending on the price movement.

Bar charts can be plotted for any time frame, such as minute, hour, day, month, etc. If you plot a daily bar chart, an individual bar in that chart will represent the price movement of one day. Likewise, if you plot an hourly bar chat, an individual bar will represent price movements in one hour, and so on for other time frames.

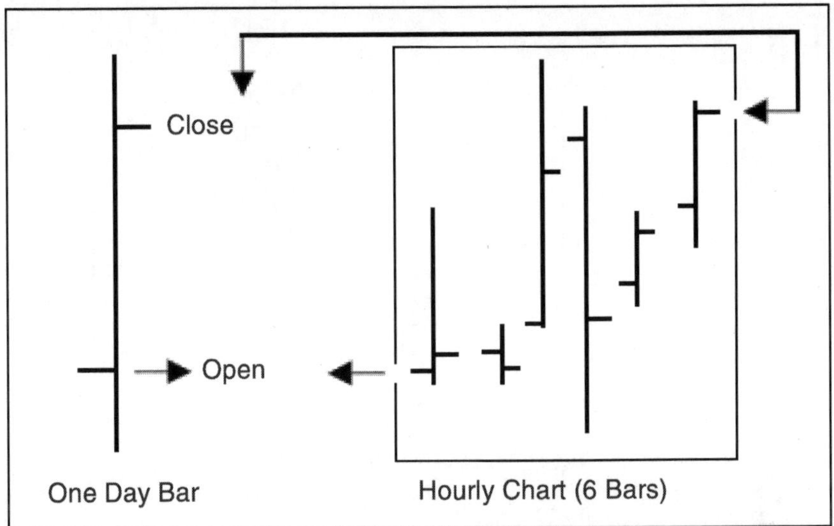

Figure 14.5: **A daily bar and hourly bars for the same trading day**

Figure 14.5 displays a daily bar and hourly bars for the same day, considering a six-hour trading day.

As you can observe, the open of the daily bar is the same as the open of the first hourly bar and the close of the daily bar is same as the close of the last hourly bar. The high and low of daily bar were made in the third and fourth hourly bars respectively. A daily bar ignored the intraday price movements which can be clearly seen in an hourly bar chart. You can go down to as low as one minute chart, depending on the period that you would be trading in. The shorter the time frame, the more information it gives of price movements.

Candlestick

Candlestick charts also show the open, high, low and close prices for a period, just as a bar chart does. However, the difference is in the way open and close prices are displayed. In a bar, the open and close are shown by a tick on the left and right sides of the bar, whereas in a

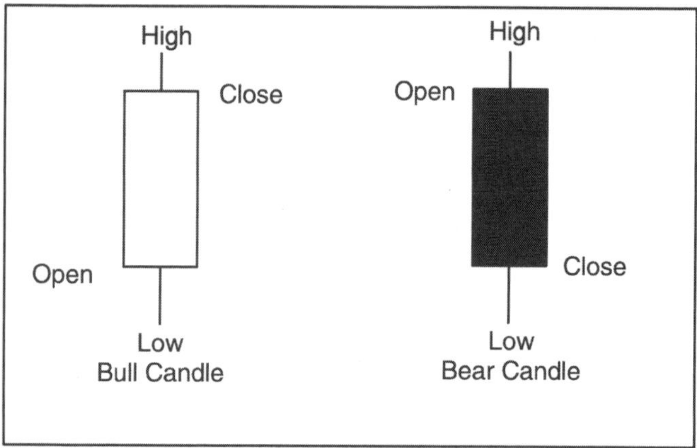

Figure 14.6: **Bull and bear candles**

candlestick, the open and close prices are displayed by a rectangular body (*see* Figure 14.6).

Two variations of candles are formed depending on the open and close prices. The high and low are indicated in a similar way by bars on the top and bottom. The variation comes in by the relationship of open and close prices and depends on whether the close price is higher or lower than open price. If the close price is higher than the open price, then the body of the candle will be white or hollow. If the close price is lower than the open price, then the body of the candle will be black or filled. The white or hollow candle is a bull candle because the closing is higher than the open indicating a bullish sentiment. The black or filled candle is a bear candle because the closing is lower than the open indicating a bearish sentiment.

The open and close form the body of the candle and the high and low form the wicks, also known as shadows (*see* Figure 14.7). In coloured charts, green and red colours are normally used. The bullish candle is depicted in green while a bearish candle is depicted in red. You can even put the colour of your choice for depicting bull and bear candles; charting software allow you to select the colours you want. The next image (Figure 14.8) is a candlestick chart, as it is plotted using the candles.

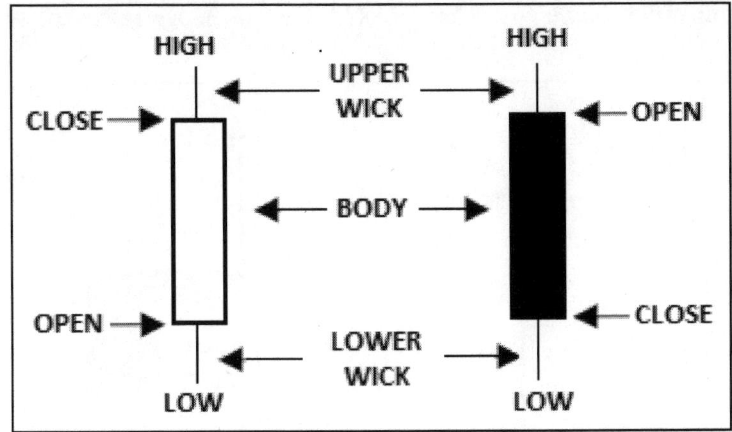

Figure 14.7: **Candle formation parameters**

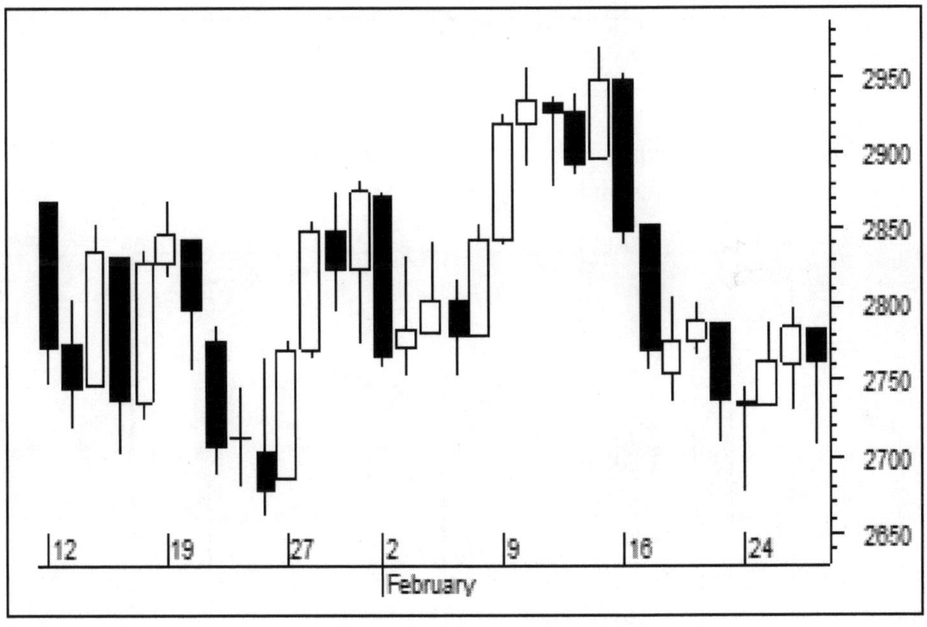

Figure 14.8: **A candlestick chart**

Figure 14.9 shows how a bar looks like when changed to candlestick.

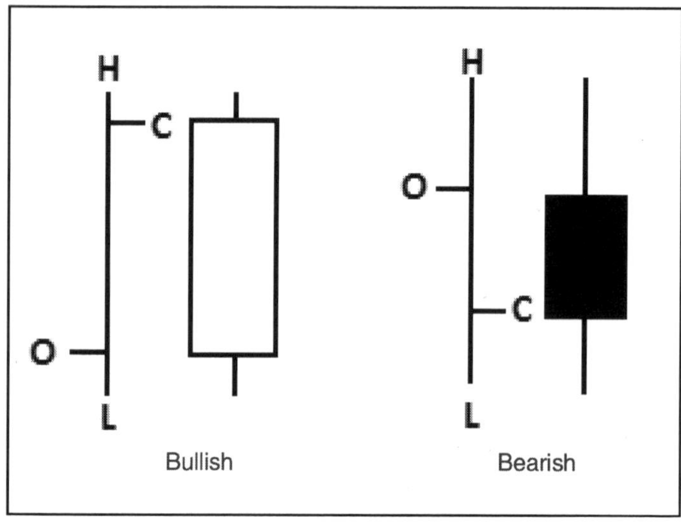

Figure 14.9: **How bars look when changed to candles**

As shown in Figure 14.10, candlesticks can take any shape depending on the open, high, low and close prices.

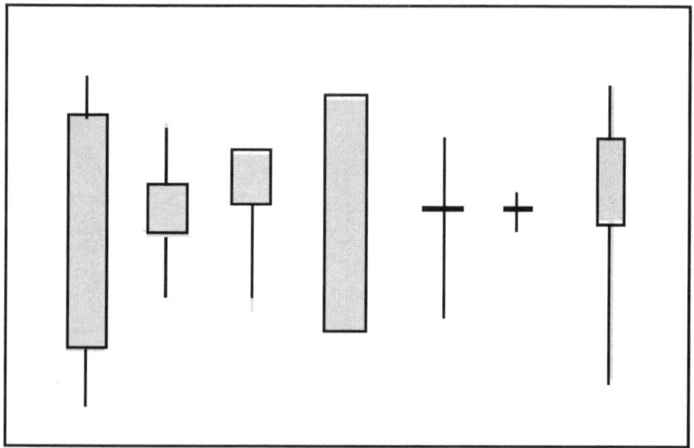

Figure 14.10: **Different shapes of candlesticks**

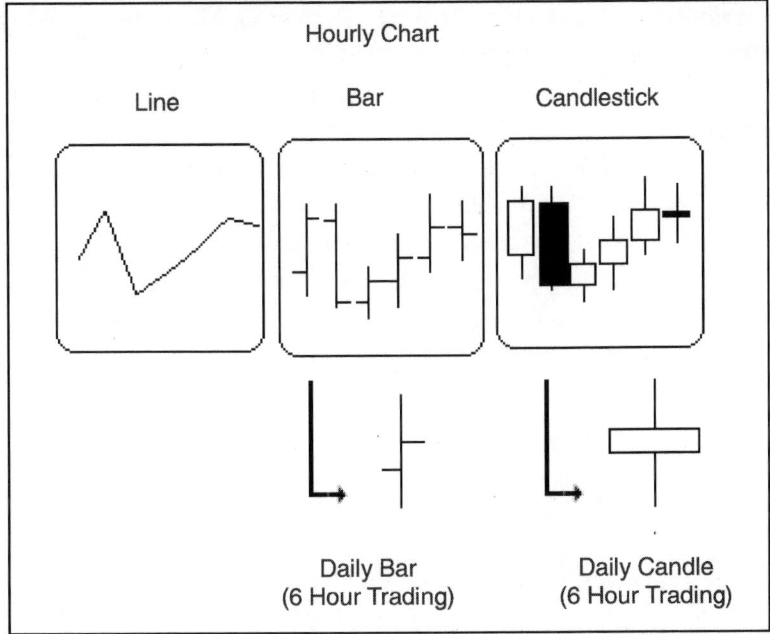

Figure 14.11: **A six hourly line, bar and candlestick chart for the same security and how it looks when converted to daily bar and candlestick.**

Figure 14.11 shows hourly line, bar and candlestick charts assuming a six-hour trading day. When such a day is considered for daily charting, a single bar and a single candle will depict the price action of six bars and six candles, respectively.

Candlestick charts are visually more appealing and easier to interpret as compared to bar charts. Each candlestick provides a complete picture of the price action for a period and is very easy to analyse. You can compare the relationship between the open and close as well as the high and low by simply looking at a candle.

Candlesticks are not just a way of price presentation. They are one of the most interesting tools in the hands of traders and a proper understanding of candlesticks is, therefore, a must.

The body of the candle, which shows the relationship between the open and close prices, is the essence of a candlestick. The importance of the candlestick can be judged from the fact that it is the oldest form of analysis and has been around for more than three centuries, long before any organised financial markets were established. Many traders use only candlesticks for short term trading and swing trading.

Detailed explanation of candlesticks and how to study them is contained in Chapter 18.

If you don't have a charting software by now, do buy one before you proceed. There are many charting software available in the market and you can choose any one that suits your objective and budget.

I expect your mail if you are not clear on any point till now (and anytime in the future). Do not proceed further if there are any doubts in your mind, send a mail and I will remove your doubts, if any.

Chapter 15

Support and Resistance

IN ANY FINANCIAL MARKET — STOCKS, COMMODITIES, CURRENCIES, etc. — prices move because of the actions of buyers and sellers. If there are more buyers than sellers, the price will move up, and if there are more sellers than buyers, the price will move down. It is as simple as that.

However, as the prices move higher, they become less attractive to buyers but more attractive to sellers. Similarly, as the prices move down, they become less attractive to sellers but more attractive to buyers. Therefore, when prices move up, there are fewer buyers and more sellers. Correspondingly, when prices fall, there are more buyers and fewer sellers.

Support

As the name suggests, support is something that stops the price from falling further (*see* Figure 15.1). When the price is falling, there are certain price levels at which the number of buyers increases and a further fall in price is halted.

Resistance

Resistance is something that stops the price from rising further. (*see* Figure 15.2). When the price is rising, there are certain price levels at which the number of sellers increases and a further rise in price is halted.

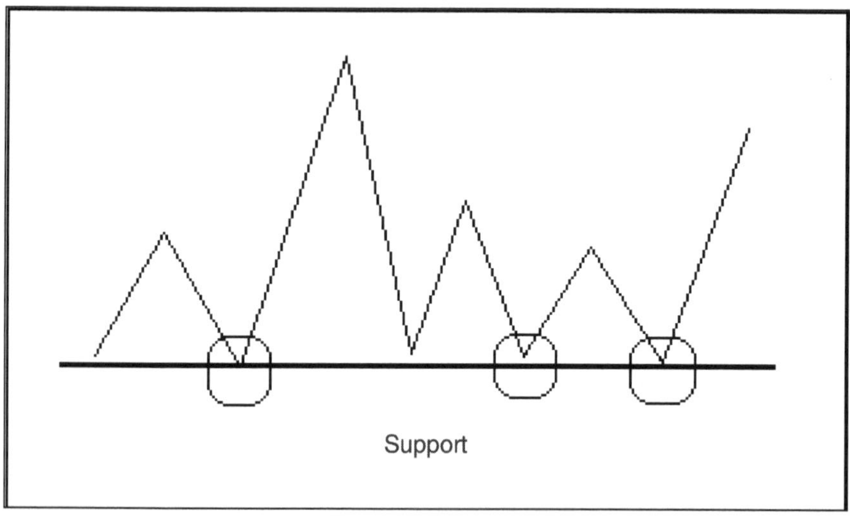

Figure 15.1: **Support**

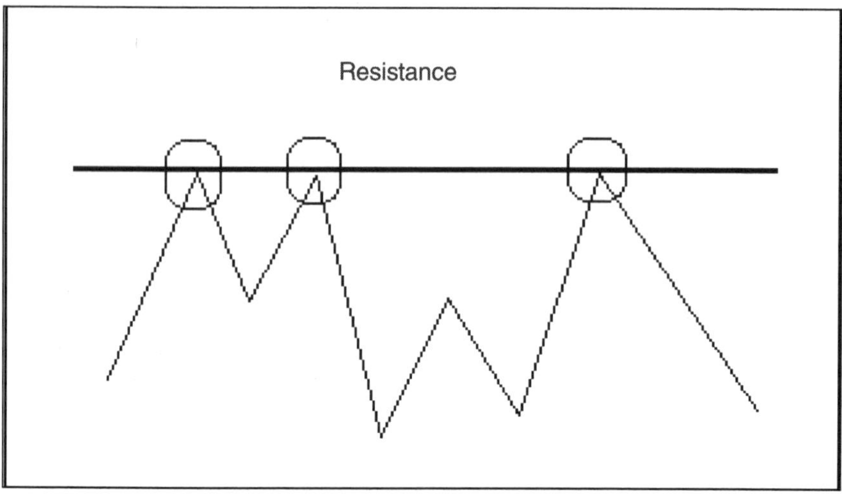

Figure 15.2: **Resistance**

Why do Support and Resistance Occur?

You might be wondering why and how do support and resistance develop. Support and resistance occur because of supply and demand. For example, when prices increase, the number of sellers also increases; in other words, more investors are willing to sell at these higher prices. At the same time, the number of buyers reduces; in other words, fewer investors are willing to buy at higher prices. A point comes when the price starts to fall. Whenever this level reoccurs, people start selling because they remember that the previous time, the price fell from that level. It is said that markets have a memory, and the previous highs and lows are always remembered.

Technical analysis is the only analytical tool that gives importance to human psychology. The first support or resistance point may be made due to a number of reasons such as an investor placing a large buy or sell order. However, this level becomes important to the market for purely psychological reasons, which creates support and resistance around such levels. This provides an excellent trading opportunity; that is what technical analysts look for.

Drawing Support and Resistance

Support

To draw a support line, you need two clear lows around the same price level. Join these lows and extend the horizontal line into the future. This line will act as support for further price movement. Whenever the price falls to this line, it is likely to bounce back. Although just two points are required to draw a support, it should be considered stronger than before each time the price rises from the support line.

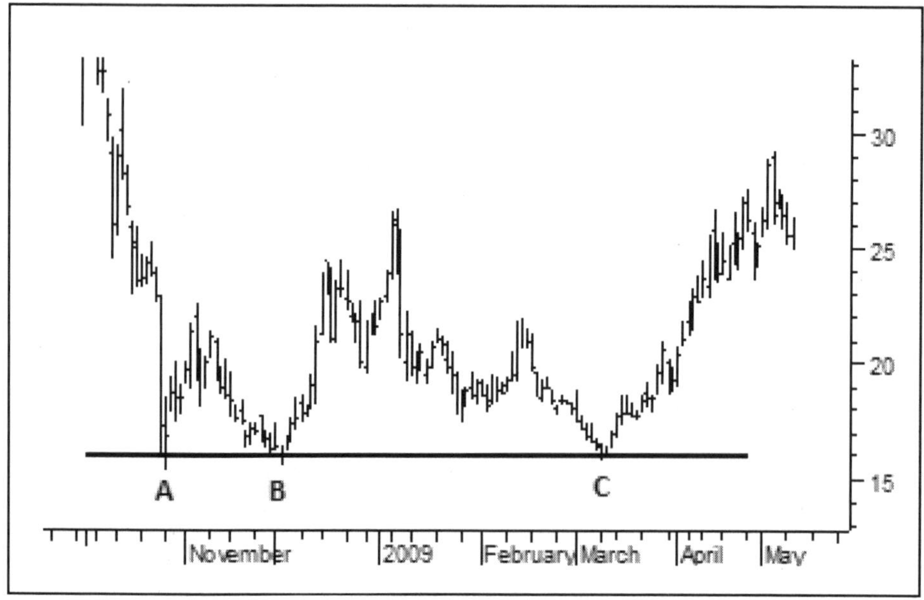

Figure 15.3: **A support line on an actual chart**

Once the support line is drawn by connecting the low points A and B, it can be used as support for future price movements. As you can observe from Figure 15.3, when the price started falling, it could not fall below point C, and bounced back from there.

Resistance

To draw a resistance line, you need two clear highs around the same price level. Join these highs and extend the horizontal line into the future. This line will act as resistance for future price movements and whenever the price rises to this line, it is likely to fall back. Although only two points are required to draw a resistance, each time the price falls back from the resistance line, the resistance line should be considered stronger than before.

Once the resistance line is drawn by connecting the high points A and B, it can be used as resistance for future price movements. As you can

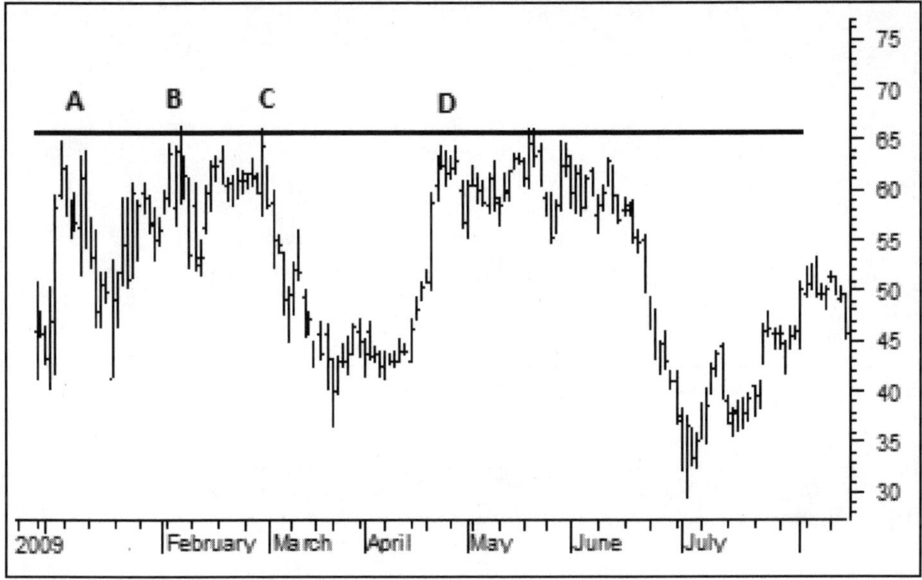

Figure 15.4: **A resistance line on an actual chart**

observe from Figure 15.4, when the price started to rise, it could not cross point C and declined from there. Point D again acted as a resistance increasing the trading strength of the resistance price.

These lows and highs used for drawing the support and resistance respectively should not be too close. There should be a reasonable gap with a minimum of eight- to ten-periods of trading between the highs and lows.

Support and Resistance Zones

Support and resistance are usually indicated by a single price level. You may hear a phrase like — 'gold has support at $800.' However, in reality, one price level cannot be depicted as support or resistance. When you look at any chart, you will, or must have realised that finding one particular price for support or resistance is impossible. This is because no such price exists. It is actually a zone or an area that acts as support or resistance. Therefore, support of gold at $800 does not mean exactly $800 but all the prices close to $800. The price may fall to $797 before rising, or it may never reach $800 and start to rise from $802.

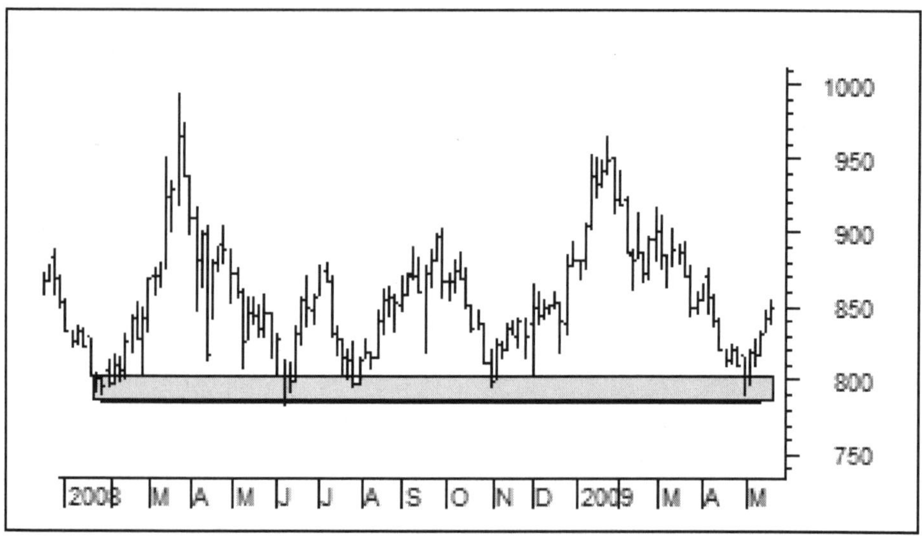

Figure 15.5: **Support zone**

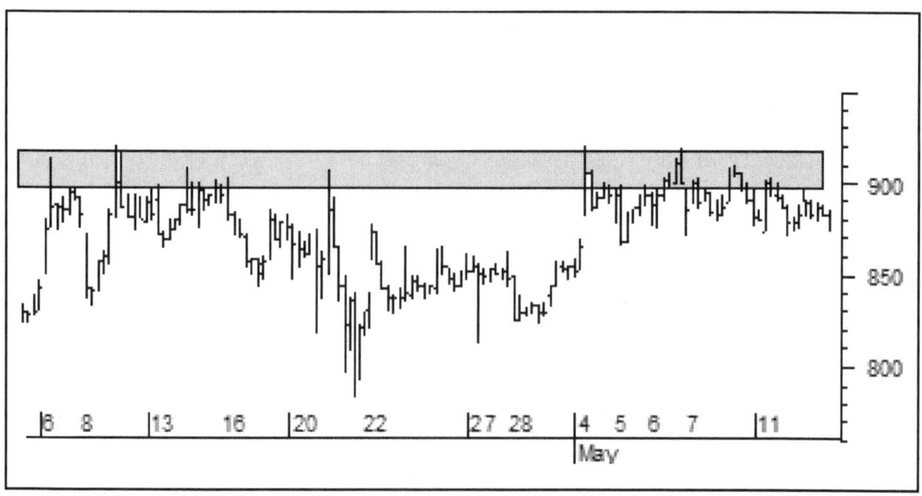

Figure 15.6: **Resistance zone**

Figures 15.5 and 15.6 show the support and resistance zones.

Trading on support and resistance is simple. Buy at support and sell at resistance. If you are a risk taker, you may enter a trade as soon as the price reaches the support or resistance zones. On the other hand, if you are very conservative about risk, you may buy only when the price reaches the lower part of the support zone, or sell when the price reaches the higher part of the resistance zone. Both have their advantages and disadvantages, and once you complete the book, you will find it much easier to spot the right entry point.

Support and Resistance Break

We have seen that prices rise from support and fall from resistance. However, at some point, the price will pass through the support or resistance zones. This is known as break of support and resistance, which means that the support level was not able to stop the price from falling, or the resistance level was not able to hold the price from rising further.

So, what happens when the support or resistance is broken? When a support level is broken and the price falls below the support, that support will change to resistance for future price movements. Similarly, when the resistance level is broken and the price rises above the resistance, that resistance will change to support for future price movements (*see* Figures 15.7 and 15.8).

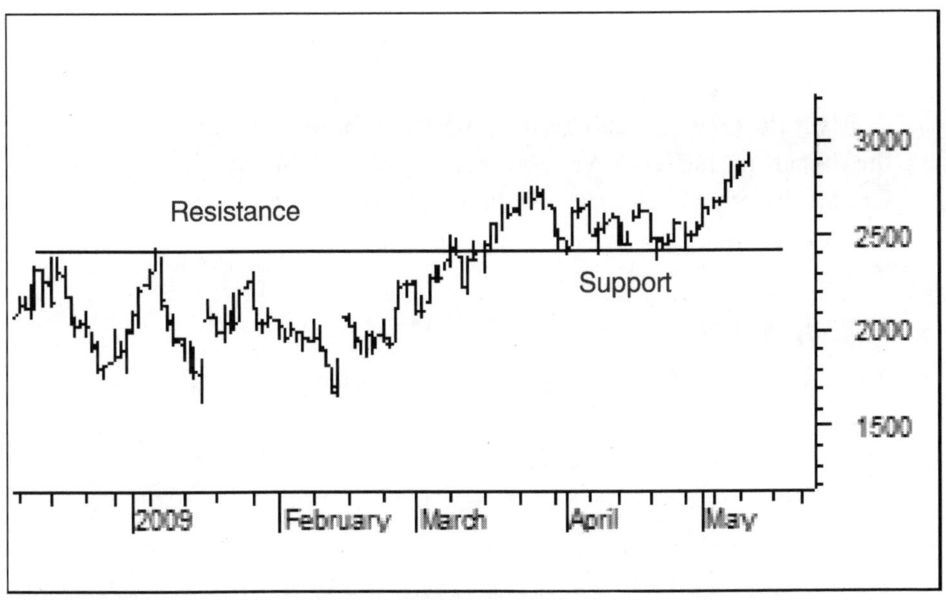

Figure 15.7: **Change of resistance to support**

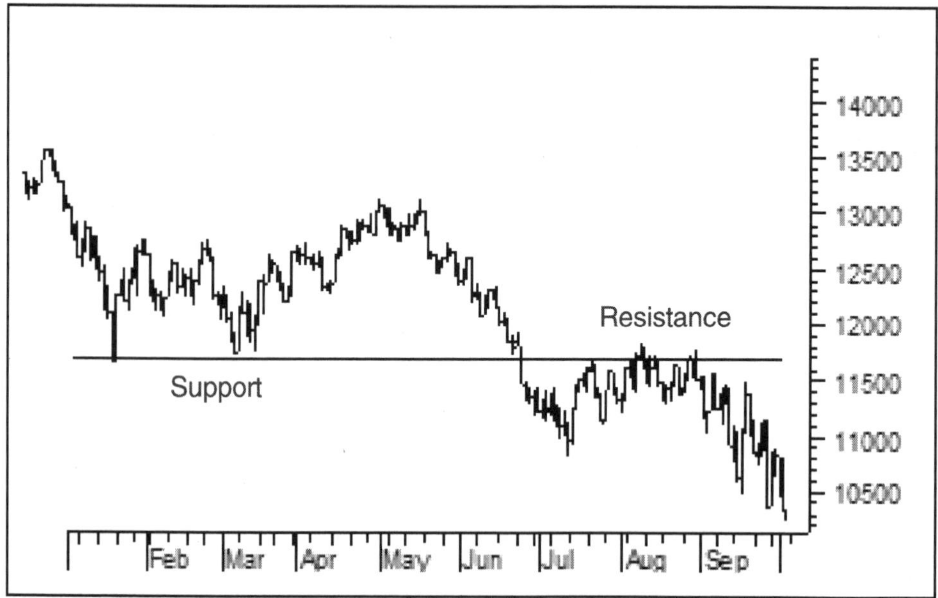

Figure 15.8: **Change of support to resistance**

However, just a few trades above the resistance or below the support zones don't constitute a breakout.

After breaking the support, it is important for the price to close below the support for the breakout to be considered valid. Similarly, it is important for the price to close above the resistance after breakout for it to be considered valid.

Trading Range

When both the buyers and sellers are not confident about the future market direction, the price moves in a narrow range. The upside is capped by resistance and the downside by the support (*see* Figure 15.9). The price moves within these support and resistance lines until the market gets clarity about the direction.

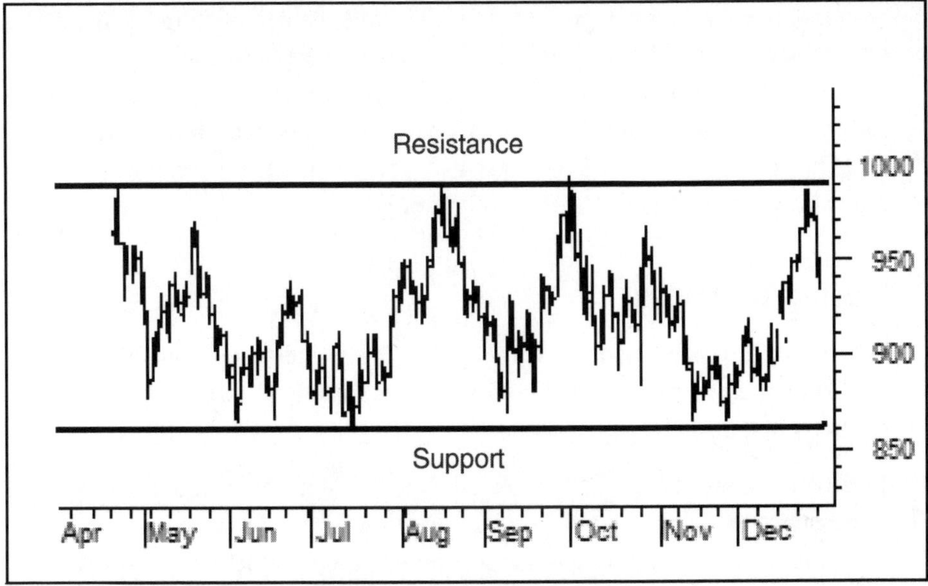

Figure 15.9: **Trading range**

This is known as a range bound market or a trading market, as there are enough opportunities to trade on both the buy and the sell side.

Importance of Support and Resistance

Support and resistance are the most basic tools and may seem rather easy for any worthwhile analysis, but the fact is that they give you price levels that are respected by the markets. Investors and traders are people and they have memories. If you follow a particular stock, you will remember any price level from where the stock rises or falls even though you may have never seen a chart. The market too remembers these price levels and moves accordingly. Therefore, any analysis you do must start with identifying support and resistance levels.

If a security is approaching an important support level, it can serve as an indication of increased buying pressure and a potential reversal. If a security is approaching a resistance level, it can indicate increased selling pressure and potential reversal. If a support or resistance level is broken, it is a sign that the relationship between supply and demand has changed.

A resistance breakout signals that bulls have gained the upper hand, while a support breakout signals that bears have become strong.

The important point to remember is that you should not expect to find support and resistance on every price chart. On many occasions, you will not find any clear support or resistance points. In such a circumstance, move on with your analysis using other tools.

Trading Strategies

When you buy, it is also known as going long, and when you sell, it is also known as going short. You will come across these terms throughout the book and elsewhere.

1. Buy at support and sell at resistance — Whenever the price approaches the support, opt for a buy position. If you have an open short position, close the trade at support and / or take a new buy position. Correspondingly, whenever the price reaches a resistance zone, opt for a sell position. If you have an open buy position, close the trade at resistance and / or take a new sell position.
2. When the support is broken and the price closes below the support zone, the first thing that you must check is the volume. If the volume has also increased on breakout and the price closes below support, then it is a strong breakout. If you had entered into a long position on support, book your loss. You can also create a new short position. For any future price movement, the support that was broken will become resistance, and whenever the price reaches that level, you can create a short position.

   Trade likewise if the resistance is broken. Check the volume; if the volume has increased and the price too has closed above resistance, close your short positions, which you might have entered into at resistance, and opt for a fresh long position. The resistance that was broken will act as support for any future price movements.
3. If you had opted for a buy position at support, you will book a loss if the support is broken, and enter into a sell position. However, sometimes it may so happen that once you take a sell position after support breakout, the market will again change direction and cross the previous support level. This is known as "whipsaw". A whipsaw occurs

when the market unexpectedly moves up and down in a confusing manner. Whipsaws move the market in such a way that traders, whether long or short, are forced to take many stop losses because the market keeps moving back and forth around a certain price level.

Whenever this situation arises, close all your positions and get out of the market. This is the time to be patient; simply wait for the market to get over the confusion and take a direction.

There is no particular reason for whipsaws to occur, but they will be a part of your trading life. So don't get irritated; just stop trading until the time is right. One way that you can limit encountering whipsaws is to trade only on strong support and resistance.

Option Strategies

- **At Support:** Buy call options or sell put options with any strike price below the support.
- **At Resistance:** Buy put options or sell call options with any strike price above the resistance.

Chapter 16

Trend

TECHNICAL ANALYSIS IS BASED ON THE ASSUMPTION that prices move in a trend. The concept of trend is the foundation of technical analysis; it is the core around which most of the studies are done.

Trend is simply the direction of the price movement. It can be up, down or sideways. As the market starts to move in one direction, the trend gains strength because of the human psychological need to find comfort in doing what everyone else is doing (herd mentality).

If the market starts to rise, the number of buyers will increase, and if the markets start to fall, the number of sellers will increase. Technical analysts use this aspect of human nature to understand the trend and profit from it. Always remember, "Trend is your friend".

Does this mean that you should always follow the crowd? The answer is "No". As you will learn in the forthcoming chapters, technical analysis also gives you the ability to judge when a trend has weakened. This gives you an edge to profit from existing and future positions much before anyone even understands what is happening.

Types of Trends

Trends are of three types — uptrend, downtrend and sideways.

Uptrend (Bullish Trend)

An uptrend occurs when the general direction of the price is up. The uptrend is confirmed when each successive peak is higher than the previous

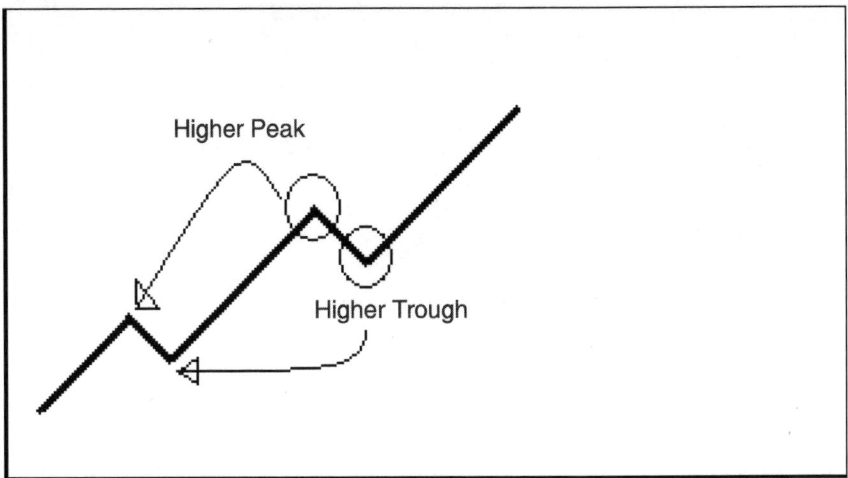

Figure 16.1: **Uptrend**

peak, and each successive trough is higher than the previous trough (*see* Figure 16.1). In technical analysis terms, this is also known as higher high and higher low. The security will be in an uptrend till it continues to make higher highs and higher lows.

Downtrend (Bearish Trend)

A downtrend occurs when the general direction of the price is down. Downtrend is confirmed when each successive peak is lower than the previous peak, and each successive trough is lower than the previous trough (*see* Figure 16.2). In technical analysis terms, this is known as lower high and lower low. The security will be in a downtrend till it continues to make lower highs and lower lows.

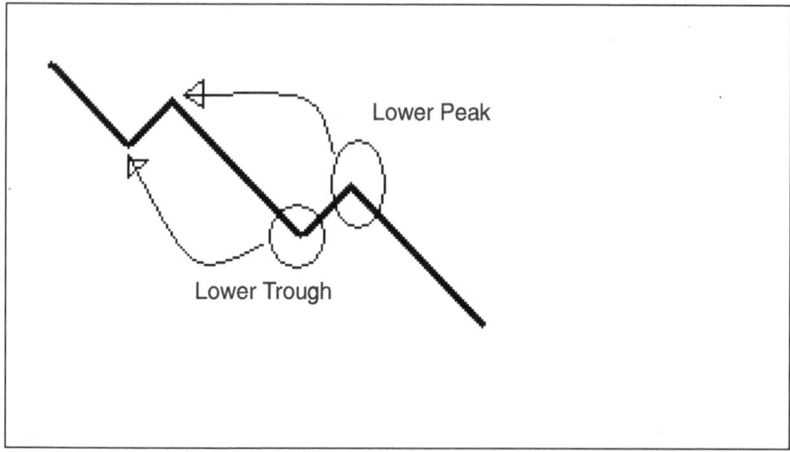

Figure 16.2: **Downtrend**

Sideways Trend

A sideways trend occurs when the price is not able to move in any particular direction, and merely moves up and down in a small range (*see* Figure 16.3). Since there is absence of any trend, this is also known as flat, trendless or non-trending market.

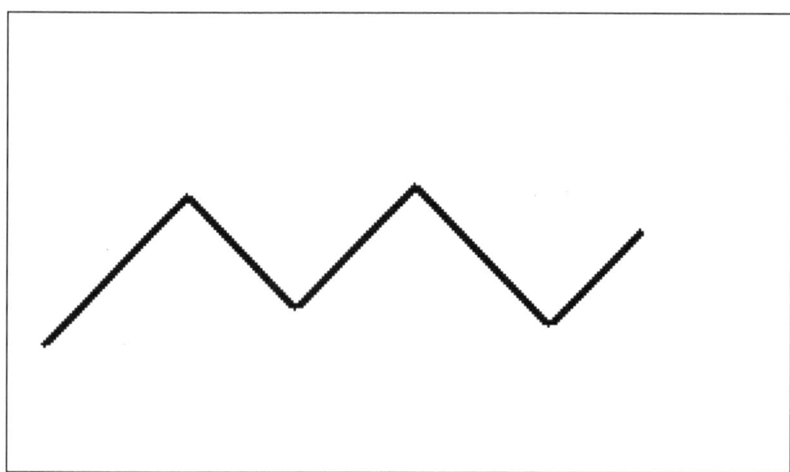

Figure 16.3: **Sideways trend**

Whatever the trend, prices don't move in a straight line. They move in a zigzag manner, sometimes going up and sometimes going down. The direction of the peaks and troughs creates the trend. If there are more buyers, the upside movements will be bigger and more in number, and if there are more sellers, the downside movements will be bigger and more in number.

Correction (Pullback)

Correction, or pullback, is the term used when prices reverse in trending markets and temporarily move against the trend. Correction of the uptrend signifies a phase of declining prices. Correction of the downtrend signifies a phase of rising prices.

Trend Classification

Trends are classified into three broad categories as shown in Figure 16.4:

1. long-term trend,

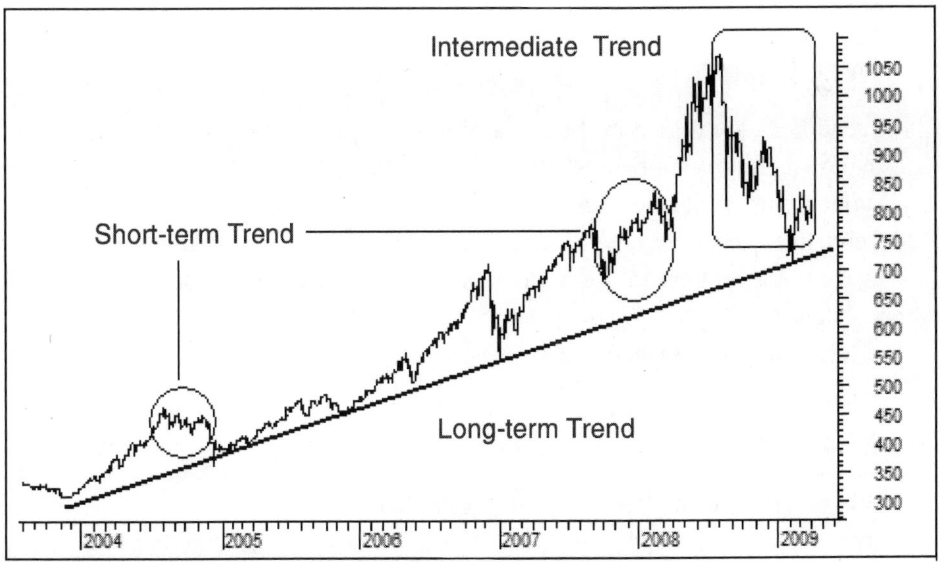

Figure 16.4: **Trend classification**

2. intermediate trend, and
3. short-term trend.

There is no clearly defined period for classifying a trend, but trends that last longer than a year are generally categorized as long-term trends or major trends. Trends that last a few months are generally categorized as intermediate trends, and trends lasting a few weeks are termed as short-term trends.

A long-term trend is composed of several intermediate trends, which often move against the direction of the major trend. If the major trend is upward and there is a downward correction in price movement followed by a continuation of the uptrend, the correction is considered to be an intermediate trend. Within major and intermediate trends, many short-term trends unfold, which can take any direction.

It is important to remember that longer the time the trend continues, the more important it is. For example, an hourly trend is less significant than a daily trend, which again is less significant than a monthly trend.

An hourly trend is best suited for a day trader, but it should be seen in context with a daily trend.

Trend Lines

Trend lines are drawn in the same way as support and resistance lines — by connecting two or more price points. The difference is that while the support and resistance lines are horizontal and depict the price level, trend lines are drawn by connecting successive highs or lows making every point on a trend line a different price level acting as support or as resistance.

There are two types of trend lines.

Uptrend Line

When the price movement results in higher highs and higher lows, it is considered an uptrend. An uptrend line is drawn by connecting two or more of the low points. The second low must be higher than the first low for the trend line to have a positive slope, or in other words, for a trend line to be rising (*see* Figure 16.5).

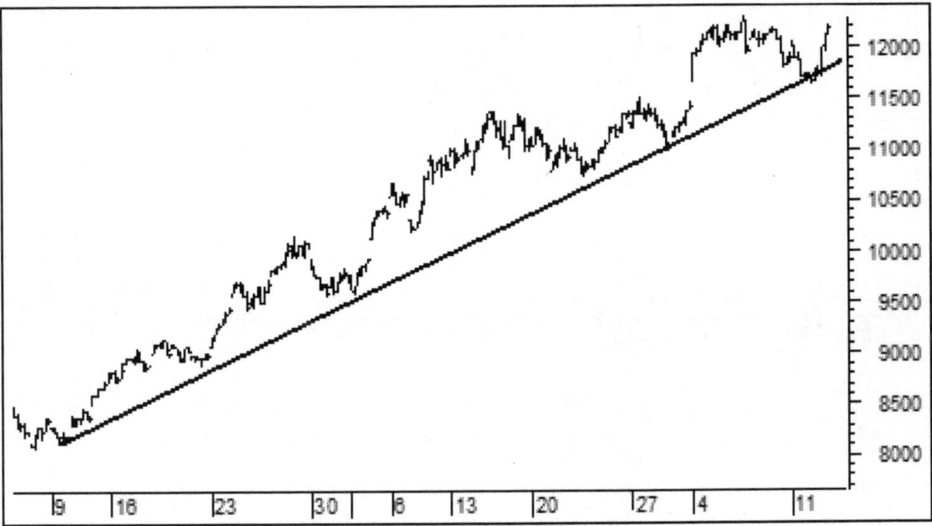

Figure 16.5: **Uptrend line**

An uptrend line acts as a support and indicates that with the passage of time, buyers are ready to buy at higher prices. A rising trend line accompanied by increasing volume indicates a clear bullish sentiment. As long as prices remain above the trend line, the uptrend is considered strong and intact.

Downtrend Line

When the price movement results in lower highs and lower lows, it is considered a downtrend. A downtrend line is drawn by connecting two or

Figure 16.6: **Downtrend line**

more high points. The second high must be lower than the first high for the trend line to have a negative slope, or in other words, for the trend line to be falling (*see* Figure 16.6).

A downtrend line acts as a resistance and indicates that, with the passage of time, sellers are ready to sell at lower prices. A falling trend line accompanied with increasing volume indicates a clearly bearish sentiment. As long as prices remain below the trend line, the downtrend is considered strong and intact.

An uptrend line provides support to prices and a downtrend line offers resistance. This support and resistance is known as trend line support and trend line resistance.

Trend Line Break

If a trend line breaks, it indicates that the trend is weak. Once the trend line is broken, the market may enter a trading range after which the trend may continue. It may also lead to a complete trend reversal.

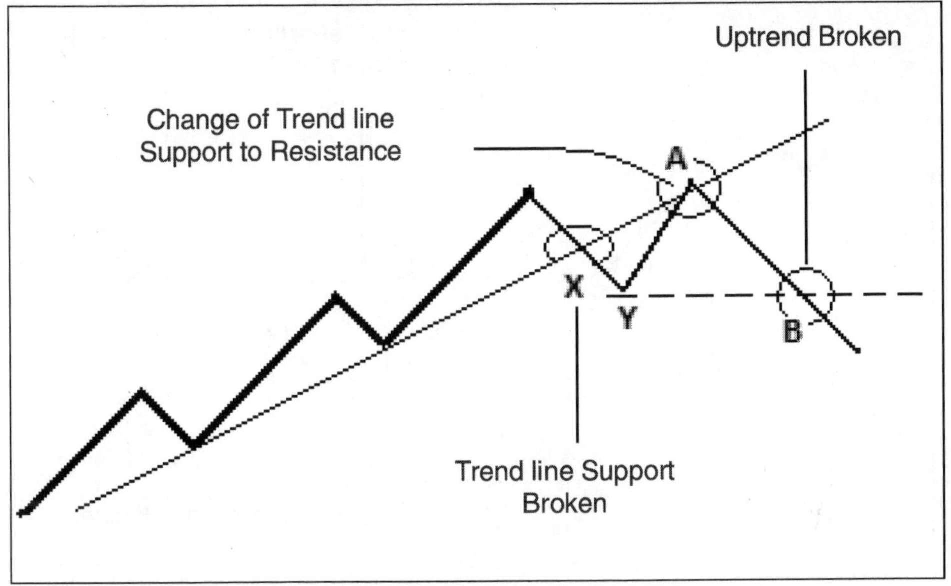

Figure 16.7: **Uptrend line break**

Uptrend Line Break

In Figure 16.7, points X, Y, A and B are crucial price levels. The price falling below X indicates weakness of uptrend as the trend line is broken. After making a low at point Y, the price rises but finds resistance at point A and starts falling again. This is another clear indication of trend weakness. At point B, the price falls below the previous low indicating a change from uptrend to downtrend.

Downtrend Line Break

In Figure 16.8, points X, Y, A and B are crucial price levels. The price rising above X indicates weakness of downtrend as the trend line is broken. After making a high at point Y, the price falls but finds support at point A, and starts rising again. This is another clear indication of trend weakness. At point B, the price rises above the previous high indicating a change from downtrend to uptrend.

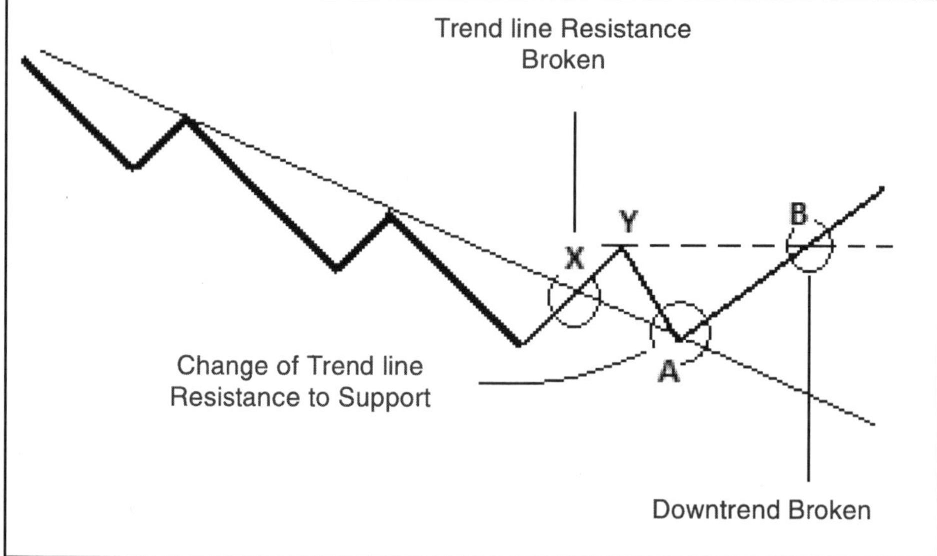

Figure 16.8: **Downtrend line break**

Trend Trading

1. Always trade in the direction of the trend. If it is an uptrend, initiate a buy position at or close to the uptrend line. If it is a downtrend, initiate a sell position at or close to the downtrend line.
2. A breakout of the uptrend line is confirmed only when the price closes below the trend line. A breakout of the downtrend line is confirmed only when the price closes above the trend line. In less active markets, wait for two closes to confirm the breakout. Clear your long positions after the breakout of the uptrend line and short positions after the breakout of the downtrend line.
3. A break of the trend line does not always indicate a change in trend; don't hurry to interpret it as one; instead wait for a confirmation of the change in trend — Prices crossing point B as shown in Figures 16.7 and 16.8.
4. After a major downtrend, there is usually a long duration of sideways or range-bound trading before the start of a new uptrend. However, a change from an uptrend to a downtrend takes much lesser time and the market may not even get to see a sideways trading period.

Trend Channel

Channelling is a very useful trading tool. A channel is made by drawing another line parallel to the trend line, connecting the tops or bottoms (*see* Figure 16.9). In an uptrend, if a parallel line can be drawn at the price tops, the trend channel is the area between the two lines. The second line i.e. the parallel line is called the "return line" because it is from this line that the price is likely to return towards the trend line.

Similarly, in a downtrend, if a parallel line can be drawn at the price bottoms, the trend channel is the area between the two lines.

Trend channels are mostly formed in highly traded securities. Securities with low trading volumes will hardly see any channel formation. It is common for a security to breach the return line momentarily due to momentum in the direction of the trend. In fact, the channel line or return line may never form in many securities due to volatility and market conditions.

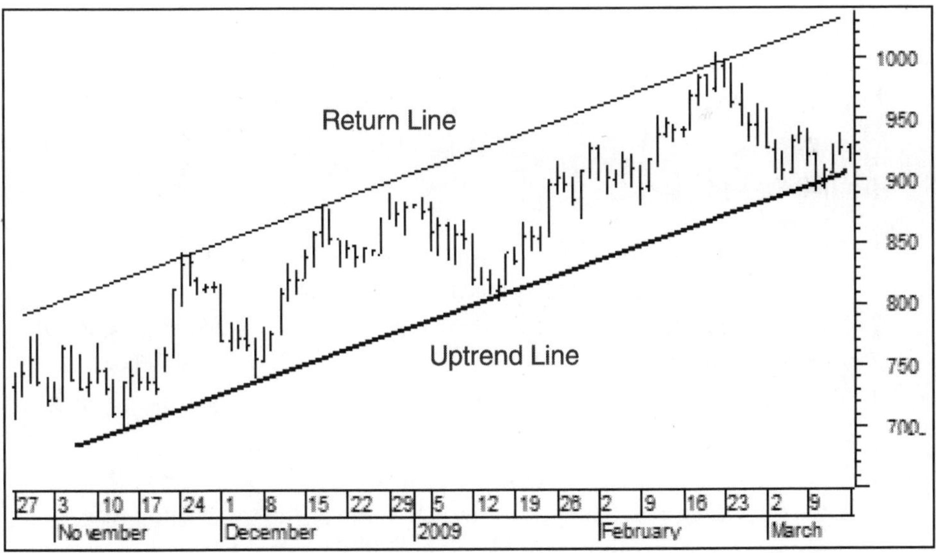

Figure 16.9: **Trend channel**

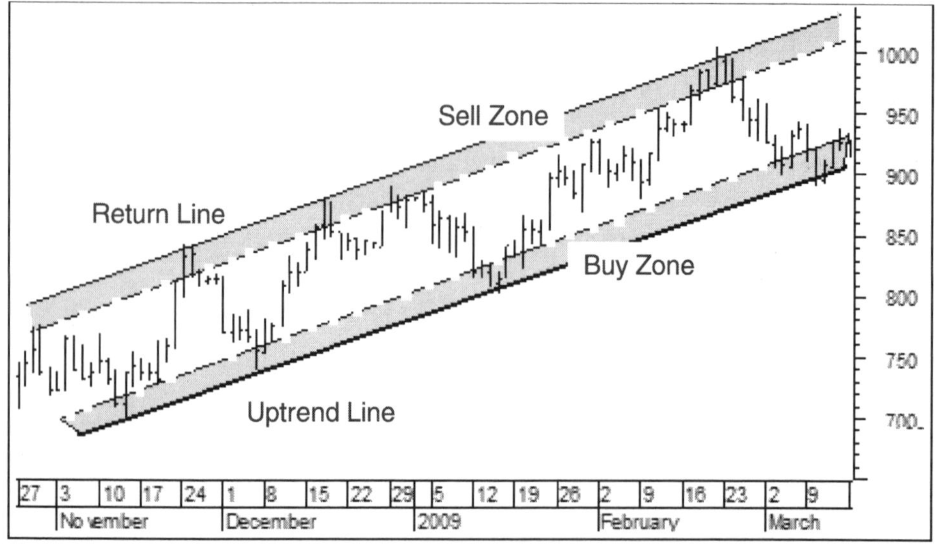

Figure 16.10: **Buy and sell zones in a channel**

Figure 16.10 shows the buy and sell zones in a channel. Even if you are not interested in a channel and are just looking for prices close to the trend line, it is always better to identify the sell zone in an uptrend and buy zone in a downtrend when trading.

Trading Trend Channels

1. Take a new position when the price reaches the trend line, and close the position when the price reaches the return line.
2. If the price fails to reach the trend line, it indicates that the trend is gaining strength.
3. If the price fails to reach the return line, it indicates that the trend is losing strength.
4. If the price crosses the return line with ease and closes there, it indicates a strong trend. The price may not come to the trend line again; in this case, the return line should be considered for making a new entry in the direction of the trend.

Volume

Volume plays an important part in understanding trends, support and resistance. The following are important volume signals that you must watch out for while analyzing trends.

Volume and Price Movement

Trend Confirmation

- Rising prices accompanied by rising volume confirm a strong uptrend.
- Falling prices accompanied by rising volume confirm a strong downtrend.

Trend Weakness

- Rising prices but falling volume indicate weakness of the uptrend.
- Falling prices and falling volume indicate weakness of the downtrend.

Volume, Peaks and Troughs

Trend Confirmation

- Higher peaks accompanied by higher volume at peaks indicates a strong uptrend.
- Lower troughs accompanied by higher volume at troughs indicates a strong downtrend.

Trend Weakness

- Higher peaks associated with lower volume at peaks indicates weakening of uptrend.
- Lower troughs associated with lower volume at troughs indicates weakening of downtrend.

Volume and Accumulation

After a strong downtrend, if prices move in a sideways direction but the volumes start to pick up as time passes, it is an indication of accumulation. This shows that long-term buyers have started accumulating the stocks and it would just be a matter of time before an uptrend starts.

Volume and Distribution

After a strong uptrend, if prices move in a sideways direction but volume starts to pick up, it indicates distribution. Long-term investors have started to sell their holdings and a trend reversal from an uptrend to a downtrend may happen.

Volume and Breakouts

In a non-trending or a range-bound market, volume may indicate the possibility of a breakout:

- Stable prices and higher volume close to resistance indicate an upward breakout.
- Stable prices and higher volume close to support indicates a downward breakout.
- High volume immediately after the breakout indicates a strong breakout.
- Low volume immediately after the breakout indicates a false breakout.

Trend lines and support / resistance should be an essential part of your analysis. These are the simplest, yet most effective of technical analysis tools. In fact, trend lines and support / resistance are perhaps the only technical analysis tools that can, by themselves, be used for trading on their own.

Arithmetic and Semi-Log Scale

The price scale along the Y-axis can be displayed in two ways — arithmetic and semi-logarithmic (semi-log). Most charts are plotted on arithmetic scale, but when you are looking at long-term trends, or when the prices have moved sharply, it is better to use the semi-log scale.

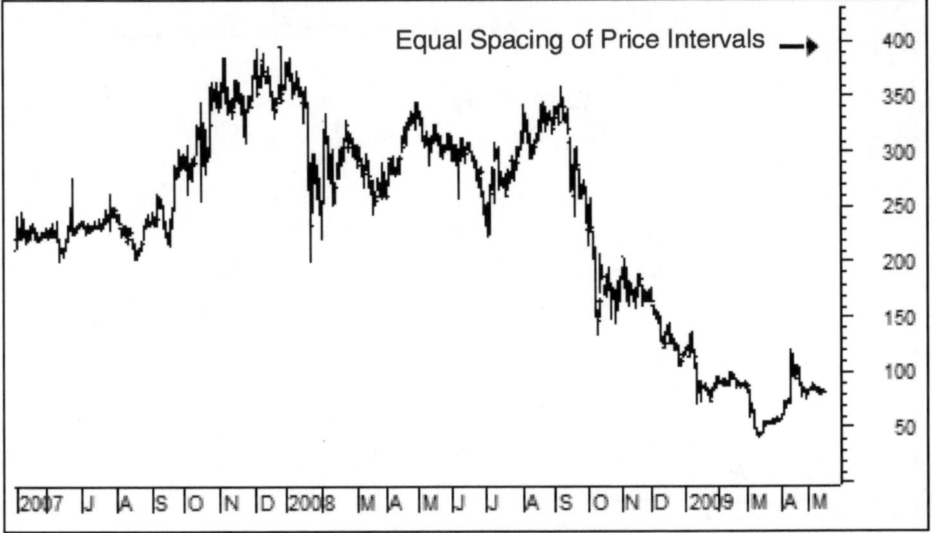

Figure 16.11: **Arithmetic scale**

Arithmetic Scale

A chart based on the arithmetic scale measures the progressions from the lowest price data to the highest in equal increments (*see* Figure 16.11). Therefore, if a chart has ₹ 10 price intervals, then each interval is the same length on the vertical Y-axis. If a security goes from ₹ 10 to ₹ 110, each ₹ 10 will be plotted by equal distance. This gives a wrong picture, as the rise from ₹ 10 to ₹ 20 is 100% whereas the rise from ₹ 100 to ₹ 110 is just 10%.

Figure 16.11 shows the price fall of a stock from 400 to 50 price units in arithmetic scale.

Semi-log Scale

The semi-logarithmic scale is based on percentage price movement and measures the lowest to highest price data points in percentage terms. On a semi-log scale, a rise from ₹ 10 to ₹ 20 would show bigger move than a rise from ₹ 100 to ₹ 110. Hence, a chart based on a semi-log scale

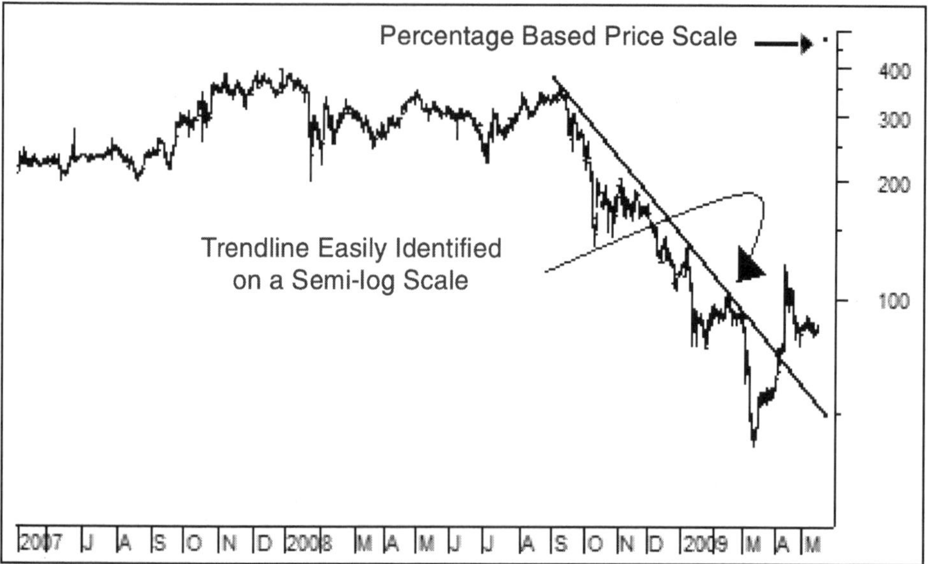

Figure 16.12: **Semi-log scale**

presents price movement more accurately than does a chart based on an arithmetic scale. It can also cover a wider range of prices than a chart of the same size based on the arithmetic scale. Figure 16.12 is same as the previous one but in a semi-log scale.

There is little difference between the two so long the price range displayed in the graph is narrow. Even in a long-term yearly chart, if there isn't much change in the price, it would not matter which scale you are using. However, you should use the semi-log scale to study long-term trends and securities with big price movements in a short time.

Point and Figure Chart (P&F)

There is a special type of charting technique known as point and figure. Until now, you have seen that a chart depicts price movement with the passage of time. In point and figure, the element of time is ignored and only the price movements are plotted. Two variations of the gold chart for the same period are shown in Figure 16.13, a bar chart and point and figure chart.

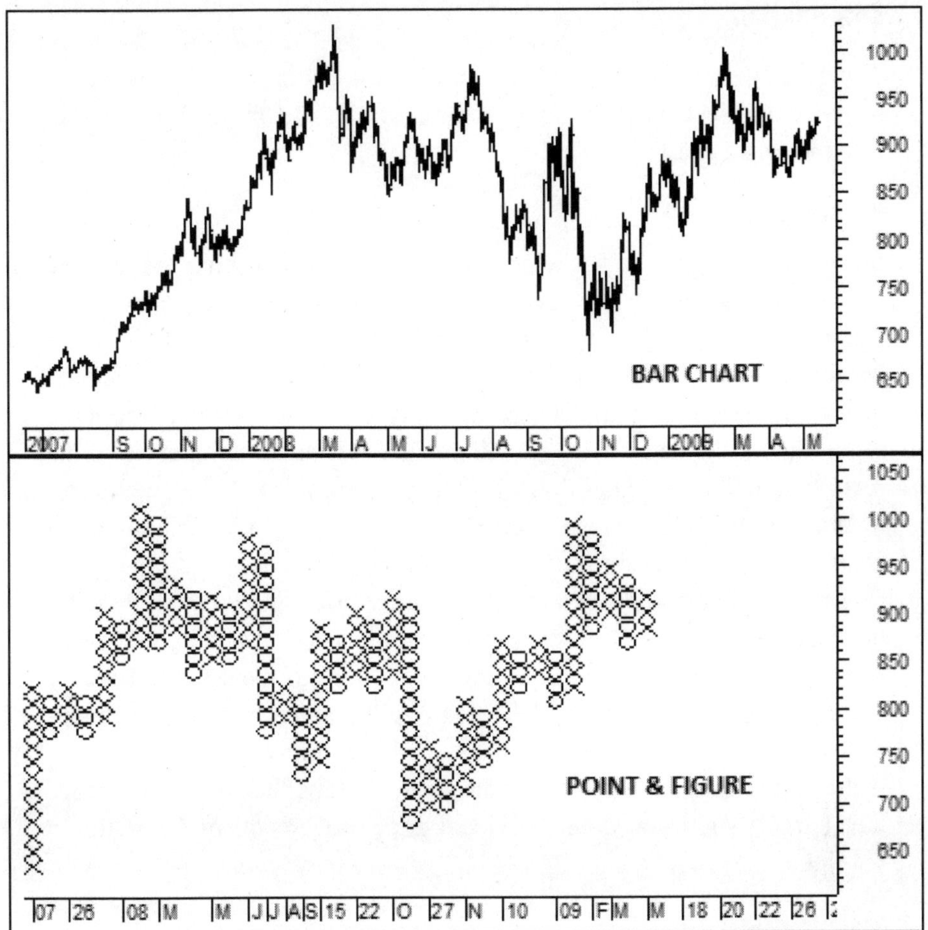

Figure 16.13: **Bar chart and point and figure chart**

Point and figure chart depicts price movement in a unique way. The chart has columns of Xs and Os. The rising prices are depicted by "X" and the falling prices by "O". The columns can only contain either an X or an O, but never both.

The timeline shown in the point and figure chart is just for reference as time is not a part of chart construction as mentioned.

Construction

There are two parameters required for plotting a point and figure chart — box size and reversal size. These parameters will be defined by you before plotting a chart.

Box Size

In a point and figure chart, the price is plotted only after it has moved by a certain amount. Box size is the amount a security's price has to move before an "X" is added on the top of a column, or before an "O" is added below a column. For example, if you are trading on a security with a price of ₹ 100, you can keep a box size of ₹ 1. It means that when a security is rising and moves up by ₹ 1, you will put an X above the column and if the security is falling and goes down by ₹ 1, you will put an O below the column. If the price moves less than ₹ 1, you will not do anything and the chart will remain the same no matter how much time passes.

The box size is dependent on the security price and you can increase or reduce the box size according to your trading. For instance, a box size of ₹ 1 is suitable for security quoting at ₹ 100. So if the security rises by ₹ 4 above the previous high, the column will contain four Xs which signifies four individual price movements of ₹ 1 within a ₹ 4 rise. Similarly, if the security falls by ₹ 4 below the previous low, the column will contain four Os signifying four individual price movements of ₹ 1 within a ₹ 4 fall.

Reversal Amount

What happens when the price reverse and starts to fall after an up move or rise after a down move? As mentioned above, the columns can only contain either Xs or Os. Therefore, the price cannot be plotted in the same column and a new column will be started when the price reverses direction.

The reversal amount is the pre-defined amount the security price must reverse before the commencement of a new column. The reversal amount is usually three times the box size. Therefore, if you are using a ₹ 1 box size, a reversal amount will be ₹ 3. That is, if the security price has been increasing steadily, there would be a column of Xs. The security price

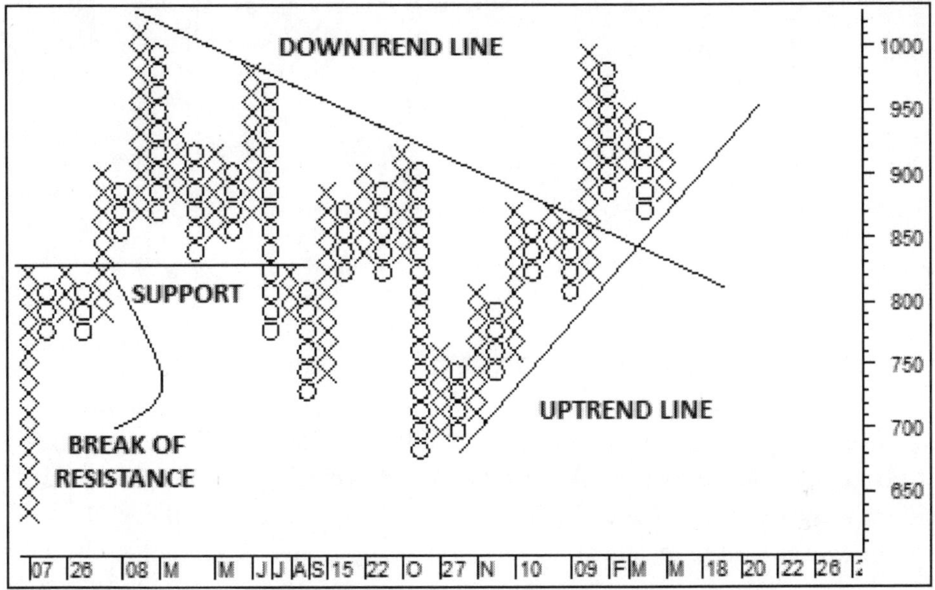

Figure 16.14: **Analysing P&F chart using support / resistance and trend lines**

must drop by ₹ 3 before a new column of Os can be started. If the security price drops less than ₹ 3, the chart will remain the same no matter how much time passes.

With a box size of ₹ 1 and a reversal amount of ₹ 3, the chart will only change when the price moves outside this range of ₹ 4. For example, if the security is rising, a new X will be added each time the security rises by ₹ 1. The new column of Os can only be started if the security falls by ₹ 3. If prices remain within this range, the chart will remain the same no matter how long it takes.

Thus, in point and figure charts, minor price movements are ignored and only the significant price movements are registered. P&F charts are, therefore, ideal for determining the support and resistance levels and identifying trends (*see* Figure 16.14).

A point and figure chart is analyzed in the same way as other charts. The signals from point and figure charts are delayed but it is a better confirmation of trend continuation or reversal. There are other charts like 'Kagi' that are constructed on the same principle. All good charting software have the option to create these charts.

Chapter 17

Dow Theory

MODERN DAY TECHNICAL ANALYSIS HAS ITS FOUNDATION IN THE DOW THEORY, based on stock market study by Charles H. Dow (1851-1902). Much has changed since the time of Charles Dow and there are both supporters and critics of the Dow Theory. However, you should be aware of the principles of Dow Theory, because not only is it the building block of Western style technical analysis, but also because many concepts of the Dow Theory are still being used.

The Dow Theory was derived from a series of editorials written by Charles Dow in *Wall Street Journal* between 1900 until the time of his death in 1902. The Dow Jones Industrial Index and the Dow Jones Rail Index (now Transportation Index) were created by Charles Dow to measure how well the economy was doing, as the indices covered two major sectors — manufacturing and transport. Dow believed that the stock markets were the best place to judge the economy and business environment.

Dow Theory Principles

Markets Discount Everything

All possible information that can affect the stock price is always discounted and reflected in it. Only those events that are impossible to predict or know are not priced. An average investor may not have any access to important information or future projections that may influence the market, but somebody does, and it will be reflected in the price.

The basic premise of technical analysis is study of price, and all other factors such as fundamental, political, macro and micro economic data as well as the risk component of a stock are considered to be incorporated into the price.

Overall Market Moves in Three Trends

Primary Trend

It is the major underlying trend of the market and lasts for a few months to a few years. It is the most important trend as all price movements are affected by the primary trend. Once a primary trend is identified, it will continue until there are confirmed reversal signals. The primary trend could be a primary uptrend or a primary downtrend. Speculators may control prices for some time but a primary trend can never be manipulated for long.

Secondary Trends

These are the corrections to the primary trend and move against it. Within a primary trend, there may be many secondary trends occurring at different intervals of time.

Thus, within a primary uptrend, there will be many short downtrends. Likewise, within a primary downtrend, there will be many short uptrends. Secondary trends are considered a good sign for the progression of a healthy primary trend.

Minor Trends

These are very short-term trends spanning not more than a few days to a couple of weeks. They can move in the direction of primary or secondary trend.

In Dow Theory, the primary trend is considered the most important followed by the secondary trend. Minor trends or daily fluctuations are ignored as they are considered market noise or movements that are haphazard and risky to trade. Primary trends have three phases.

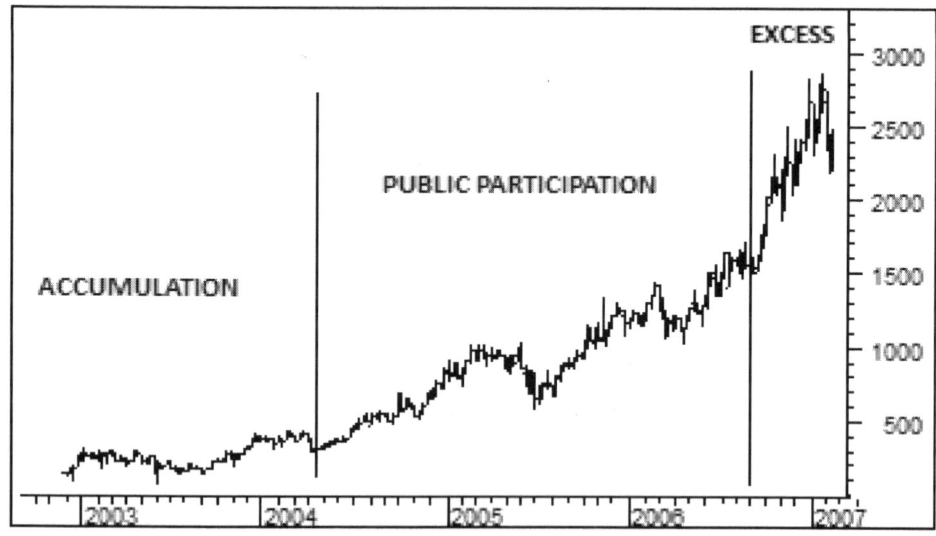

Figure 17.1: **Three phases of the primary uptrend**

Primary Uptrend (Bull Market) — Figure 17.1

Accumulation Phase

This is the first phase of an uptrend where long-term investors start to accumulate stocks. The accumulation phase also marks the end of a downtrend. At this point, there is widespread panic and most investors have given up hope of any sort of uptrend in prices. The news and analysis are negative about the markets but it is also the time when stocks are available at the most attractive prices.

Accumulation phase is difficult to spot and most people will see it as just a pause after which the downtrend will resume. The consolidation of price and increasing volume on up ticks are some of the important clues to the beginning of an accumulation phase.

Public Participation Phase

As the consolidation phase extends, the fear of prices moving down subsides and the market starts to move up. The business condition improves and higher earnings are reported by corporate. This attracts more investors and a clear uptrend in prices is visible. At this point, the general public starts to invest.

This is usually the longest phase and constitutes broad based participation from across the investor community. Technical analysts initiate long positions as an uptrend is confirmed.

Excess Phase

This is the last phase of a bull market primary trend. By this time, the bear market is long forgotten and the market is just seen as going up. There is widespread euphoria and any words of caution are ridiculed. New investors, who are mesmerized by the returns, enter in large numbers. Everyone from the public to analysts see higher levels ahead.

This is the time when stocks become overvalued and judicious investors who had entered in the accumulation phase start to sell their holdings.

Primary Downtrend (Bear Market)

The Distribution Phase

This phase marks the beginning of a downtrend. The market views are still positive and a general sentiment of optimism prevails. However, the signs of market topping out start to appear. It also marks the end of the excess phase where the long-term investors had started to liquidate their portfolio. As the market declines, it is seen as an opportunity to buy stocks.

Public Participation Phase

As prices start to drift lower, the public realizes that the uptrend has been stalled and euphoria is replaced by caution. The business environment deteriorates and lower earnings are reported. The prices fall further and people start to participate in the downward move.

The Panic Phase

This is the last phase of the primary bear market and is characterized by panic and despair. The sentiments turn completely negative and large sell-offs are common. The companies are downgraded, earnings estimates lowered and everyone sees much lower levels of the market.

In this phase, investors who had bought in excess phase of the bull market start to sell in panic, and judicious investors start to accumulate stocks.

Indices Must Confirm Each Other

According to the Dow Theory, a primary uptrend or a downtrend cannot be in place until both the industrial average and the transport average move in tandem. For an uptrend to be confirmed, both the indices must be in uptrend, and for a downtrend to be confirmed, both the indices must be in downtrend. The reason is that if major sectors of the economy are not in agreement, a trend cannot be forecasted.

Trends are confirmed by Volume

A trend should be supported by volume. In an uptrend, volume must increase as the price rises, and reduce as the price falls. In a downtrend, volume must increase as price falls, and decrease as price rises. Any change in volume pattern is an indication of trend weakness.

Primary Trend Will Continue Until a Confirmed Reversal

The Dow Theory states that though the market may move anywhere in the short duration, it will finally resume in the direction of the primary trend. Trading in the direction of the trend is the crux of the Dow Theory. Trend can only be deemed to have ended when there are definitive signals such as lower lows and lower highs after uptrend or higher highs, and higher lows after downtrend.

The following three assumptions upon which technical analysis is based are the outcome of the Dow Theory:

1. Markets discount everything.
2. Price moves in trends.
3. History repeats itself — Investors' reaction remains almost the same towards price fluctuations, moving between euphoria and hope to panic and despair. The psychological factors are crucial as a similar situation that happened in the past will tend to activate a similar reaction. The outcome is a repetitive nature of price movements, which sometimes form clear patterns that can be analyzed and traded.

Chapter 18

Candlestick Study

A CANDLESTICK IS MORE VISUALLY INFORMATIVE THAN A BAR, even though both show the open, high, low and close of a security for a certain period. The body of the candlestick depicts the relationship between open and close prices, and the analysis is mostly based on the shape of the body.

The bars, on the other hand, give equal importance to high and low prices. These high and low prices most often represent market noise and do not hold much significance. The advantage of candlesticks is that they visually indicate the importance of open and close prices compared to the high and low.

Candlesticks make it easy to read price action and allow traders to understand market sentiment within seconds. Candlesticks are perhaps the quickest way to identify different types of price action, and this makes them an integral analysis tool for day traders.

Candlesticks help in one of the most difficult aspects of trading to predict clear swing points. When combined with other technical analysis tools, they provide a high level of accuracy in entry and exit levels.

Do not confuse continuation and reversal patterns in candlesticks to look for trend continuation or reversal. Candlesticks are short-term indicators used mostly for intraday or swing trading. Of course, candlesticks will be the first to indicate a possible change in trend if they occur at important trendline support and resistance levels.

A candlestick gives you insight into investors psychology and indicates whether a pattern foretells a bullish or bearish move. However, it is preferable to use candlesticks in combination with other tools.

Shapes of Candlesticks

Candlesticks can take different shapes depending on the price movement. A candle with a long body indicates strong buying or selling activity. The volume in a long bodied candle is usually high. A short candle indicates subdued trading activity with not much change in price movement. The volume is usually quite low in a short candle (*see* Figure 18.1).

A long white candle indicates strong buying pressure while a long black candle indicates strong selling pressure. Whenever a long white candle is formed after a period of continuous price declines, it indicates a support area from where the prices are likely to rise. You can enter with a buy position keeping the low or open price as the stop loss point. Whenever a long black candle is formed after a period of continuous price rise, it indicates a resistance area from where prices are likely to start falling. You can initiate a sell position keeping the high or open as the stop loss point. When a long candle, bullish or bearish, is formed after a congested price range, it indicates the breakout of price from a trading range. You can enter in the direction of the candle. However, a long bullish candle after a strong uptrend, and a long bearish candle after a strong downtrend should not be traded. These may indicate a heightened

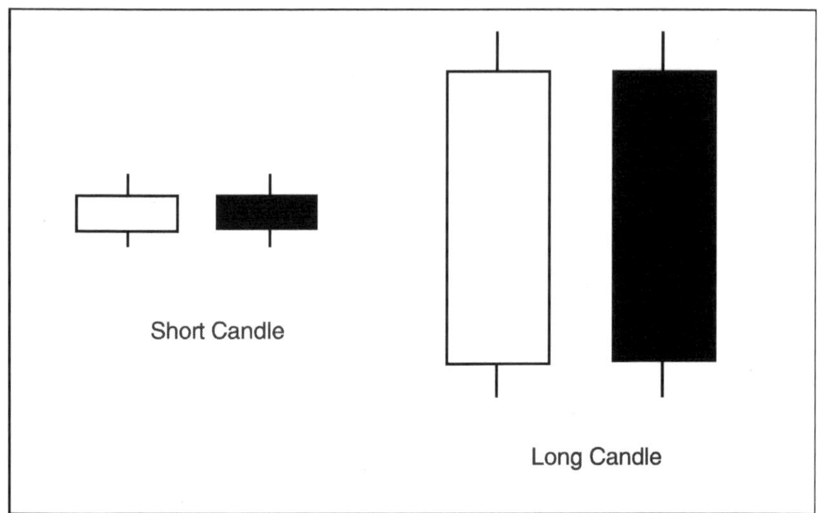

Figure 18.1: **Shapes of candlesticks**

optimism or panic state before the trend changes. Wait for the market to settle down before taking an entry.

Wicks

Wicks of a candle provide important insights into trading activity. A candle may have long wicks with small body or it may have no wicks at all (*see* Figure 18.2).

A candle with long wicks and small body indicates that the trading was active but finally no real consensus was built. A long upper wick indicates that buyers did try to control the market but were unsuccessful in keeping the prices higher. A long lower wick indicates that the sellers tried to control the market but were unsuccessful. If a candle with a long upper wick is formed after a downward movement, you should be alert as it is a sign of buyers returning to the market and it could be a reversal point. In the same way, if a candle with a long lower wick is formed after an upward movement, it signals increasing selling activity and the prices may fall.

A candle without any wicks is known as Marubozu. Neither the upper nor the lower wick is formed. Marubozu represents a very strong price movement. A white Marubozu indicates that buyers dominated the trading session from the beginning and the sellers were almost absent. A

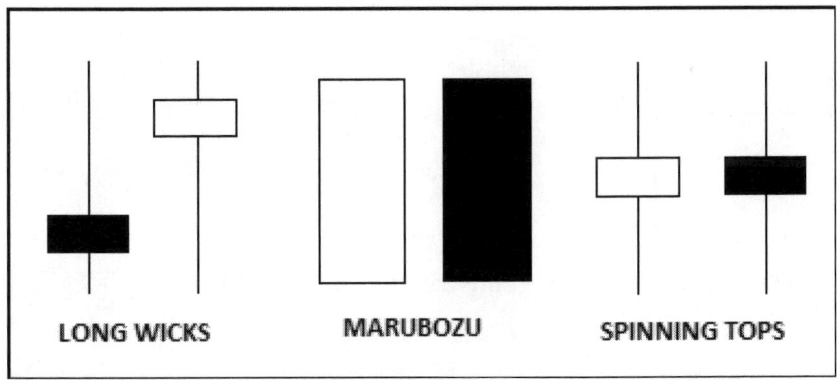

Figure 18.2: **Wicks of a candle**

black Marubozu indicates that sellers dominated the trading session from the beginning and the buyers were almost absent.

Candles with long upper and lower wick, and a small body in the middle, are known as spinning tops. These candles indicate indecision in the market as both bulls and bears were equally active.

Doji

A Doji is formed when the open and close prices are equal. The upper and lower wicks may be of any length but the body is virtually non-existent — *see* Figure 18.3. Dojis provide crucial information about market sentiments on their own and are also a part of many important candlestick patterns. Although the ideal Doji should have the same open and close prices, those candlesticks are also considered Dojis that have a negligible difference in open and close prices.

Dojis are clear indication of market indecision and can be a helpful tool when trying to find the tops and bottoms of a security. Neither the bulls nor the bears are convinced enough to push the market in their direction. In a non-trending market when the volatility is very low, the Doji are of no special use and will be formed frequently. However, their relevance is greatest when they are formed after a sustained up or downtrend. If a Doji is formed after an uptrend or a long bullish candle, it indicates a weakening of buying pressure. Likewise, a Doji after a

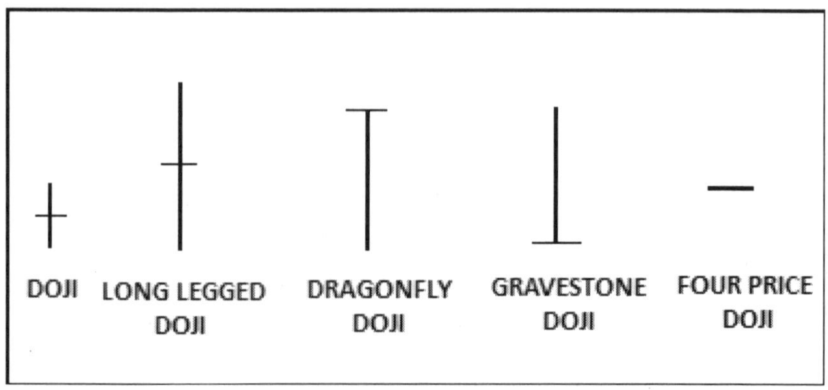

Figure 18.3: **Dojis**

downtrend or a long black candle indicates a weakening of selling pressure. Trading on Doji formation should be done after confirming with other technical tools. For example, the formation of a Doji around a strong support or resistance is a good entry point but if no other technical tool is giving a clear direction, then you should wait for new candles to be formed before taking an entry.

There are four major kinds of Doji:

1. **Regular Doji:** A regular Doji has small upper and lower wicks and is usually formed in a lacklustre trading market when most of the traders are out of the market. It is a very small candle with the same open and close prices indicating the absence of strong market participation. You should be careful when a regular Doji is formed after a strong trend as it may also indicate a pause before the ongoing trend resumes. It is, therefore, wise to trade only after there is some sort of confirmation of trend reversal or continuation.
2. **Long-legged Doji:** Long-legged Doji has long upper and lower wicks that are almost equal in length. It indicates that the prices had a much higher swing and traded well above and below the opening price but in general, nothing much happened. Long-legged Doji shows a bigger struggle between the bulls and bears. The higher market participation is a sign that the market will not stay in a trading range for long, and is bound to take some direction soon.
3. **Gravestone Doji:** Gravestone Doji forms when the open, low and close prices are the same, but the high is too far off creating a long upper wick. A Gravestone Doji indicates that while buyers dominated the trading session and pushed prices higher, but by the end of the session, sellers resurfaced and brought the prices back to the opening level, i.e. the session low.

   Gravestone Doji is a bearish reversal pattern when it comes after an uptrend. During the session, the market opens and starts to rally continuing the previous bull run. However, after making a high, the market starts to fall. By the end of the session, the prices fall to the low and close there. This is an indicator that the bulls are losing strength and the bears are taking control.
4. **Dragonfly Doji:** Dragonfly Doji forms when the open, high and close prices are the same, and the low is far off, creating a long lower wick.

A Dragonfly Doji indicates that sellers dominated the trading session and pushed the prices lower, but by the end of the session buyers resurfaced and brought the prices back to the opening level, i.e. the session high.

Dragonfly Doji is a bullish reversal pattern when it occurs after a downtrend. During the session, the market opens and starts to fall continuing the previous bear run. However, after making a low, the market starts to rise. By the end of the session, the market finishes flat on the high of the session. This is an indication that the bears are losing strength and the bulls are taking control.

Apart from these, there is another kind of Doji, named four-priced Doji. It is a rare formation and is usually formed in markets that have price limits or circuits. The price may open on the limit level and trade there the whole day creating a four-priced Doji.

You should not use a Doji as a stand-alone buy or sell signal except in the case of dragonfly or a gravestone Doji. It should be used as a supporting tool to other indicators.

Patterns

There are many pattern formations, both reversal and continuation, consisting of one, two or more candles. The following section contains an explanation of only those patterns that have high reliability. As mentioned earlier, the candlestick reversal or continuation patterns should not be taken to mean trend reversal or continuation. Candlestick patterns help you to identify a top, a bottom or a pause in price movement, but they must be supported by other technical tools for confirming overall trend reversal or continuation.

Reversal Patterns

One Candle Patterns

One-candle patterns are not so reliable to trade on their own and should be considered as a supporting tool to other technical indicators.

1. Hammer

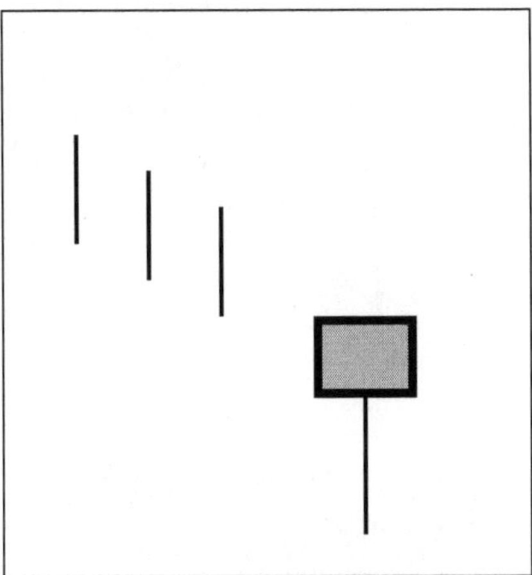

Figure 18.4: **Hammer (Bullish)**

- **Identification:** It consists of a small real body at the upper end of a trading range with a long lower wick. There is no upper wick and the colour of the body does not matter, but the pattern is slightly more reliable if the real body is white. The longer the lower wick, the more bullish is the pattern (Figure 18.4).
- **Trading:** Hammer indicates a possibility of reversal due to increased buying activity after a downtrend or within a retracement of an uptrend. A buy can be initiated keeping the low as stop loss. The buy signal is confirmed if a strong white candle with increased volume follows the pattern.

2. Shooting Star

- **Identification:** It consists of a small real body at the lower end of the trading range with a long upper wick. There is no lower wick and the colour of the body does not matter, but the pattern is slightly more

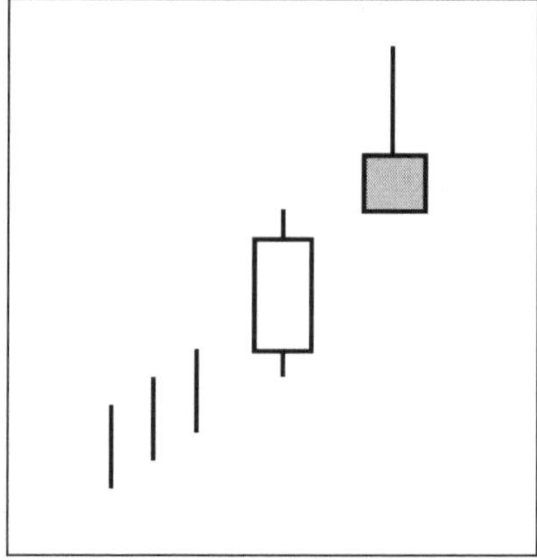

Figure 18.5: **Shooting Star (Bearish)**

reliable if the real body is black. The longer the upper wick, the more bearish the pattern (Figure 18.5).

- **Trading:** A shooting star indicates the possibility of a reversal due to increased selling activity after an uptrend or within a retracement of a downtrend. A sell can be initiated keeping the high as the stop loss point. The sell signal is confirmed if a black candle with increased volume follows the pattern.

Two Candle Patterns

1. Bullish Engulfing

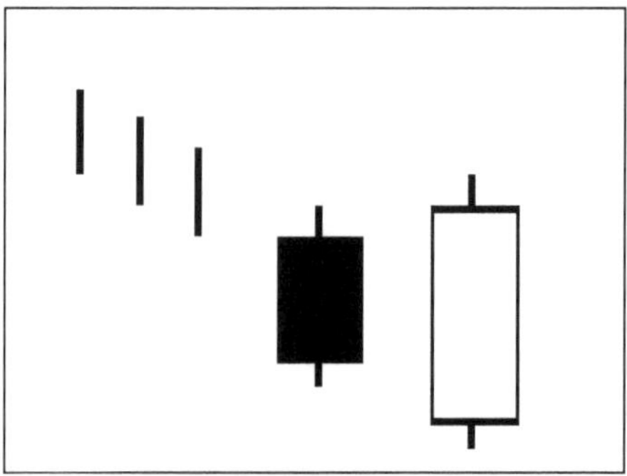

Figure 18.6: **Engulfing (Bullish)**

- **Identification:** It consists of two candles. The first candle is black which signifies continuation of the previous downtrend. The second candle opens with a gap down, but prices rally and close above the first candle's open, making it a bullish candle that completely engulfs the body of the first candle (Figure 18.6).
- **Trading:** Bullish engulfing is quite common but constitutes a strong pattern if it occurs after a downtrend and is in the oversold zone. Initiate a buy position. Look for volumes to confirm the signal.

2. Bearish Engulfing

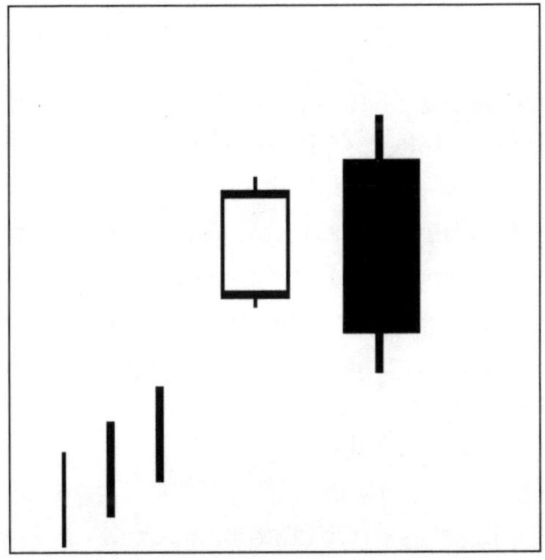

Figure 18.7: **Engulfing (Bearish)**

- **Identification:** It consists of two candles. The first candle is bullish which signifies the continuation of the previous uptrend. The second candle opens with a gap up, but the market falls and it closes below the first candle's open, making it a long black candle that completely engulfs the body of the first candle (Figure 18.7).
- **Trading:** Just like bullish engulfing, bearish engulfing too is quite common, but constitutes a strong pattern if it occurs after an uptrend and is in the overbought zone. Initiate a sell position. Look for volume to confirm the signal.

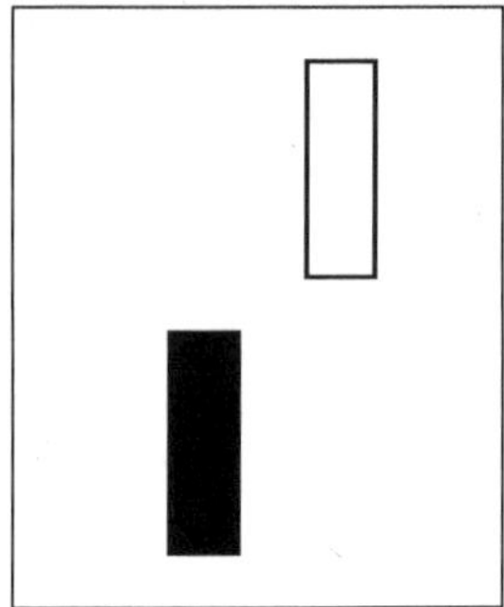

Figure 18.8: **Bullish Kicking**

3. Bullish Kicking

- **Identification:** It consists of two Marubozu candles. The first is a black Marubozu, which is followed by a white Marubozu that opens with a gap up (Figure 18.8).
- **Trading:** Bullish kicking is a very strong pattern. The fact that the security has gapped up and rallied to close at its high is a strong bullish signal regardless of the previous trend. Initiate a buy position keeping the high of the black candle as a stop loss point. Use volume on the white candle to confirm the signal.

4. Bearish Kicking

- **Identification:** It consists of two Marubozu candles. The first is a white Marubozu, which is followed by a black Marubozu that opens with a gap down (Figure 18.9).

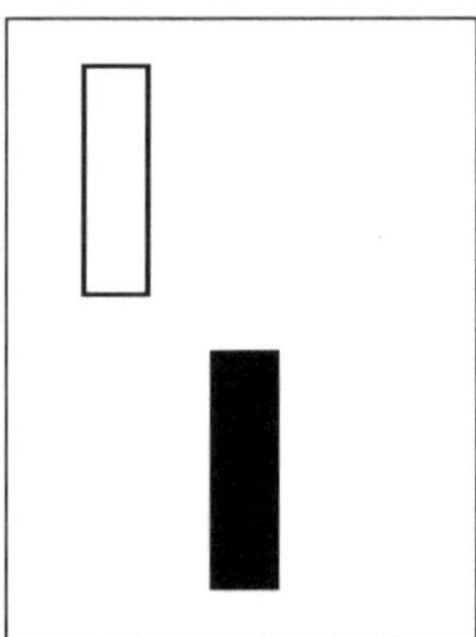

Figure 18.9: **Bearish Kicking**

- **Trading:** Bearish kicking is a very strong pattern. The fact that the security has gapped down and crashed to close at its low is a strong bearish signal regardless of the previous trend. Initiate a sell position keeping the low of the white candle as a stop loss point. Use volume on the black candle to confirm the signal.

5. Piercing Line

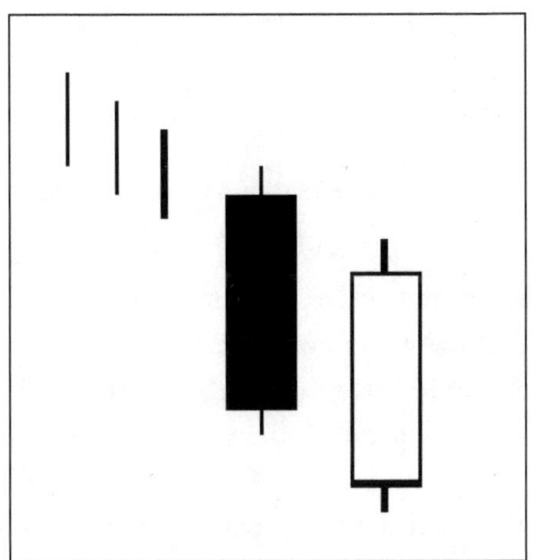

Figure 18.10: **Piercing Line (Bullish)**

- **Identification:** It consists of two candles. The first candle is black, which signifies continuation of the previous downtrend. The second candle opens with a gap down but prices rally and close above the midpoint but within the range of the previous black candle's body (Figure 18.10).
- **Trading:** The piercing line is a reliable reversal pattern as it indicates more actual buying rather than a sudden profit booking or optimism like in a bullish engulfing move. The pattern is stronger if the gap down occurs at support and the white candle is accompanied by a surge in volume. Initiate buy positions.

6. Dark Cloud Cover

- **Identification:** It consists of two candles. The first candle is white which signifies continuation of the previous uptrend. The second candle

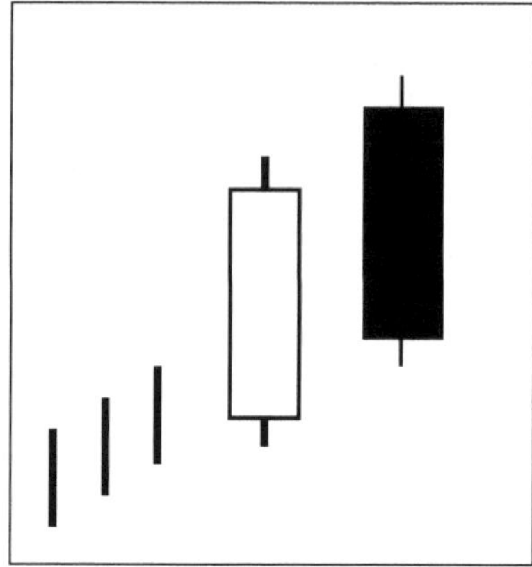

Figure 18.11: **Dark Cloud Cover (Bearish)**

opens with a gap up but prices fall and close below the midpoint, but within the range of the previous white candle's body (Figure 18.11).

- **Trading:** The dark cloud cover is a reliable reversal pattern as it indicates more actual selling rather than a sudden profit booking or panic like in a bearish engulfing move. The pattern is stronger if the gap up occurs at resistance and the black candle is accompanied by a surge in volume. Initiate sell positions.

6. Harami

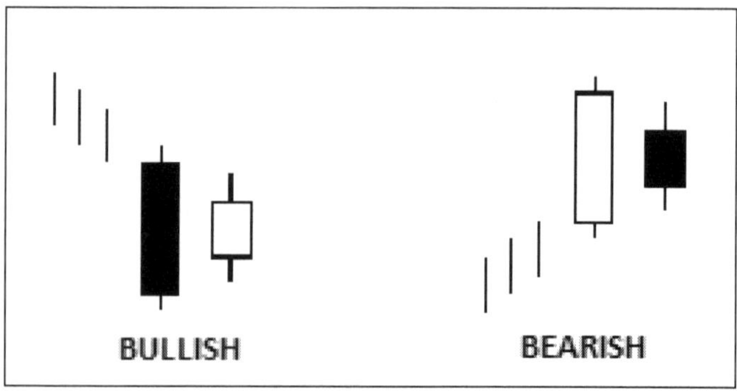

Figure 18.12: **Harami**

- **Identification:** Harami is a two-candle pattern and can be considered an opposite of engulfing. The first candle is long and the second candle has a small body that is completely contained within the range of the previous candle's body. The second candle is opposite in colour to the first candle (Figure 18.12).
- **Trading:** Harami pattern has low reliability and indicates indecision. Watch the market if it occurs after a sustained uptrend or downtrend as this might be an indication of the trend losing strength. The candles that follow the pattern will confirm the direction of the market.

Three Candle Patterns

1. Bullish Abandoned Baby

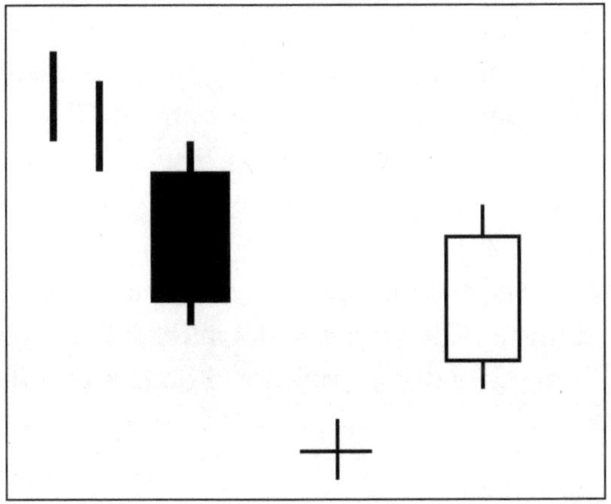

Figure 18.19: **Abandoned Baby (Bullish)**

- **Identification:** It consists of three candles. The first candle is black, signifying the continuation of the previous downtrend. The second candle is a regular Doji that forms with a gap down. The third candle is white that forms with a gap up. The wicks of two adjacent candles do not overlap (Figure 18.19).
- **Trading:** This pattern is rare but strong. Go long keeping the low of the third candle as a stop loss. You can also buy call options or sell puts.

2. Bearish Abandoned Baby

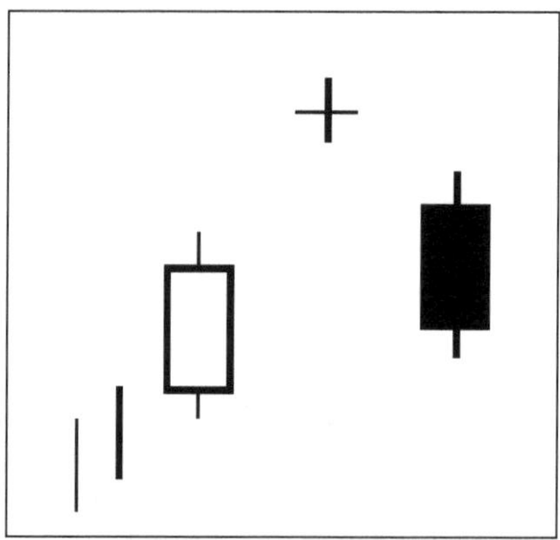

Figure 18.20: **Abandoned Baby (Bearish)**

- **Identification:** It consists of three candles. The first candle is white signifying the continuation of the previous uptrend. The second candle is a regular Doji that forms with a gap up. The third candle is black that forms with a gap down. The wicks of two adjacent candles do not overlap (Figure 18.20).
- **Trading:** This pattern is rare but strong. When it occurs after an uptrend, or in retracement during a downtrend, go short keeping the high of the third candle as a stop loss. You can also buy put options and sell calls.

3. Morning Doji Star

- **Identification:** It consists of three candles. The first candle is black signifying the continuation of the previous downtrend. The second candle is a regular Doji that forms with a gap down. The third candle is white that forms with a gap up and closes in the top half of the first candle. The wicks of two adjacent candles overlap (Figure 18.21).
- **Trading:** This pattern is rare but strong. When it occurs after a downtrend, or in pull back during an uptrend, go long keeping the low of the third candle as a stop loss. You can also buy call options or sell puts.

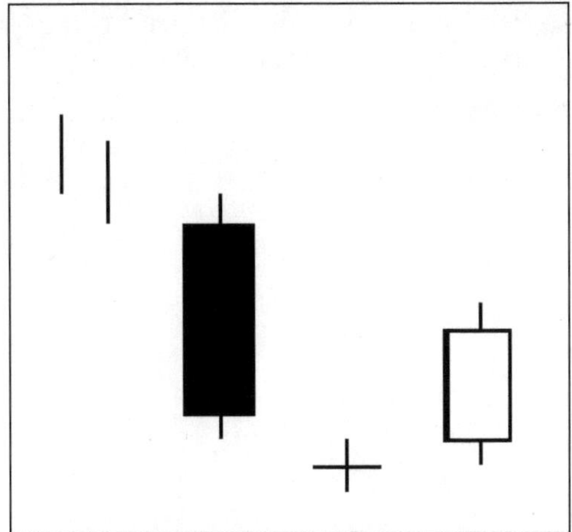

Figure 18.21: **Morning Doji Star (Bullish)**

4. Evening Doji Star

- **Identification:** It consists of three candles. The first candle is white signifying the continuation of the previous uptrend. The second candle is a regular Doji that forms with a gap up. The third candle is black that forms with a gap down and closes in the bottom half of the first candle. The wicks of two adjacent candles do overlap (Figure 18.22).

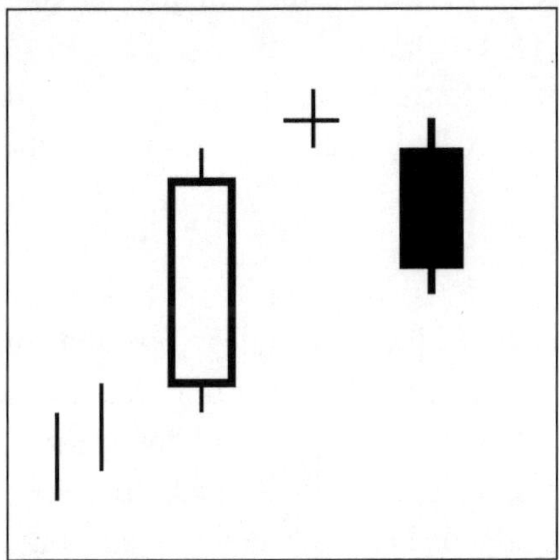

Figure 18.22: **Evening Doji Star (Bearish)**

- **Trading:** This pattern is rare but strong. When it occurs after an uptrend, or in retracement during a downtrend, go short keeping the high of the third candle as a stop loss. You can also buy put options or sell calls.

5. Morning Star

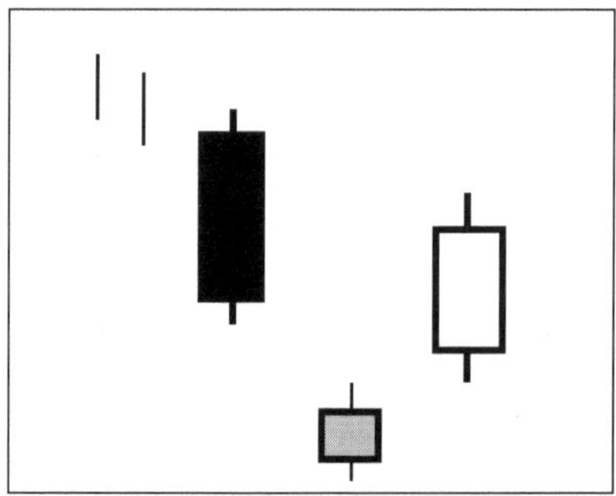

Figure 18.23: **Morning Star (Bullish)**

- **Identification:** It consists of three candles. The first candle is black signifying the continuation of the previous downtrend. The second candle has a small body that forms with a gap down. The third candle is white that forms with a gap up and closes in the top half of the first candle. The colour of the second candle is not important (Figure 18.23).
- **Trading:** When this pattern occurs after a downtrend, or in a pull back during an uptrend, go long keeping the low of the third candle as a stop loss.

6. Evening Star

- **Identification:** It consists of three candles. The first candle is white signifying the continuation of the previous uptrend. The second candle has a small body that forms with a gap up. The third candle is black that forms with a gap down and closes in the bottom half of the first candle. The wicks of two adjacent candles may overlap (Figure 18.24).
- **Trading:** When this pattern occurs after an uptrend, or in retracement during a downtrend, go short with the high of the third candle as a stop loss.

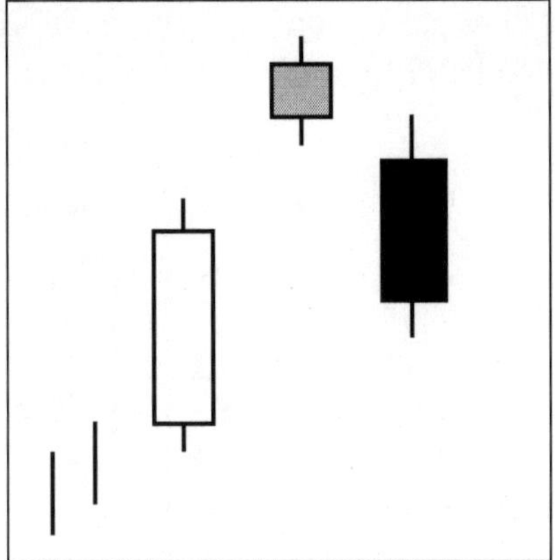

Figure 18.24: **Evening Star (Bearish)**

7. Three Black Crows

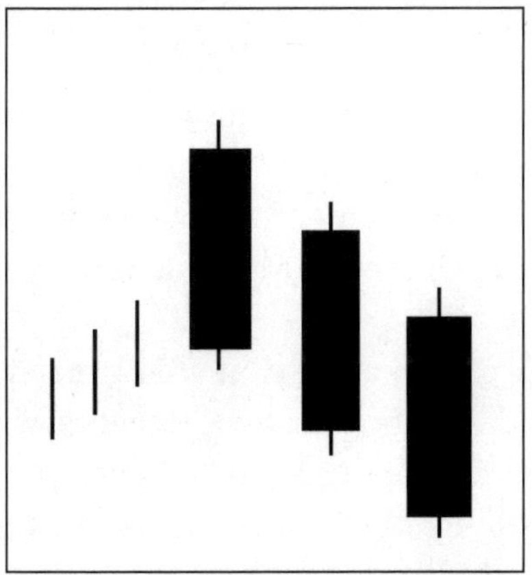

Figure 18.25: **Three Black Crows (Bearish)**

- **Identification:** It consists of three long black candles with small upper and lower wicks. The first candle is followed by a second black candle that opens within the body of the first candle and closes below the close of the first candle. The third candle forms in the same way (Figure 18.25).
- **Trading:** When this pattern appears in an uptrend or within a retracement of a downtrend, it indicates strong chances of reversal. Go short

in the security or buy put options and sell calls. If volume accompanies the move, the reliability of the pattern increases significantly.

8. Three White Soldiers

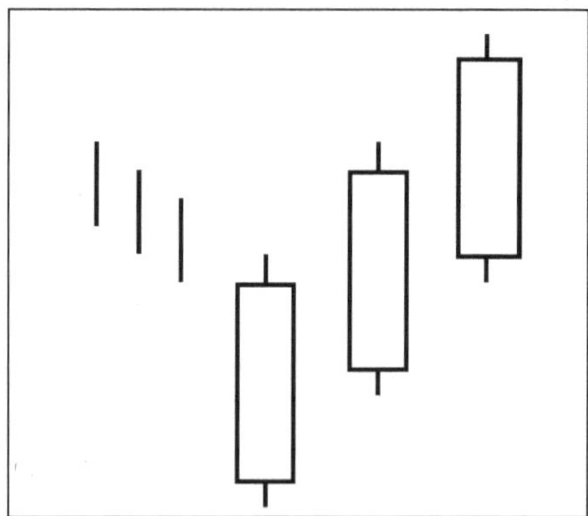

Figure 18.26: **Three White Soldiers (Bullish)**

- **Identification:** It consists of three long white candles with small upper and lower wicks. The first candle is followed by a second white candle that opens within the body of the first candle and closes above the close of the first candle. The third candle forms in the same way (Figure 18.26).
- **Trading:** When this pattern appears in a downtrend or within a retracement of an uptrend, it indicates strong chances of reversal. Go long in the security or buy call options and sell puts. If volume accompanies the move, the reliability of the pattern increases significantly.

Multiple Candle Patterns

The combination of multiple white and black bodied candles sometimes develops into strong patterns that are obvious only to the candlestick investor.

Two such patterns are Dumpling Top and Fry-Pan Bottom. These two patterns take time to develop and provide insights to a reversal that can be used by long-term investors.

1. Dumpling Top

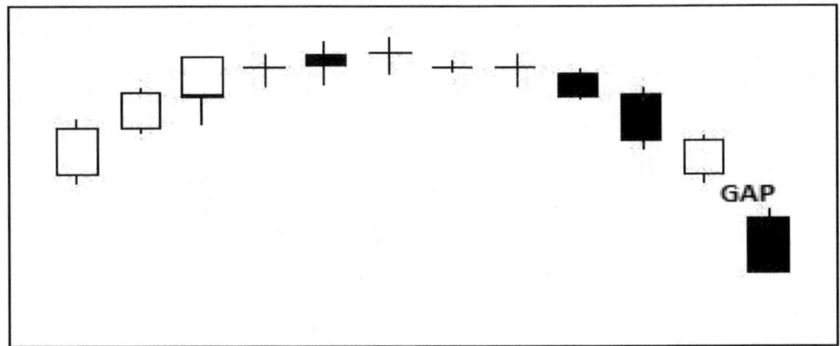

Figure 18.27: **Dumpling Top**

- **Identification:** The dumpling top consists of multiple candles with small real bodies that form after an uptrend. It makes a top that seems rounded in shape and is confirmed after gap down formation of a candle (Figure 18.27).
- **Trading:** Dumpling top gives clear signs of trend reversal. You can go short after the gap down formation of a candle, keeping the low of previous candle as the stop loss point. The signal is strong if the gap down occurs at the support. You can also buy put options and sell calls. The sudden rise in volume during the formation of the candle after the gap enhances the reliability of the pattern.

2. Fry-Pan Bottom

- **Identification:** The Fry-pan Bottom consists of multiple candles with small real bodies that form after a downtrend. It makes a bottom that seems rounded in shape and is confirmed after a gap up formation of a candle (Figure 18.28).
- **Trading:** Fry-pan Bottom gives clear signs of trend reversal. You can go long after the gap up formation of a candle keeping the high of the previous candle as the stop loss point. The signal is strong if the gap up occurs at resistance. You can also buy call options and sell puts. The sudden rise in volume during the formation of the candle after the gap enhances the reliability of the pattern.

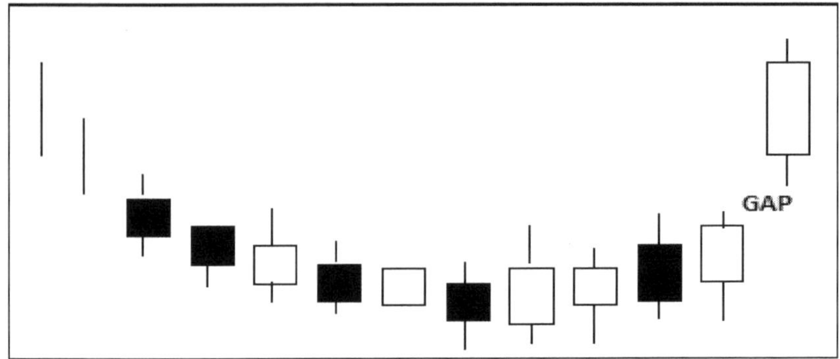

Figure 18.28: **Fry-pan Bottom**

Continuation Patterns

1. Rising Three (Bullish)

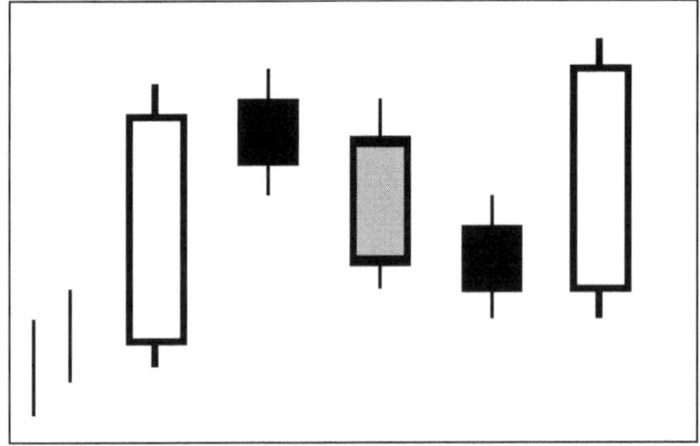

Figure 18.29: **Rising Three (Bullish)**

- **Identification:** This pattern consists of five candles. The first one is a long white candle signifying the continuation of the previous uptrend. It is followed by three relatively small candles with low volumes that move against the overall trend but stay within the range of the first candle. The fifth candle is white that closes above the close of the first candle and continues the uptrend (Figure 18.29).
- **Trading:** This is a very strong continuation pattern and a brief pullback is nothing more than a consolidation of the uptrend. Initiate buy positions in the security or buy call options and sell puts.

2. Falling Three (Bearish)

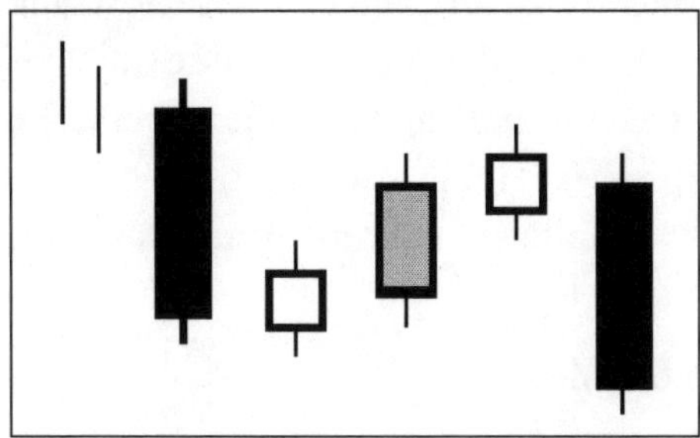

Figure 18.30: **Falling Three (Bearish)**

- **Identification:** This pattern consists of five candles. The first one is a long black candle signifying the continuation of the previous downtrend. It is followed by three relatively small candles that move against the overall trend but stay within the range of the first candle. The fifth candle is black that closes below the close of the first candle and continues the downtrend (Figure 18.30).
- **Trading:** This is a very strong continuation pattern and a brief pullback is nothing more than a consolidation of the downtrend. Initiate sell positions in the security or buy put options and sell calls.

3. Matt Hold

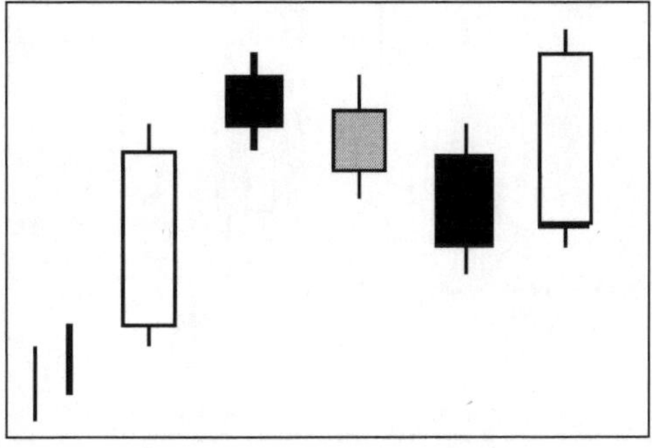

Figure 18.31: **Matt Hold**

- **Identification:** This pattern consists of five candles. A long white candle in an uptrend is followed by a relatively small black candle, which gaps in the direction of the trend. The next two candles continue the brief pullback and are small candles that stay within the range of the first candle. The fifth candle is a long white one that closes above the close of the first candle and continues the uptrend (Figure 18.31).

- **Trading:** The bullish Mat Hold is similar to the bullish rising three and a buy position can be initiated after the formation of this pattern.

Number of Middle Candles

In the above continuation patterns, the number of middle candles may be more than three, but the signals will be the same.

The important thing to look out for is volume. The volume in the three middle candles should drop, and when the fifth candles form in the direction of the trend, the volume should be substantially high. When volume increases with price movements in direction of the candlestick signal, whatever the pattern may be, it adds to the strength of the signal.

Figure 18.32 shows a few candlestick patterns.

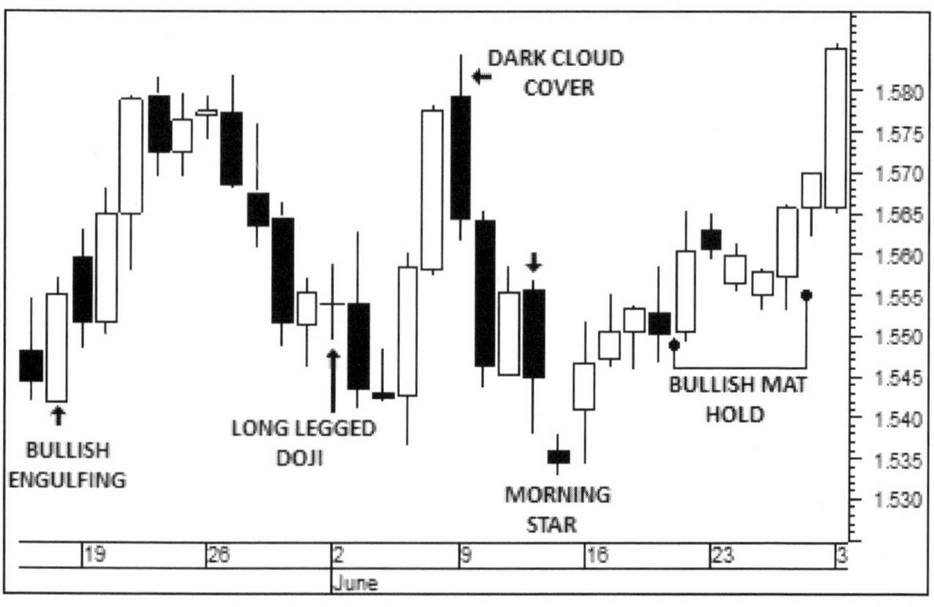

Figure 18.32: **Showing some candlestick patterns**

Chapter 19

Gaps

A GAP IS AN AREA IN A PRICE CHART where no trading has happened. Upside gaps occur when the price opens much higher and the lowest price traded is above the previous period's high. Downside gaps occur when the price opens much lower and the highest price traded is below the previous period's low (*see* Figure 19.7).

An unexpected event or news, like earning figures, political activity, etc. after the market close, is a major reason for gap formation as investors try to adjust to the new situation. There may be purely psychological factors, too. If a security closes at the highest or the lowest point after a big price move, it may open with a gap.

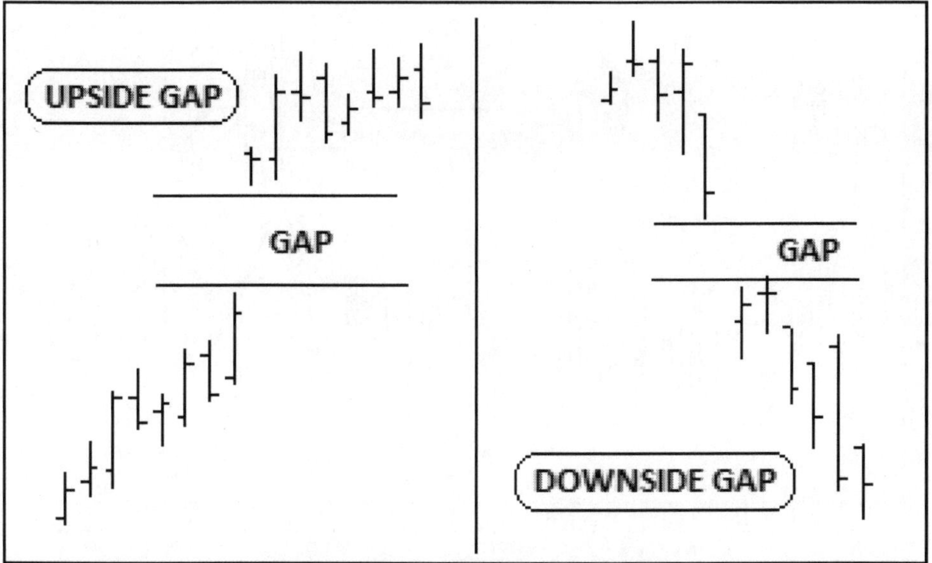

Figure 19.1: **Upside and downside gaps**

Gaps rarely occur in a continuous market as any news is priced in immediately. That is why gaps are rare in the currency market but frequent in daily charts of stock and commodity markets.

There are four basic types of gaps:

- Common gaps.
- Breakaway gaps.
- Continuation or runaway gaps.
- Exhaustion gaps.

Common Gaps

Common gaps occur in a range bound or congested market (*see* Figure 19.2). Since the market is not moving in any particular trend, common gaps do not hold much importance and should be ignored.

Common gaps are usually filled and thus provide the only trading opportunity if you wish to trade them. Filling the gap or closing the gap means that the price retraces to the levels that existed before the formation of the gap. If a common gap forms close to resistance, you can enter

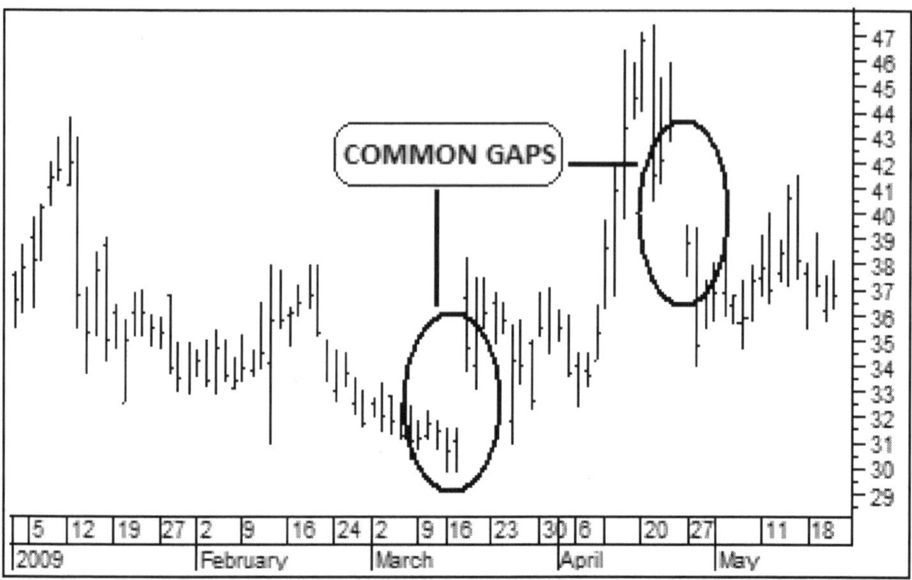

Figure 19.2: **Common gaps**

a sell position while if it forms close to support, you can buy the security. The volume does not change much from the previous levels when a common gap is formed.

Breakaway Gaps

Breakaway gaps occur when the price breaks out of the trading range with a gap (*see* Figure 19.3).

The volume increases significantly after the gap opening because traders who are placed on the wrong side book losses at any price they can get and new positions are initiated in the direction of the gap. The price may or may not make new highs in an upside breakout and new lows in a downside breakout, but the gap is usually not filled. The breakout from the trading range indicates the start of a new trend in the direction of the gap.

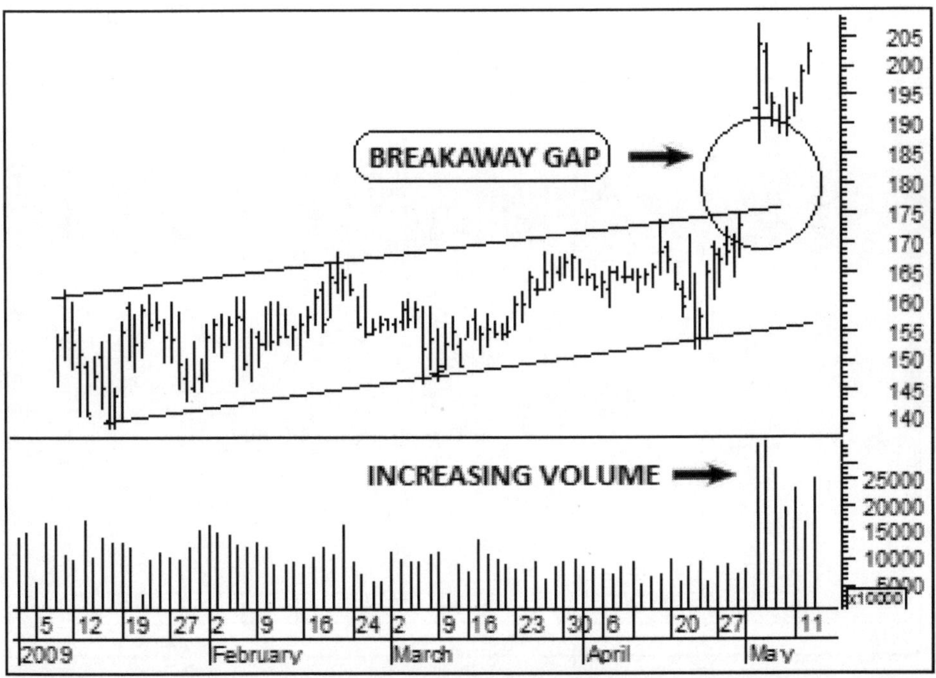

Figure 19.3: **Breakaway gap**

Trading strategy

- **Upside Breakaway Gap:** Go long, keeping the lower end of the gap as a stop loss zone.
- **Downside Breakaway Gap:** Go short, keeping the higher end of the gap as a stop loss zone.

A gap formed after the breakout from a chart pattern such as a triangle should be considered much stronger than a gap that forms after a trading range not associated with any chart pattern.

Be careful if the volume has increased abnormally just before the gap formation as it may indicate profit booking after the gap. In such a situation, wait for some time for the market to settle before you take a position.

Continuation or Runaway Gaps

Runaway gaps occur in the middle of a strong trend and are followed by new highs in the case of an uptrend and new lows in a downtrend

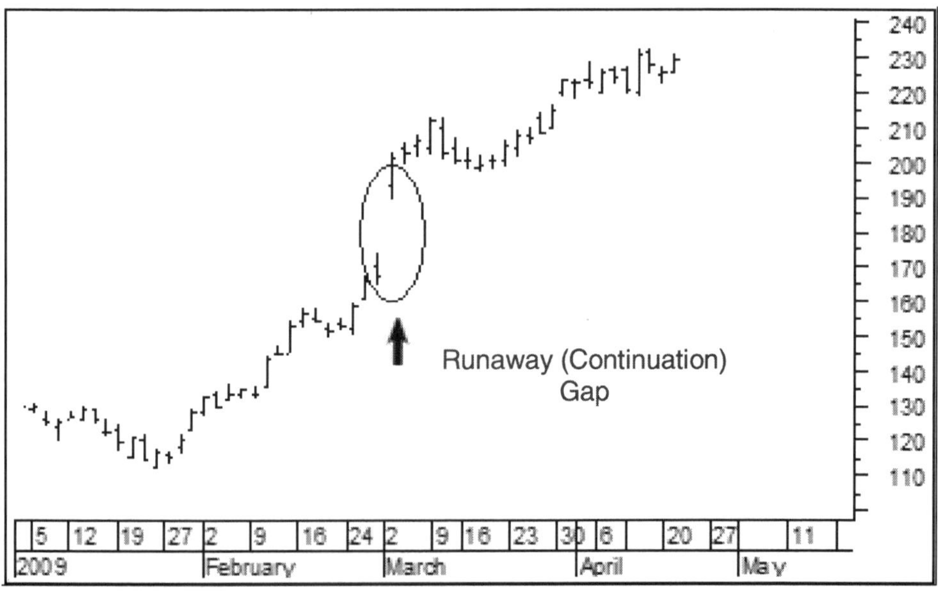

Figure 19.4: **Runaway (continuation) gap**

(*see* Figure 19.4). They are also known as continuation gaps because they indicate the continuation of the ongoing trend.

Continuation gaps are formed because of a sudden increase in trading activity of a security. In a bull trend, any positive news, no matter how insignificant, is enough to create a gap up opening, and during a bear trend, any negative news, no matter how insignificant, is enough to give a gap down opening. These situations compel the traders and investors who were waiting on the sideline for a retracement, to enter the markets as they give up any hope of retracements. In an uptrend, the gap indicates fresh investments, while in a downtrend, a gap indicates panic liquidation. In either case, it is clear that the trend will continue and is not going to change soon. Volume increases significantly after gap formation.

Trading Strategy

These gaps are useful for projecting price targets as they usually form in the middle of a trend:

- **Upside Runaway Gap:** Go long but be careful if no new highs are made in subsequent trading sessions. Close your buy position and be out of the market as this may indicate that the trend is too weak to continue.
- **Downside Runaway Gap:** Go short but be careful if no new lows are made in subsequent trading sessions. Close your sell position and exit the market as this may indicate that the trend is too weak to continue.

Exhaustion Gaps

Exhaustion gaps occur at the end of a strong uptrend or downtrend in the direction of the trend (*see* Figure 19.5). They signify the final move in the direction of the trend before it ends. The difference between an exhaustion gap and a runaway gap is that no new highs or lows are made in an exhaustion gap and the gap is filled soon. The volume increases substantially at gap formation.

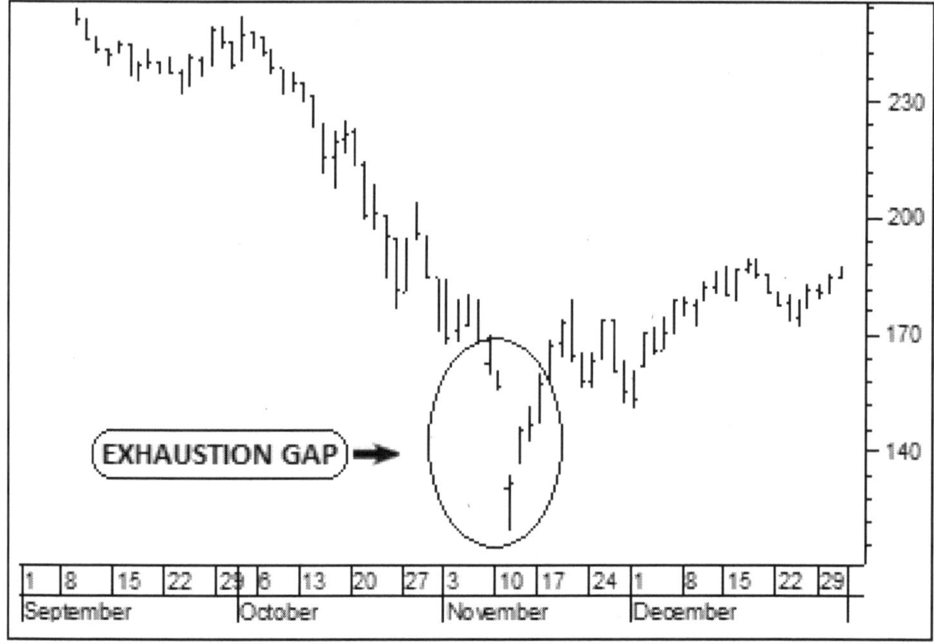

Figure 19.5: **Exhaustion gap**

In an uptrend, they indicate irrational euphoria, and in a downtrend, irrational panic. However, once an exhaustion gap is formed, markets see reality and start retracing.

Exhaustion gaps and runaway gaps are difficult to differentiate at formation. So if you had taken a position after a gap thinking it to be a runaway gap, close the position if no new highs or lows are being made as it may turn out to be an exhaustion gap.

Trading Strategies

- **Upside Exhaustion Gap:** Close all buy positions and go short. Keep a stop loss around the high made after the gap formation.
- **Downside Exhaustion Gap:** Close all sell positions and go long. Keep a stop loss around the low made after the gap formation.

Island Cluster

Island cluster is a powerful reversal signal (*see* Figure 19.6). It is identified by an exhaustion gap followed by a few ranged trading sessions — and then a breakaway gap occurring in the opposite direction to the exhaustion gap. The trading sessions form a sort of an island and are known as island cluster.

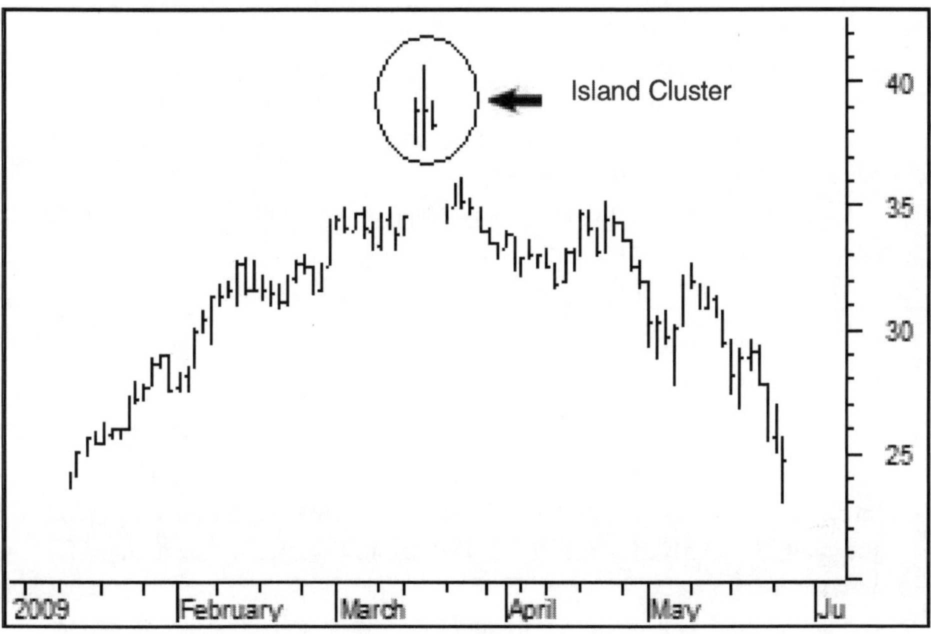

Figure 19.6: **Island cluster**

Trading strategy

- **Upside Island Cluster:** Close all buy positions and go short. Keep the upper end of the gap as a stop loss zone.
- **Downside Island Cluster:** Close all sell positions and go long. Keep the lower end of the gap as a stop loss zone.

Chapter 20

Chart Patterns

THE PRICE MOVEMENT PLOTTED ON A CHART sometimes forms different identifiable shapes known as chart patterns. These patterns indicate the trading activities of buyers and sellers, which helps to analyze the future movements and probable price targets.

Chart patterns can occur in any time-frame, within intraday price movements to long-term yearly charts.

Patterns fall into three broad categories:

- continuation patterns,
- reversal patterns, and
- neutral patterns.

Continuation patterns indicate that the ongoing trend is likely to continue; reversal patterns indicate a complete reversal of the ongoing trend and neutral pattern may lead to continuation, reversal or formation of a new short-term trend.

Support and resistance levels and trendlines are the base of pattern formation and all trading strategies of support, resistance and trendlines should be implemented while analyzing chart patterns.

The major difference between chart patterns and candlestick patterns is that candlestick patterns indicate a short-term reversal or continuation whereas chart patterns indicate a trend reversal or continuation.

Reversal Patterns

Head and Shoulders

The head and shoulders pattern looks just as the name indicates — a head in the middle and shoulders on either side (*see* Figure 20.1). When this pattern is formed after an uptrend, it is known as head and shoulders top, and when formed after a downtrend, it is known as head and shoulders bottom (or inverted head and shoulders).

Head and shoulders pattern is a very powerful and reliable reversal pattern.

Head and Shoulders (Top)

A Head and Shoulders (Top) reversal pattern forms after an uptrend. The pattern contains three successive peaks with the middle peak called the head, being the highest, and two lower peaks on either side of the head called shoulders.

An important aspect of the pattern is the neckline. The neckline is formed by drawing a line connecting two reaction low points of the formation (*see* Point L1 and Point L2 in Figure 20.1). The first low point occurs at the end of the left shoulder (Point L1) and the second at the end of the head formation (Point L2). The neckline can be upward or downward sloping, or it could be horizontal. However, a downward sloping neckline strengthens the head and shoulders top formation. The pattern is complete when the support provided by the neckline is broken. This happens when the security price starts to fall from the top of the right

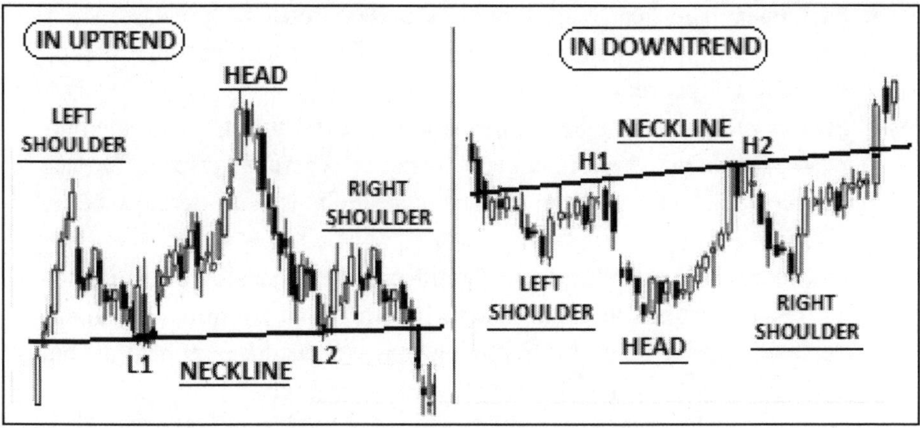

Figure 20.1: **Head and Shoulders**

shoulder and moves below the neckline. The breakout is confirmed when the security price trades and closes below the neckline.

Head and Shoulders (Bottom)

A Head and Shoulders (Bottom), or an inverted head and shoulders reversal pattern forms after a downtrend. The pattern contains three successive troughs with the middle trough (the head) being the lowest, and two higher troughs on the left and right side are the shoulders.

An important aspect of the pattern is the neckline. The neckline is formed by drawing a line connecting two reaction high points of the formation (Point H1 and Point H2 in Figure 20.1). The first high point occurs at the end of the left shoulder (Point H1) and the second at the end of the head formation (Point H2). The neckline can be upward or downward sloping, or it could be horizontal. However, an upward sloping neckline strengthens the inverted head and shoulders formation. The pattern is complete when the resistance provided by the neckline is broken. This happens when the security price starts to rise from the low point of the right shoulder and moves above the neckline. The breakout is confirmed when the security price trades and closes above the neckline.

Pattern Formation Criteria

- **Prior Trend:** The head and shoulders pattern must be preceded by a strong trend. If the pattern occurs in a trading or non-trending market, it should be ignored.
- **Head:** A clearly visible head formation is sufficient criteria for the purpose of trading, but a longer head formation where the price difference between the head and the shoulders is high, is considered a better chart pattern.
- **Shoulders:** The classic head and shoulders pattern consists of symmetrical left and right shoulders, but such formations are rare. The shoulders will usually be of different widths as well as different heights, but still be counted as shoulders and traded accordingly.

Price Objective

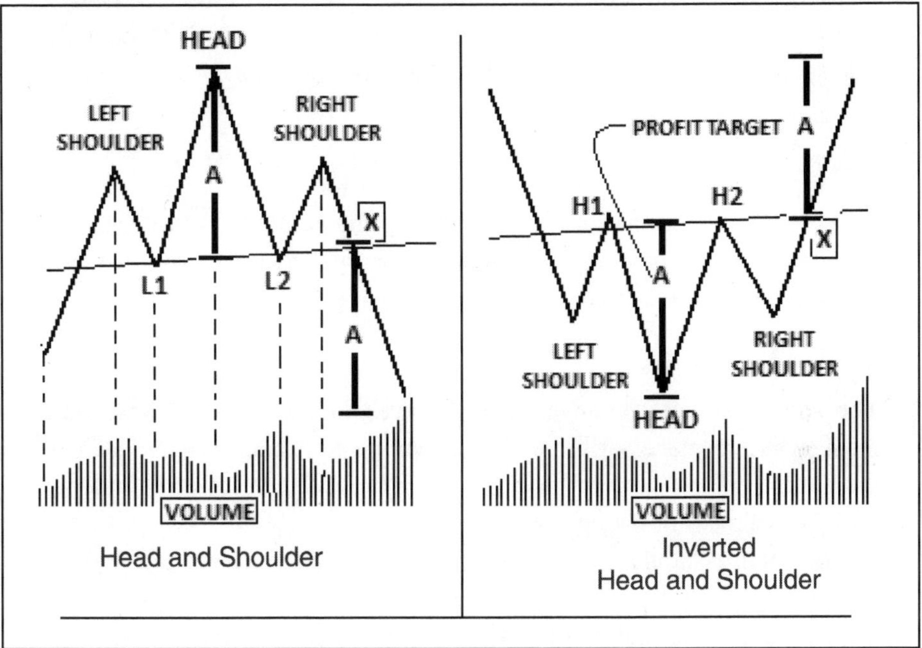

Figure 20.2: **Price target in Head and Shoulder patterns**

Head and Shoulders Top

The vertical distance from the highest point of the head to the neckline, indicated by the letter A in Figure 20.2, is the profit target that you should look for. Once the price breaks down from the neckline support (Point X), it is expected to fall to at least the distance equal to A.

Head and Shoulders Bottom

The vertical distance from the lowest point of the head to the neckline, indicated by the letter A in Figure 20.2, is the profit target that you should look for. Once the price breaks out from the neckline resistance (Point X), it is expected to rise to at least the distance equal to A.

The head and shoulders pattern is a trend reversal pattern. You should define your profit objective depending on other factors too rather than just follow the price objective of the pattern. For instance, if a clear head and shoulders pattern has formed in a long-term chart, you can look for much higher profit as the new trend may continue for a longer time increasing your chances of getting much higher returns. In such situations, you can look for trend reversal signals rather than merely follow the price objective of the chart pattern to close your position.

Volume

Volume plays a crucial part in confirming the strength of the head and shoulders pattern. Changes in volume as the pattern progresses can help identify the pattern even before it is complete.

Head and Shoulders Top

The volume during the advance to the peak of the left shoulder should ideally, but not necessarily be higher than in the advance to the peak of the head. The new high of the head being formed with lower volume indicates weakness of the uptrend.

The volume should increase as the prices fall from the top of the head. It is another indication that the market is more inclined to selling.

The volume during the advance to the peak of the right shoulder should be quite low and increase substantially as the prices fall after making the high of the right shoulder. The sudden increase in volume at breakout will confirm the trend reversal from uptrend to downtrend.

In short, during the second half of the pattern, prices should rise with decreasing volume but fall with increasing volume.

Head and Shoulders Bottom

The volume during the decline to the trough of the left shoulder should ideally, but not necessarily be higher than in the decline to the trough of the head. The new low of the head being formed with lower volume indicates weakness of downtrend.

The volume should increase as the prices rise from the low of the head. It is another indication that the market is more inclined to buying.

The volume during the decline to the trough of the right shoulder should be quite low and increase substantially as the prices rise after making the low of the right shoulder. The sudden increase in volume at breakout will confirm the trend reversal from downtrend to uptrend.

In short, during the second half of the pattern, prices should fall with decreasing volume but rise with increasing volume.

Trading

- **Head and Shoulders Top:** Sell at breakout of the neckline and keep a clear stop loss if the price again crosses and closes above the neckline.
- **Options:** Buy put options. Sell call options with strike price above the head.
- **Head and Shoulders Bottom:** Buy at breakout of the neckline and keep a clear stop loss if the price again crosses and closes below the neckline.
- **Options:** Buy call options. Sell put options with the strike price below the head.

In Figure 20.3, the price target was achieved but there are two clear caution signs. The neckline is upward sloping and the right shoulder is higher than the left shoulder. In such situations, it is better not to rush and sell after the breakout. Wait for a few trading sessions to pass. It is likely that

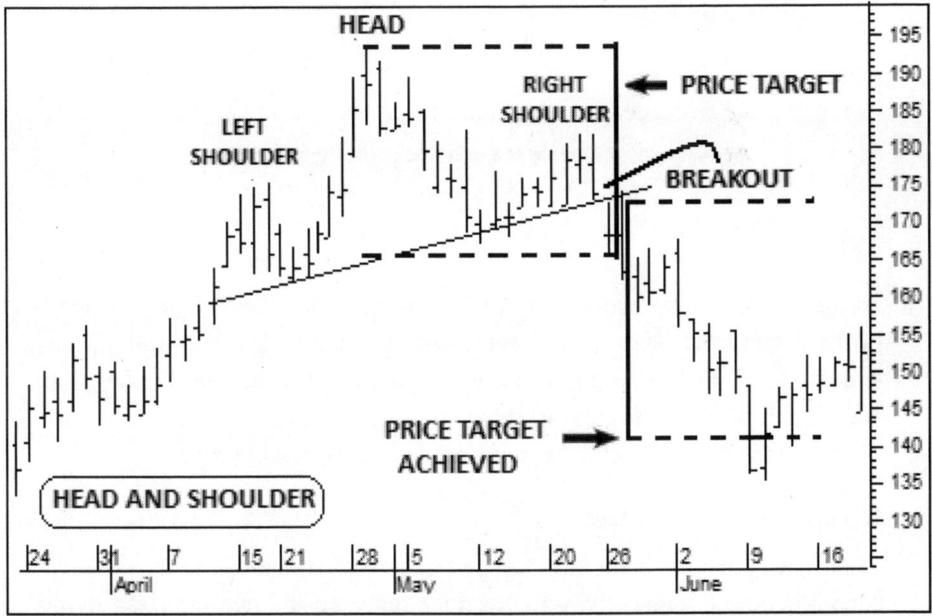

Figure 20.3: **A head and shoulders formation requiring cautious approach**

the price will rise and find resistance around the neckline. Take short position there keeping the price levels above the neckline as a stop loss.

Double Top and Double Bottom

Double tops and double bottoms are perhaps the most frequently occurring patterns but their relevance as trend reversal patterns is nevertheless high if properly identified.

The double top resembles the letter "M" and the double bottom resembles the letter "W" (*see* Figure 20.4).

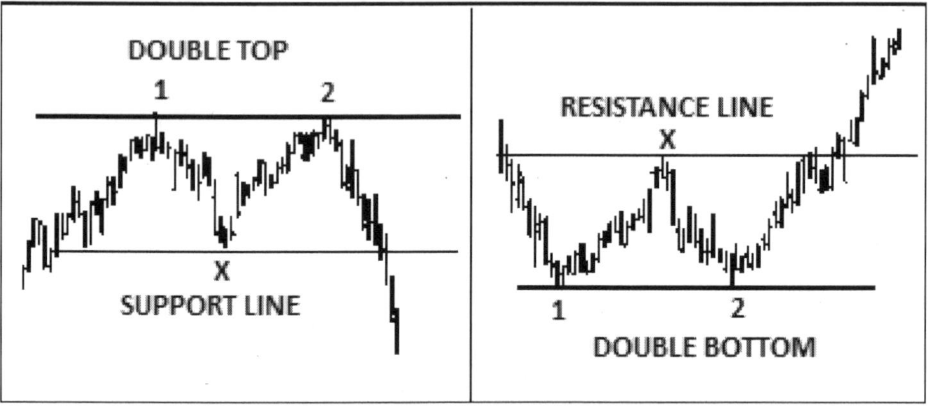

Figure 20.4: **Double top and double bottom patterns**

Double Top

A double top occurs after an uptrend and consists of two clearly defined peaks around the same price levels and a reaction low, or trough, between them. The lowest point of the trough (X) is the support level which is used for drawing the support line (*see* Figure 20.4).

Important points to keep in mind while trading double top:

1. Distance between the Tops

Trade cautiously those double top patterns where the tops are too close to each other. The longer the time distance between the two tops, the more reliable is the pattern (*see* Figure 20.5).

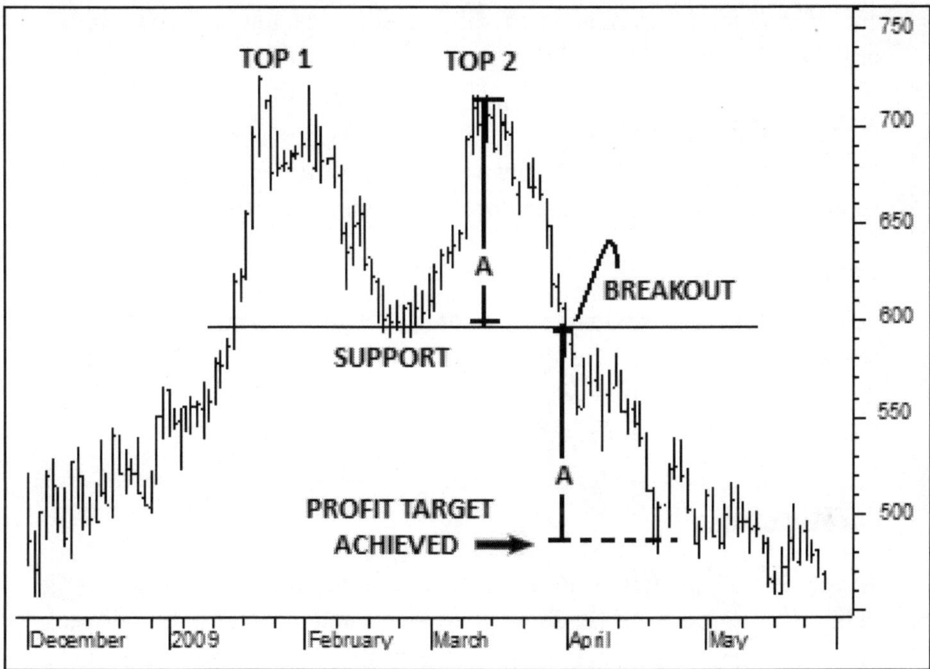

Figure 20.5: **Price target in a double top pattern**

2. Price Decline After the First Top

This is a very important aspect of double top formation. A deep trough between the two tops increases the reliability of the pattern. In general, look for at least 10% price correction from the high of the tops.

3. Volume

Volume on the second top should be lower than the first top. Volume should also increase as the prices start to fall after the high of the second top.

4. Breakout

Determining whether the decline from the second peak is the indication of a valid double top developing or simply a temporary correction of an uptrend is difficult. As a rule, you should follow the trend, and in case of a double top, you should wait for a clear breakout of support level before considering it as a reversal. High volume after breakout indicates validity of the double top.

5. Pullback after Breakout

In a double top, a pull back to the previous support line is common. If the support line acts as a resistance, the double top is confirmed.

Trading Strategies

Sell at breakout keeping the stop loss level just above the low of the trough or support line. The price target after the breakout will be equal to the vertical distance between the high of the peaks and the support line (indicated by A in Figure 20.5).

Double Bottom

A double bottom occurs after a downtrend and consists of two clearly defined troughs around the same price levels and a reaction high or peak between them. The highest point of the peak (X) is the resistance level that is used for drawing the resistance line (Figure 20.4).

Following are the important points to be kept in mind while trading double bottom:

1. Distance between Troughs

Trade cautiously those double bottom patterns where the troughs are too close. The longer the time gap between the two troughs, the more reliable is the pattern.

2. Price Rise after the First Trough

This is a very important aspect of the double bottom formation. A high peak between the two troughs increases the reliability of the pattern. In general, look for at least 10% price correction from the low of the troughs.

3. Volume

Volume at the second trough should be lower than it was at the first one. Volume should also increase as the prices start to rise after the low of the second bottom.

4. Breakout

Determining whether the rise from the second trough is the indication of a valid double bottom developing, or simply a temporary correction of a downtrend, is difficult to guess. As a rule, you should follow the trend and, in the case of a double bottom, you should wait for a clear breakout of resistance level before considering it as a reversal. High volume after breakout indicates the validity of a double bottom.

5. Pullback after Breakout

In double bottoms, a pull back to the previous resistance line is common. If the resistance line acts as a support, the double bottom is confirmed.

Trading strategies

Buy at the breakout keeping the stop loss just below the high of the peak or resistance line. The price target after the breakout will be equal to the vertical distance between the low of the bottoms and the resistance line, Point X in Figure 20.4.

Triple Top and Triple Bottom

Triple Top

Triple top is a strong reversal pattern that occurs after a sustained uptrend. It consists of three peaks around the same price levels and two reaction lows between them (*see* Figure 20.6). The trading strategy and price target are similar to those in the double top pattern. The highest high and the lowest low are taken as the range of the pattern and the price target will be equal to this range after the breakout. In a tradable pattern, the volume decreases at each successive peak and increases at the second trough and at the breakout.

Triple Bottom

Triple bottom is a strong reversal pattern that occurs after a sustained downtrend. It consists of three troughs around the same price levels and

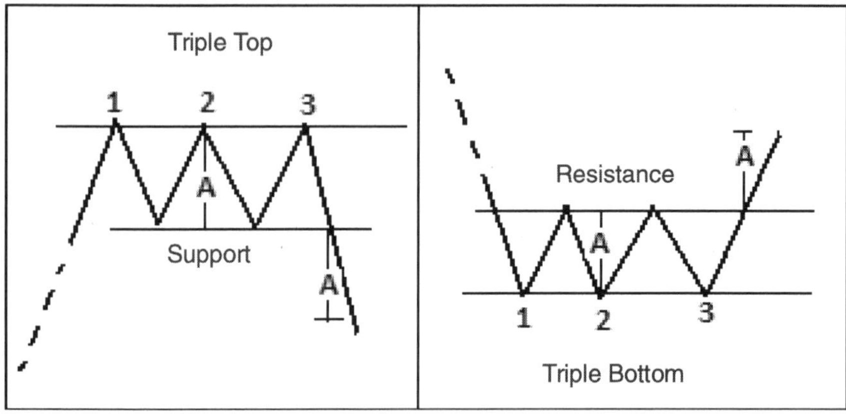

Figure 20.6: **Triple top and triple bottom**

two reaction highs between them (*see* Figure 20.6). The trading strategy and price target are similar to those in the double bottom pattern. The lowest low and the highest high are taken as the range of the pattern and the price target will be equal to this range after breakout. In a tradable pattern, the volume decreases at each successive trough and increases at the second high and at the breakout.

Rounded Top and Rounded Bottom

These are patterns with gradual and fairly symmetrical change in the trend direction where the reversal is prolonged and rounded in shape, like a letter "U" (*see* Figure 20.7). These can be the best reversal patterns as they indicate a gradual distribution, or accumulation, of assets.

A Rounded Top forms as investor sentiment shifts gradually from bullishness to bearishness, which is reflected in dropping volumes towards the top. After a period of ranged trading at the top, there is a gradual downturn and the shift to a bear trend, indicated by an increase in trading volumes.

A Rounded Bottom forms as investors sentiment shifts gradually from bearishness to bullishness, which is reflected in dropping volumes towards the bottom. After a period of ranged trading at the bottom, there

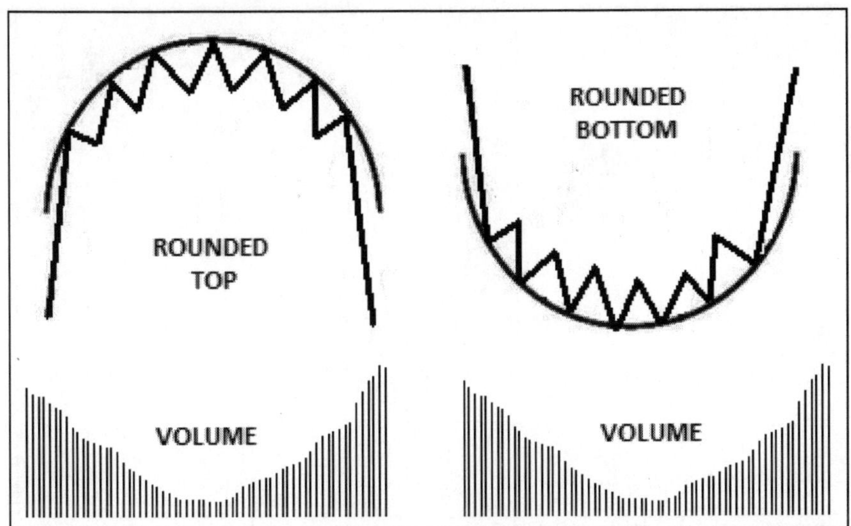

Figure 20.7: **Rounded Top and Rounded Bottom**

is a gradual upturn and the shift to a bull trend, indicated by an increase in trading volume.

There are no specific price targets and you should carry on the profit until there is a clear indication of reversal, or correction, of the trend.

V-formation

V-formations are unusual reversal patterns and do not give much time for traders to react (*see* Figure 20.8). There is no consolidation phase and the trend changes from one to another without any indications or warnings.

V-formation after an uptrend is referred to as V-top reversal pattern and that after a downtrend, a V-bottom reversal pattern.

V-formations are formed with heavy volumes as traders rush to clear their loss making positions at every level and new positions are initiated.

The first part of V-formations is not difficult to trade as the traders have a clear view of the market. However, the second part is sudden and creates much confusion. The importance of short-term tools like

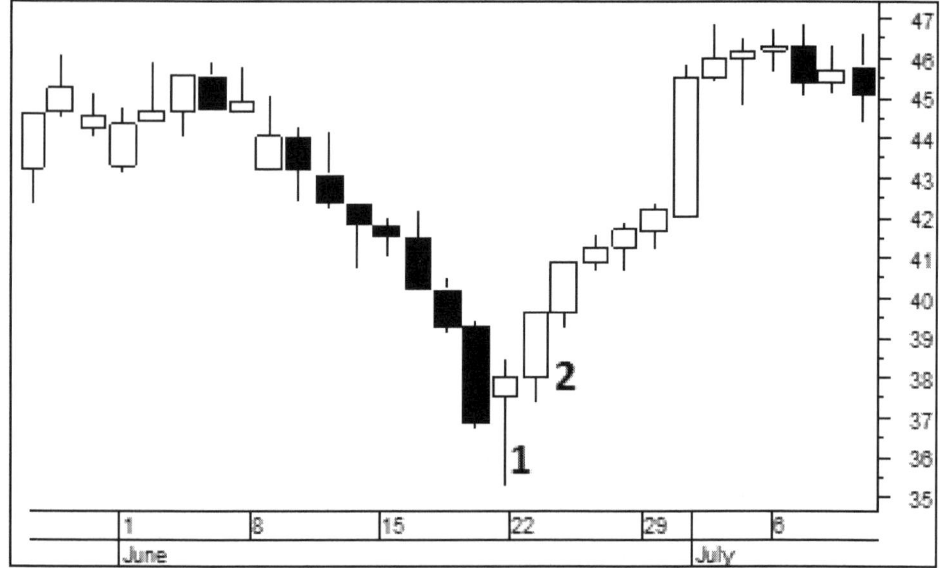

Figure 20.8: **V-formation**

candlesticks is realized in such situations. As you can observe in Figure 20.8, the candlesticks gave a clear signal of price reversal. Both Candle 1 and Candle 2 indicated a strong bullish sentiment which should be sufficient criteria for closing short positions. If you do not have a short position, then wait for the market to settle down. If you had somehow anticipated the change in price direction by some short-term tools like candlesticks, then stay in the market and ride the profit. However, if you are caught unaware and your position starts to give losses, clear the position immediately.

Neutral Patterns

Triangles

Triangles are one of the simplest, yet the most reliable of chart patterns. Triangles are neutral patterns that can lead to trend continuation or reversal. The interesting aspect of triangle patterns is that they can be traded in a range-bound market with no clear prior trend.

Triangles form when price movement starts to narrow down indicating reducing investor participation and indecisive market sentiment.

Triangles are of three types: ascending, descending and symmetrical (*see* Figure 20.9):

- **Ascending Triangle:** An ascending triangle is formed when the price makes higher lows but the highs remain unchanged. The uptrend line approaching the resistance line contracts the price movement into a smaller range with every passing trading session. It is considered a bullish pattern as higher lows indicate that the sellers are losing strength. Ascending triangles are usually observed in an uptrend and act as a continuation pattern but signal strong reversal in a downtrend.
- **Descending Triangle:** A descending triangle is formed when the price makes lower highs but the lows remain unchanged. The downtrend line approaching the support line contracts the price movement into a smaller range with every passing trading session. It is considered a bearish pattern as lower highs indicate that the buyers are losing strength. Descending triangles are usually observed in a downtrend and act as a continuation pattern but signal strong reversal in an up-trend.

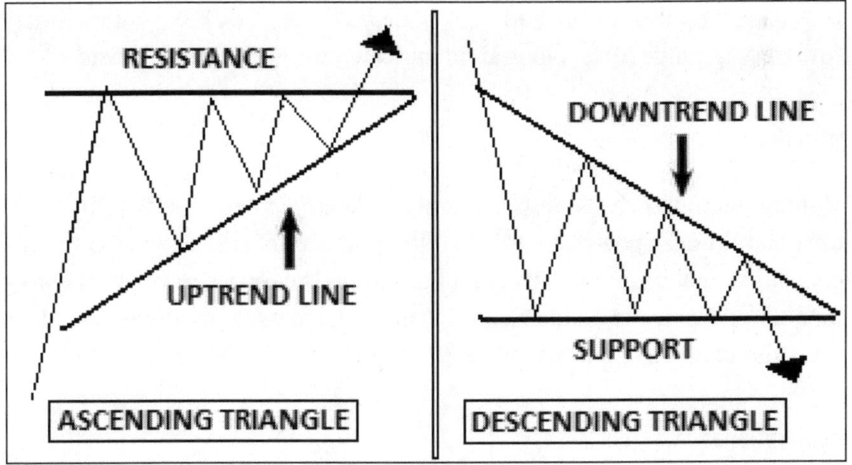

Figure 20.9: **Triangles**

- **Symmetrical Triangles:** Symmetrical triangles are formed when the price makes lower highs and higher lows. The uptrend line and downtrend line approaching each other contract the price movement into a smaller range with every passing trading session. Among all three triangle types, symmetrical triangles are the strongest indication of market indecisiveness and do not indicate any clear market sentiment.

Triangle Characteristics

Triangles are low-risk-high-reward chart patterns. It is important to understand how the psychology of traders plays out during the triangle formation. Triangles form due to decreasing trading activity that cannot continue for long. Triangles are like the silence before the storm and, at some point, traders will get restless and push the price in one direction or other. This will attract more traders as they will see some clear price direction after a long time. Due to the narrow range within a triangle, the stop loss levels are close to the entry levels but the profit target is exceptionally high.

Breakout

Breakout from the triangle pattern is the most important aspect and the first clear opportunity to trade the pattern. Prices breaking out of a narrow trading range after a long time indicate a big price move ahead.

Volume

Volume supports the significance of the chart pattern. Ideally, the volume should continue decreasing as the pattern progresses due to the increasingly fewer traders participating. At the breakout, however, the volume should show a sudden and substantial increase, as there is a clear price direction for traders to trade.

Price Target

The targeted price for a triangle is measured at the start of the triangle and is equal to the vertical distance from the first trough, or peak, to the

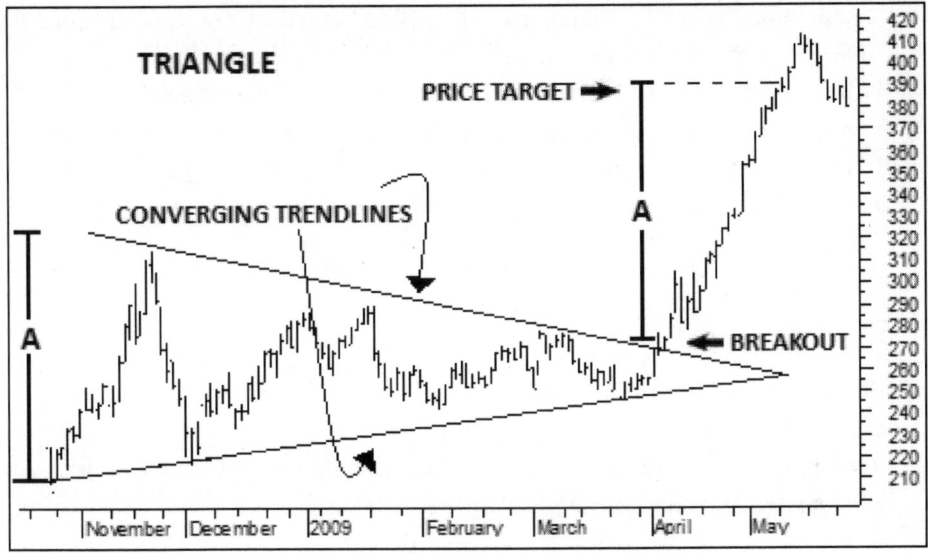

Figure 20.10: **Price target in a triangle formation**

opposite border of the triangle (indicated by the letter A in Figure 20.10). The move is then projected vertically from the point of breakout to calculate the profit target.

Trading Strategies

1. **Upside Breakout:** Buy after breakout keeping the stop loss just below the previous trough.
2. **Downside Breakout:** Sell after breakout keeping the stop loss just above the previous peak.
3. **Ascending Triangle:** If the range has narrowed too much, look at the volume pattern. If the volume shows signs of increase when prices rise, this indicates the likelihood of an upside breakout. You can go long as price approaches the resistance without waiting for the breakout, but be very careful and switch the position if there is a downside breakout with increased volume. This strategy carries some risk but gives you the edge if the breakout happens with a gap up opening.
4. **Descending Triangle:** If the range has narrowed too much, look at the volume pattern. If the volume shows signs of increase when prices fall,

this indicates the likelihood of a downside breakout. You can go short as price approaches the support without waiting for the breakout, but be very careful and switch the position if there is an upside breakout with increased volume. This strategy carries some risk but gives you the edge if the breakout happens with a gap down opening.

5. **Options:** Create a strangle or buy both out-of-the-money call and put options with strike prices close to the present price.

Wedges

Wedges are similar to symmetrical triangles and form with two converging trendlines; the difference being that the slope of both upper and lower trend line is either up or down, unlike the triangle where both trend lines have opposing slopes (*see* Figure 20.11).

Wedges are of two types:

1. **Rising Wedge:** It consists of two converging trend lines that are slanted upward. The difference between the rising wedge and a triangle is that there are higher highs and higher lows in a rising wedge and the apex of this pattern is slanted upwards at an angle.

   The lower trendline has a greater slant than the upper trendline which makes them converge at a point.

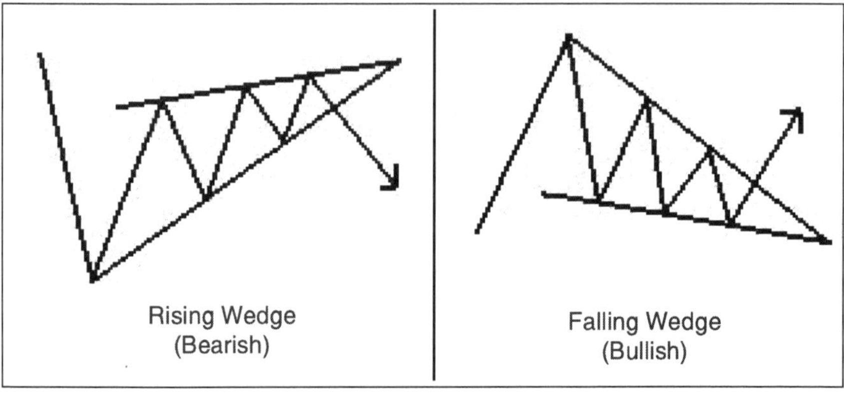

Figure 20.11: **Wedges**

2. **Falling Wedge:** It consists of two converging trend lines that are slanted downwards. The difference between the falling wedge and a triangle is that there are lower highs and lower lows in a falling wedge and the apex of this pattern is slanted downwards at an angle (*see* Figure 20.12).

   The upper trend line has a greater slant than the lower trend line that makes them converge at a point.

   Wedges are best traded as continuation patterns:

   - **Downtrend Continuation:** A rising wedge after a downtrend is a strong bearish continuation pattern. The pattern may seem bullish but it is just a correction to the previous downtrend.
   - **Uptrend Continuation:** A falling wedge after an uptrend is a strong bullish continuation pattern. The pattern may seem bearish but it is just a correction to the previous uptrend.

All trading aspects of wedges as continuation pattern like price target, volume consideration, etc. are similar to flags and pennants.

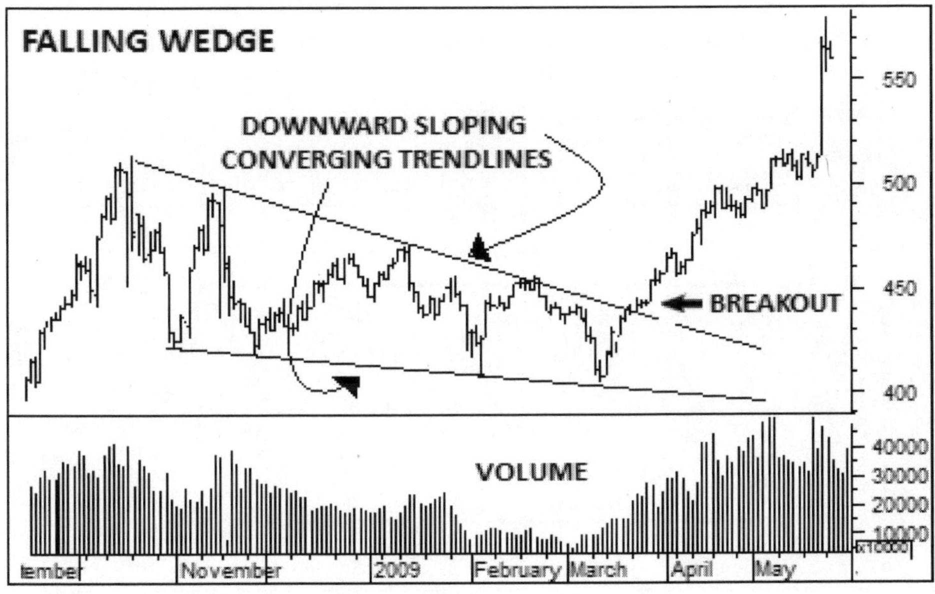

Figure 20.12: **Falling wedge as a continuation pattern**

Wedges are traded according to triangle trading guidelines when:

1. They occur in a trading market without any prior trend.
2. When a rising wedge occurs after an uptrend and falling wedge occurs after a downtrend.

Rectangles

Rectangles (*see* Figure 20.13) are sometimes referred to as trading ranges, consolidation zones or congestion areas.

A Rectangle is categorised as a continuation pattern if it forms after a strong trend. The volume should reduce considerably during a rectangle formation after a strong trend. However, rectangles can also be traded on their own depending on the direction of the breakout. The prior trend can be used as an additional tool. For example, if a rectangle forms after a strong uptrend and the volume in the rectangle shows increase during a price rise, it indicates that there may be an upside breakout. In such a situation, avoid taking short positions.

The profit target after the breakout will be equal to the height of the rectangle. However, if the rectangle forms after a strong uptrend or downtrend, and breakout occurs in the direction of the trend, then other aspects should also be seen while booking profit.

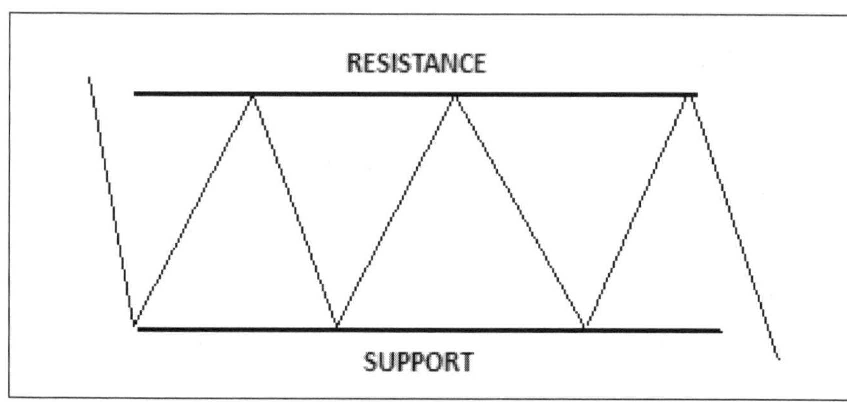

Figure 20.13: **Rectangle**

Continuation Patterns

Flags and Pennants

Flags and Pennants are extremely reliable continuation chart patterns. They occur midway in a sharp trend and do not take much time to form. Flags and pennants can be considered a short pause after a sharp uptrend, or downtrend, before the ongoing trend resumes.

Flags

Flag patterns are continuation patterns marked by a big price move followed by a short correction phase in which prices move within two parallel lines. As the name suggests, flag patterns have the appearance of a flag on a pole.

Flags are classified as bullish if they occur during an uptrend or bearish if they occur during a downtrend (*see* Figure 20.14).

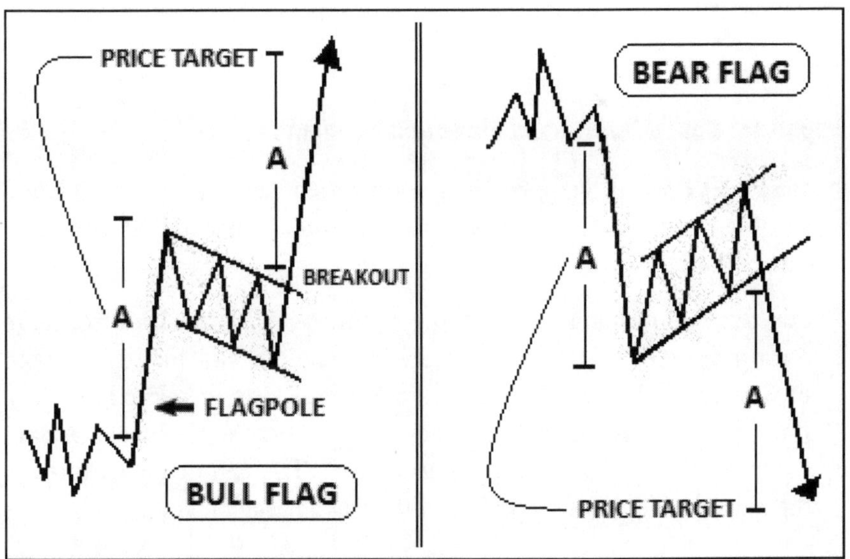

Figure 20.14: **Price targets in bull and bear flags**

A bull flag is formed if there is a sharp, almost vertical price rise followed by short consolidation in the form of downward sloping rectangle pattern. The rectangle pattern that slopes downward and moves against the uptrend strengthens the flag pattern. However, even if there is no downward slope, it is still considered a flag pattern.

A bear flag is formed if there is a sharp, almost vertical price decline followed by short consolidation in the form of an upward sloping rectangle pattern. The rectangle pattern that slopes upward and moves against the downtrend strengthens the flag pattern. However, even if there is no upward slope, it is still considered a flag pattern.

Pennants

Pennant patterns are very similar to flag patterns except that the consolidation phase after a sharp uptrend or downtrend is marked by a triangle, usually a symmetrical triangle.

Pennants are classified as bullish if they occur during an uptrend or bearish if they occur during a downtrend (*see* Figure 20.15).

Important Characteristics of Flags and Pennants

- **Sharp Price Move:** A sharp uptrend or downtrend prior to a consolidation phase is essential for flags or pennants to be considered as continuation patterns.

- **Flagpole:** The formation of flagpole signifies large price movements in a short duration of time. The flagpole is the distance that the uptrend or downtrend has covered before the price starts to consolidate in a flag or pennant formation. The start of the flagpole is a breakout from the trend line or support / resistance level. The end of the flagpole is the highest or the lowest price that the trend has achieved.

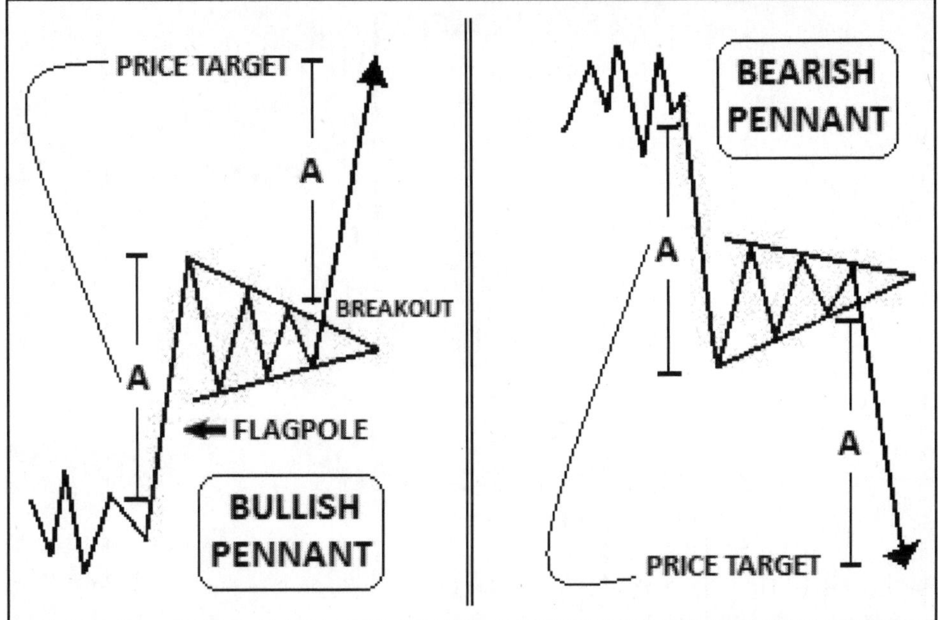

Figure 20.15: **Price target in Bull and Bear Pennants**

- **Breakout:** For a bullish flag or pennant, a break above the resistance confirms the resumption of an uptrend. For a bearish flag or pennant, a break below the support confirms the resumption of a downtrend.
- **Volume:** The price advance or decline that forms the flagpole should be accompanied by heavy volume. Low volume during the sudden and sharp move that creates the flagpole indicates that the market is not participating in the move and the prices are likely to retreat.

  After the flagpole formation, the volume should drop substantially in a consolidation phase of flag and pennant pattern.

  The volume should show a sudden increase at the breakout from a flag or pennant formation in the direction of the trend. If the breakout happens against the trend, a low volume will indicate that it is a false breakout. However, if the breakout against the trend happens with strong volumes, then the pattern has most likely failed and should not be traded.

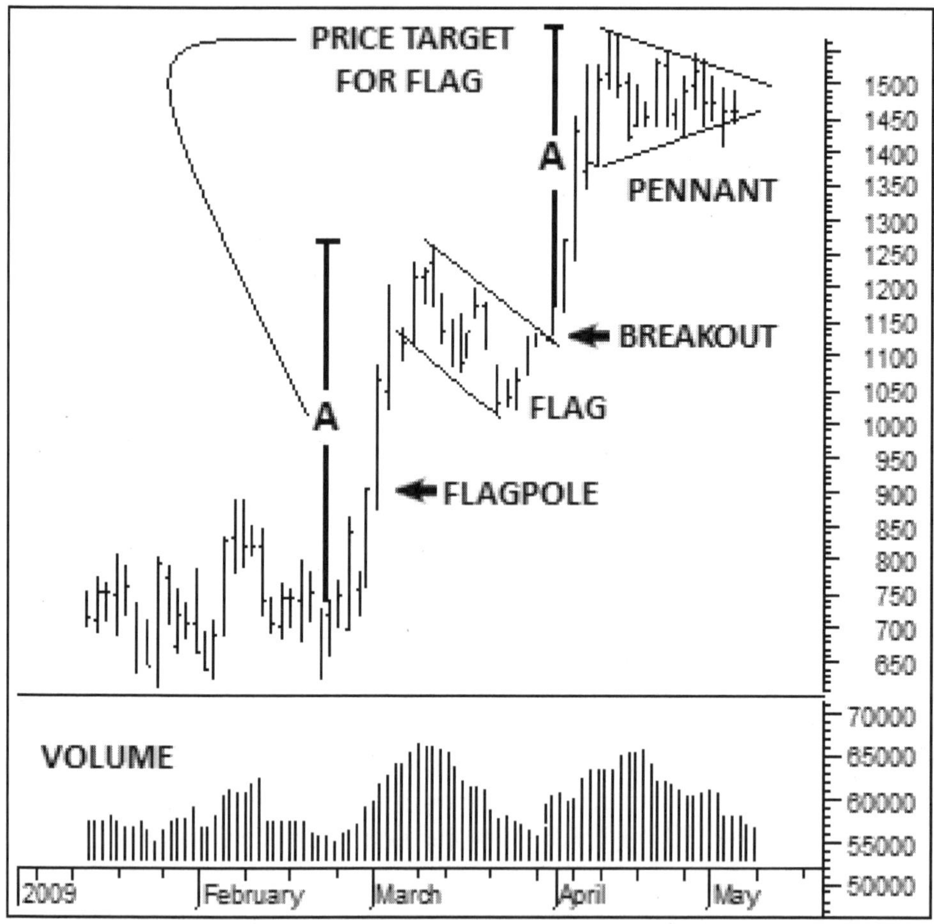

Figure 20.16: **An actual chart depicting price target in a flag formation**

- **Price Targets:** The price target after the breakout is equal to the length of the flagpole (indicated by letter A in Figure 20.16).

Trading Strategies

1. **Bullish Flag and Pennant:** Buy at the upside breakout. If the volume shows signs of increasing as price rises within a flag or pennant, a long position can be taken before the breakout.

- **Options:** Buy call options. Sell put options with strike price at the lower end of the flagpole.

2. **Bearish Flag and Pennant:** Sell at the downside breakout. If the volume shows signs of increasing as price falls within a flag or pennant, a short position can be taken before the breakout.
   - **Options:** Buy put options. Sell call options with strike price at the upper end of the flagpole.

Conclusion

Chart patterns are excellent trading tools. Remember, however, that they should be clearly identifiable at the first look. If you have to spend time to recognise the chart patterns, then they are probably not there at all. Gaps should be watched carefully if you are analyzing chart patterns. My experience suggests that gaps formed as part of a breakout after pattern formation gives strength to a chart pattern. However, if the chart pattern has started forming after a gap, then it should not be considered for trading purposes. For instance, a big gap before the left shoulder of the head and shoulders pattern makes the pattern weak and prone to failure. Similarly, a big gap should not be considered as a flagpole of a flag or pennant formation.

Chapter 21

Indicators

TECHNICAL ANALYSIS IS BASED ON PRICE AND VOLUME DATA. The tools that have been covered till now use basic data of price (open, high, low, close) and volume. Technical indicators can be considered as an advanced interpretation of price and volume data.

Price and volume data is refined through mathematical formulae and calculations to develop an indicator. The calculations range from simple to complex, but those of you who hate maths needn't worry as the only thing required is to learn how to use indicators, not how they may have been calculated.

Indicators measure different aspects of the market and are broadly divided into four types:

1. **Trend Indicators:** The most basic rule of technical analysis is to always trade with the trend, never against it. Trend indicators are designed to identify the strength and direction of a trend, providing you with a clear picture of which way to trade.
2. **Momentum Indicators:** These indicators measure the momentum, or the speed of the price movement. For example, if a ball is thrown up into the air, its speed will start to reduce as it goes higher. A point will come when it will stop rising and start falling down. Before this point is reached, the ball would still be moving up, but at reducing speed. In other words, the ball is supposed to be losing momentum. Financial markets move in the same way, and momentum indicators indicate when the speed of price rise or fall is declining. This way, a momentum indicator warns the traders about probable tops and bottoms before they are actually made.

3. **Volume Indicators:** These indicators measure the volume strength behind a price movement. A price movement associated with strong volumes is a better opportunity to trade than one associated with weak volume.
4. **Volatility Indicators:** These indicators measure market volatility and help you to plan your entry and exit based on the level of volatility.

Construction

There are two ways indicators are constructed — those that are bounded within a range and others that are not-bound. Most indicators are range-bound, i.e. where they move within a set range, say, like zero to 100. Trading signals are provided by the position of the indicator in the overall range. These indicators are also known as oscillators as they oscillate up and down within a set range and provide good overbought and oversold levels for a security. Oscillators can again be of two types — centred and banded. Centred oscillators fluctuate above and below a centre line whereas banded oscillators fluctuate above and below two bands that depict extreme price levels — or overbought and oversold levels.

The non-bounded indicators can trend, just like a security for a long period.

Indicators are also classified as leading and lagging indicators.

Leading indicators are designed to lead the price movements and are effective as predictive tools. Momentum indicators / oscillators are part of leading indicators.

Lagging indicators on the other hand, lag the price movement and are used as confirmation tools and are suited for trending markets.

The advantage of leading indicators is that they provide early signals for entry and exit and also greater numbers of trading signals. Leading indicators are best suited for ranged markets and in trending markets to trade in the direction of the major trend.

The disadvantage of leading indicators is that they are associated with bigger risks. Even though they are termed as leading indicators, they are still derived from the price, and will ultimately move according to price. They are thus prone to false signals and whipsaws, a situation when buy or sell signals are reversed in a short time.

The advantage of lagging or trend-following indicators is their ability to catch a move and stay with the trend. When markets are trending, lagging indicators can be enormously profitable and easy to use. The longer the trend, the fewer the signals and thus fewer number of trading positions involved.

The disadvantage of lagging indicators is that they are useless in non-trending markets and second, that the signals are delayed.

Technical indicators that are superimposed or placed on the price chart itself are known as "overlays", as they use the same scale as price. The rest are simply referred to as indicators and placed above or below the main price chart as a separate graph.

Chapter 22

Moving Averages

MOVING AVERAGES ARE ONE OF THE MOST FREQUENTLY USED INDICATORS due to their simplicity and effectiveness. They are used to smoothen any data series, including price, for a specified period. Moving averages are trend indicators and fall in the category of lagging indicators. There are different types of moving averages depending on the calculation parameters.

Simple Moving Average (SMA)

As the name suggests, this is the simplest to calculate. If you want to calculate the simple moving average of the last five days for a security, add the closing prices of all five days and divide the figure by five.

Taking an example, if gold's closing prices for the past five days are $850, $870, $840, $855 and $901 respectively, then the average price of gold for the last five days will be: 850+870+840+855+901/5 or 4,316/5= $863.2.

The price $863.2 will be the first point of the moving average and will be plotted after five days. The calculation is repeated for each new closing price on the chart. Therefore, if the next closing price is $890, then this new price would be added and the oldest price, which is $850, would be dropped. The new 5-day simple moving average would now be calculated as 870+840+855+901+890/5, which comes to $871.2. The averages are then joined to form a smooth curving line known as the moving average line, and it will continue to move over time.

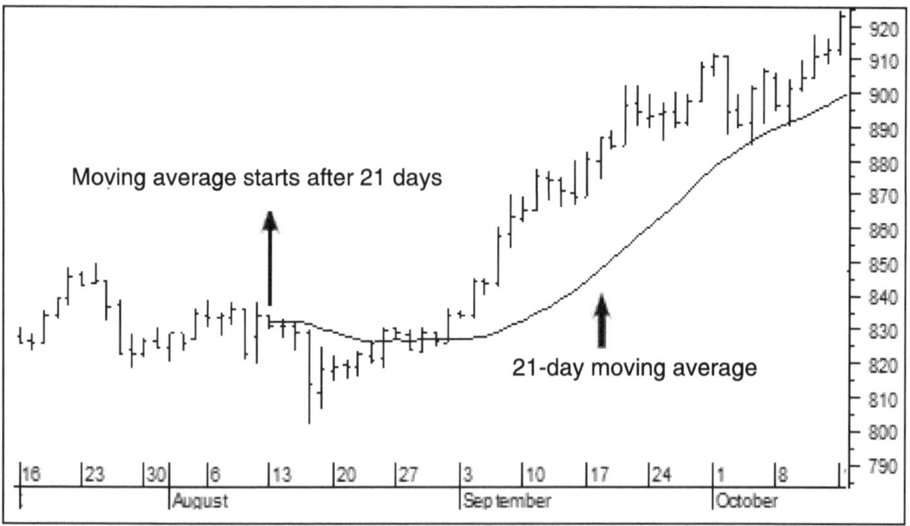

Figure 22.1: **21-day moving average**

Similarly, if you want a simple moving average of the last 21 days, add the closing prices of all 21 days and divide the total by 21. Figure 22.1 depicts a 21-day simple moving average plotted with price.

In the above example, the calculation is based on closing prices. You can calculate the moving average on other price parameters like open, high and low. However, the closing price is mostly used for calculation as it is the price at which the market finally settled on. Moving averages can be calculated for any time-frame, from minutes, hours to years. All the parameters are provided by charting software and you just have to select your preference.

Exponential Moving Average (EMA)

If you believe that the most recent price information is the most useful one on a chart, then you can use the Exponential Moving Average, also called exponentially weighted moving averages, or EMA.

In the simple moving average, all the past data is given equal importance. For instance, in a 21-day simple moving average, the closing price on Day 1 and that on Day 21 hold equal weight. This causes averages to

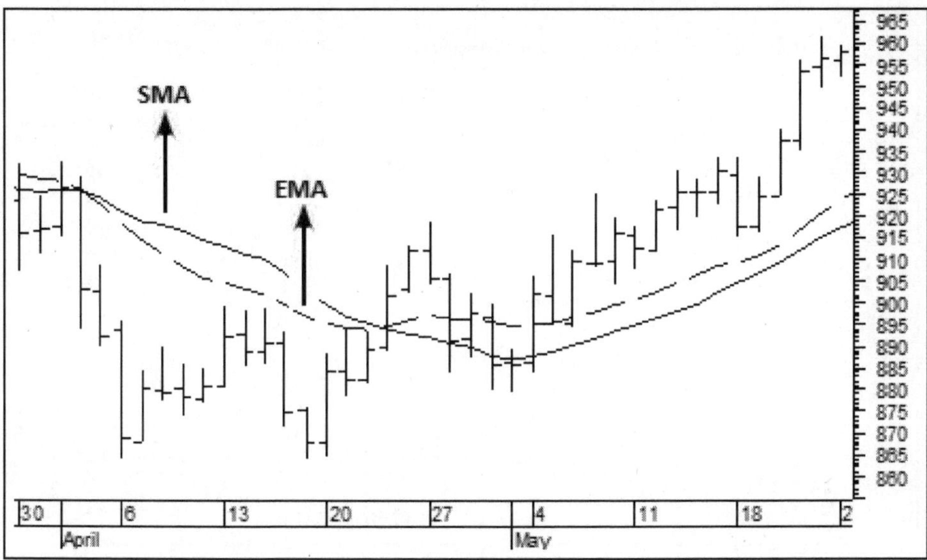

Figure 22.2: **Chart depicting SMA and EMA for the same period**

lag the price movement. To overcome this lag, exponential moving averages are used. Exponential moving averages reduce the lag by giving more weight to the latest prices relative to the earlier ones. The calculation of EMA is more complex than SMA. The important thing to remember is that the exponential moving average puts more weight on recent prices. Therefore, it reacts more quickly to new price change compared to SMA. Figure 22.2 shows the 21-day SMA and EMA. As you will observe, EMA is more price sensitive and moves closer to the price than SMA.

There are also other moving averages, like weighted moving averages, linear weighted average, volume adjusted (gives more weight to days with high volume), variable, etc. The only major difference between the various types of moving averages is the weight assigned to the prices.

One average that considers volatility in calculation is the variable moving average. It is generally believed that trending markets are less volatile and when volatility increases, it can be a sign of a trend change. A variable moving average is an exponential moving average that automatically adjusts its weighting based on volatility. It gets more sensitive to recent data as volatility increases, and less sensitive to recent data as

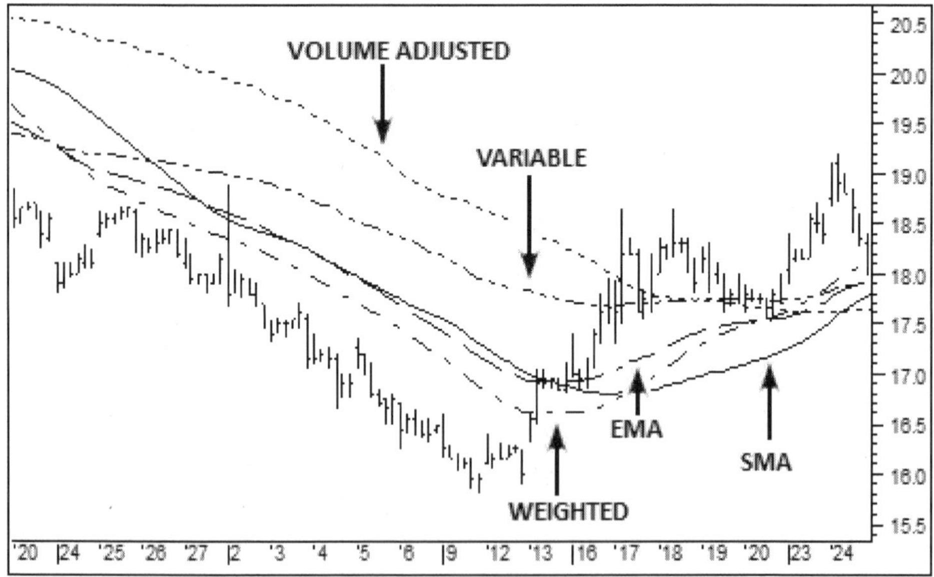

Figure 22.3: **Multiple moving averages for the same period**

volatility reduces. This aspect of a variable moving average gives an early signal as it becomes more sensitive in periods of high volatility.

Figure 22.3 is an hourly chart depicting five moving averages: SMA, EMA, weighted, variable and volume-adjusted moving averages. All the averages are for the same period, i.e. 50 hours.

Which Moving Average to Use

It is difficult to clearly decide which moving average to use. Your selection of a moving average will depend on your trading style. However, moving averages are used to smoothen the price so that volatility does not affect trading. If they are made too sensitive to price, then they lose their basic purpose. Due to this reason, simple moving average works best most of the time. However, if you wish to work on still more price sensitive averages, then EMA can be used. Avoid using moving averages other than SMA and EMA during your initial trading days as you may lose interest in moving averages due to their complexity. In fact, a majority of traders never use any other moving average apart from SMA and EMA. Study other moving averages when you have gained enough experience and are academically more inclined to technical analysis than trading.

Trading Moving Averages

Moving averages are lagging indicators and good for judging the direction of the trend. You can judge the trend from moving averages through three basic ways:

1. **Slope of Moving Average:** An upward sloping moving average indicates an uptrend; a downward sloping moving average indicates a downtrend.
2. **Price:** When the security is trading above the moving average, it is considered an uptrend; when the security is trading below the moving average, it is considered a downtrend.
3. **Multiple Moving Averages:** When two or more moving averages of different periods are used on the same chart, for example 9-day and 21-day periods SMA, their position relative to each other indicates the running market trend. When a short period moving average is below the longer period moving average, it is a downtrend; when a shorter period moving average is above the longer period moving average, it is an uptrend. The short period moving average is referred to as fast moving average; the longer period moving average is referred to as slow moving average.

Moving averages are best suited for following the trend and are not capable of predicting a change in trend as they lag price move. Since they are trend following indicators, they should only be used in a trending market and not when the markets are in a trading range. In a non-trending market, moving averages result in many whipsaws thereby causing frequent losses.

Once there is a clear indication that a security is trending, the next decision will be to decide on the number of periods to be used. You can use any number such as five, twenty, fifty, hundred, etc. as this is very subjective. However, there are certain points you should keep in mind.

If the security is not indicating a strong trend, a longer period moving average needs to be used whereas when a security is in a strong trend, a shorter period moving average will be more suitable as long ones will be ineffective. If the security is too volatile, a short period moving average, like 5 or 13, would be prone to whipsaws, and longer period moving averages will be required.

The most commonly used periods are 9, 13, 21, 50, 100 and 200. Once you start using moving averages, your trading experience and style will dictate the kind of moving average you would be using. If the price is crossing the moving average too often, increase the period. On the other hand, if the moving average is continuously too far away from the price, reduce the period. If your analysis requires quick entry and exit, use exponential moving average.

Moving averages can be traded in a variety of ways — in combination with price, and in combination with each other.

Moving Average with Price

Support and Resistance

A single moving average plotted with price provides important support and resistance levels in a trending market (*see* Figure 22.4).

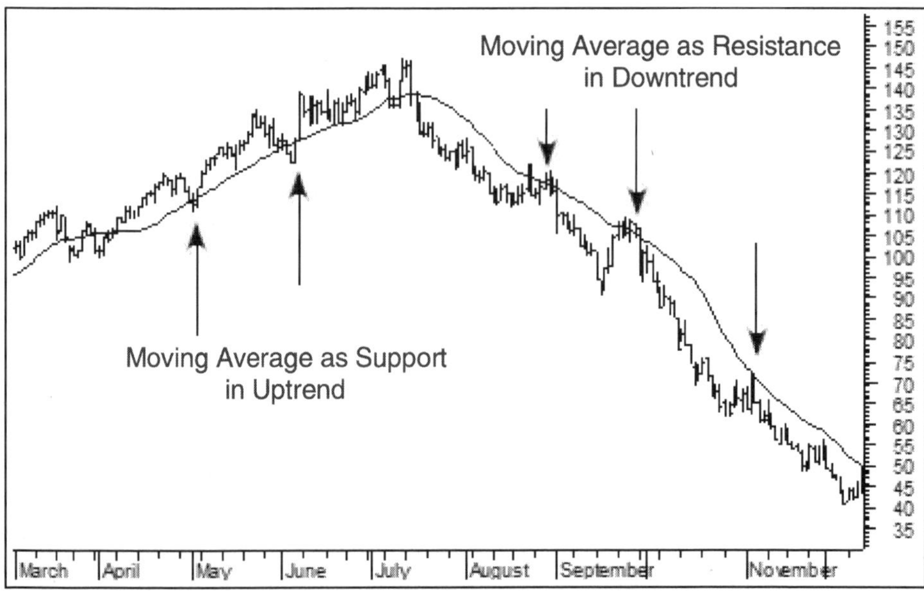

Figure 22.4: **Moving average acting as support and resistance**

Price Crossover

When price crosses the moving average, it provides buy and sell trading signals depending on the direction of the crossover. The following are the important price crossover techniques:

- Go long (buy) when price crosses the rising moving average to upside. This is a very strong bullish signal.
- Go short (sell) when price crosses the falling moving average to downside. This is a very strong bearish signal.
- Never buy on an upside price crossover when the moving average is falling, and
- never sell on a downside crossover when the moving average is rising.

Identical conditions of moving average and price may require a different approach depending on how other technical tools are used in combination. The following are two situations:

1. Contrarian trade — In a trading market when the moving averages are not showing any trend, enter a contrarian trade after crossover if the price moves too far away from the moving average. This means that if the price is rising, then sell, and if the price is falling, then buy. This is also known as fading. The logic is that since there is no clear trend, a big price move is bound to retrace to the moving average. However, you should not attempt this if there is either a chart pattern or a support and resistance breakout.

2. When moving averages are not showing any clear slope, you can still buy at an upside crossover and sell at a downside crossover. This gives you an opportunity to avoid the lag. However, it has associated risks as the market may be in a trading range triggering the stop losses with every entry. To reduce the risk, wait for at least three closes above or below the average and look for an indication of slope formation in the direction of the trade before taking an entry. Also, remember to avoid taking any position if the price has moved too far away from the moving average.

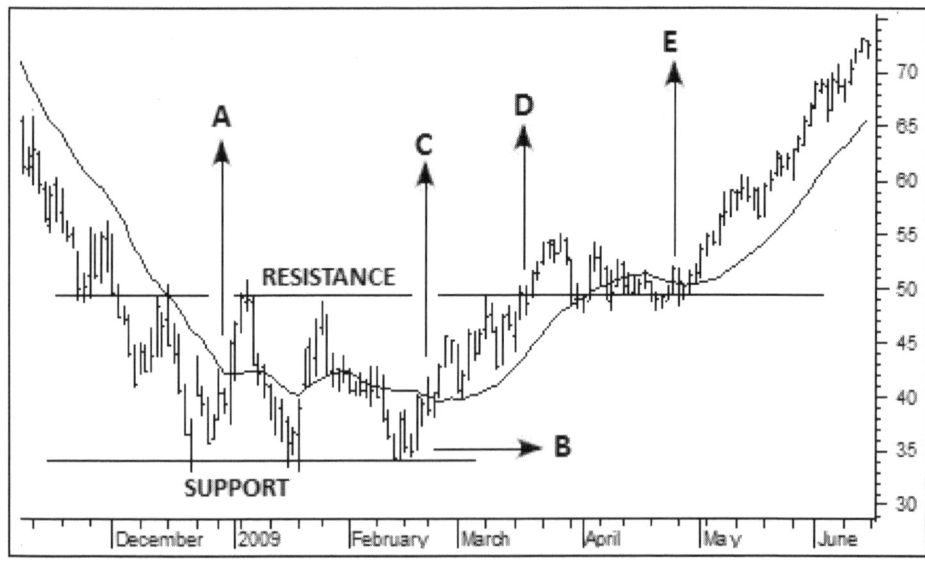

Figure 22.5: **Different market phases using moving average**

In Figure 22.5, you can observe all the three market phases — first a downtrend, then a trading range, followed by an uptrend using a 21-day moving average:

Point A: The price has crossed the moving average and the right trading strategy would be to fade the crossover and sell because of two reasons — first, there was a prior downtrend and, second, there is a clear resistance around 48-price level. Buying at crossover will only lead to a stop loss.

Point B: There are good reasons to buy at these levels because the moving average has flattened indicating a trading range, and it is also a good support level.

Point C: The crossover is happening in a clear trading market so any entry should be avoided as no moving average trading signal can be identified.

Point D: The price has crossed the resistance level accompanied by a rising moving average. It is a buy signal even though much of the price rise has already happened. Although the price is not able to move up immediately, it is holding close to the previous resistance line which is now the support, indicating the chances of an upside move. If the price closes convincingly below this line, you would book the loss.

Point E: There is an upside crossover which is also a breakout of a small triangle formation indicating a clear buy signal.

Two Moving Averages

Using price with a single moving average has its weakness due to the volatility factor of price. This can be overcome by using two moving averages in analysis — one a shorter period, and another, a longer period moving average. For a short period, you can use either 5-period, 9-period or 13-period moving averages, and for the longer period, you can use either 21-period, 34-period or 50-period moving averages. The final decision will be yours depending on the duration of your trade. You may even use a 100-period moving average as the longer one, but as you increase the length of the period, the number of trading signals will get fewer. The two-moving-average-analysis is also known as double crossover method.

Trading Signals

1. Go long when the fast moving average crosses the slow moving average to the upside.
2. Go short when the fast moving average crosses the slow moving average to the downside.

   The above two strategies yield for too many false breakouts. To avoid the risk, a variation of double crossover method known as Dead Cross and Golden Cross should be used:

   - **Dead Cross:** When the crossover happens between two moving averages that are moving in opposite directions, it is known as a Dead Cross. These types of crossovers should not be traded.
   - **Golden Cross:** When the crossover happens between two moving averages that are moving in the same direction, it is known as a Golden Cross. These types of crossovers are very reliable. Therefore, if a rising fast moving average crosses a rising slow moving average to the upside, it is a very strong "buy" signal.

3. The slow moving average acts as a support, or resistance as the case may be to the fast moving average. The fast moving average is likely to bounce off from the slow moving average as they touch each other during a strong trend. When the fast moving average is easily able to cross the slow moving average, it indicates weakening of the trend.

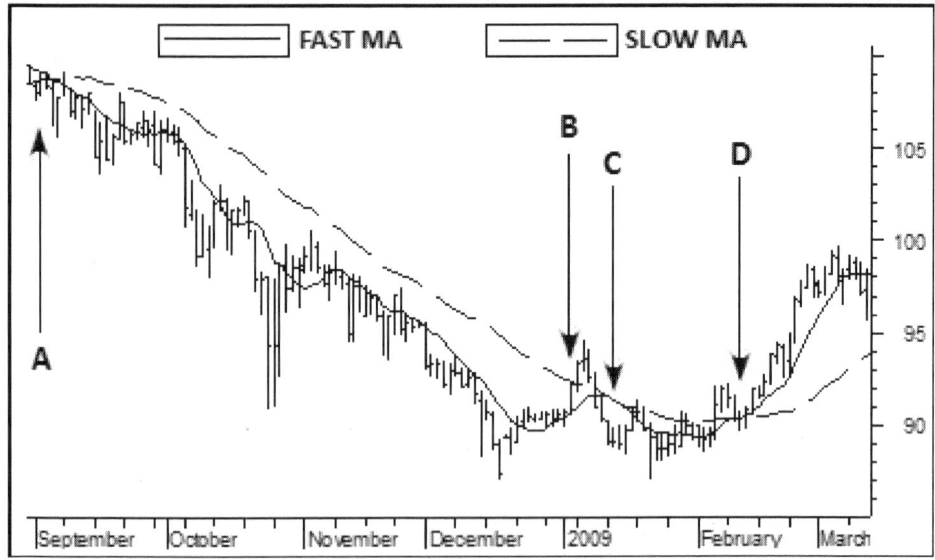

Figure 22.6: **Using two moving averages to trade**

4. When the two moving averages are running very close to each other, it indicates a complete absence of trend. Do not use moving averages for analysis in such a situation and fade any price movement that goes far away from the moving average.

Figure 22.6 shows the benefits of using a fast moving average instead of price for the purpose of analysis.

Point A: A fast moving average has crossed the slow moving average to downside giving a 'sell' signal. You can go short after the crossover point.

Point B: The price has crossed the moving averages but the fast moving average has not yet crossed the slow moving average indicating that it is not yet the right time to buy.

Point C: After touching the slow moving average, the fast moving average starts to fall again. The right entry strategy here would be to go short.

Point D: The fast moving average crosses the slow moving average to the upside. If you had gone short at point C, book the loss and go long after point D when the price breaks the previous high.

The big gap between moving averages sometimes provides a good trading opportunity. When the distance between two moving averages increases too much, trade on overbought and oversold trading signals in oscillators like RSI, explained in Chapter 23 "Oscillators".

Three Moving Averages

Using three moving averages refines the analysis and reduces the risk further. Combining three moving averages is one of the best methods to determining the strength and direction of a trend. The combination could be for short term trading (5-day, 9-day, and 13-day), swing trading (9-day, 13-day and 21-day) or long term trading (21-day, 50-day and 100-day).

When all the three moving averages are rising, it indicates a strong up-trend.

When all the moving averages are falling, it indicates a strong down-trend. The larger the gap between the moving averages, the stronger the trend.

Trading Techniques

- Go long when the middle moving average crosses the slow moving average to the upside.
- Go short when the middle moving average crosses the slow moving average to the downside.
- Close long positions when the fast moving average crosses the middle moving average to the downside.
- Close short positions when the fast moving average crosses the middle moving average to the upside.

The above strategies are just a few ways you can trade three moving averages. You must try different combinations and optimize your trading according to your style. For example, one of the ways you could trade is to go long when the fast moving average crosses the middle moving average to upside with both of them being above the slow moving average.

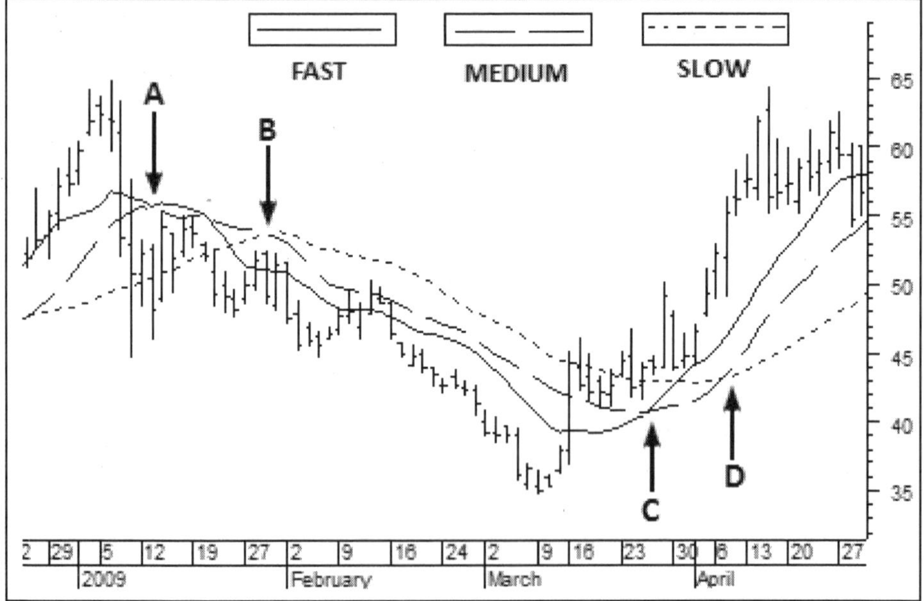

Figure 22.7: **Using three moving averages to trade**

This is a very strong "buy" signal. Figure 22.7 depicts three moving averages.

Point A: It is the first indication that the trend is changing as the fast moving average crossed the medium moving average to downside.

Point B: After point B, the downtrend is confirmed as all three moving averages are falling.

Point C: Point C indicates the end of the downtrend as the fast moving average crossed the medium moving average to upside.

Point D: After point D, the uptrend is confirmed as all three moving averages are rising.

Avoid using more than three averages, as it will make your analysis complicated and vague. The signals too will be fewer making it impractical for a trader.

Important Points about Moving Averages

1. Identify the moving average period that suits your trading style. Even when you decide to trade with the most commonly used averages such

as 9-day, 13-day, 21-day, 50-day, etc. test these moving averages before committing any money.

2. Remember that moving averages are trend following indicators that give an opportunity to make huge profits after taking risks of frequent stop losses. If your position has turned profitable, do not be in a haste to exit from the trade as you can capture a big move.
3. The 21-day moving average depicts the short-term trend; the 50-day moving average depicts the medium-term trend and the 200-day moving average depicts the long-term trend. Day traders should always use the 200-day moving average as reference as it shows the major trend the market is following. Try to look for a "buy" opportunity in securities that are above their 200-day moving average, and a "sell" opportunity in securities that are below their 200-day moving average.
4. Whichever time-frame chart you are using for trading, analyze the next closest higher time-frame chart as reference for better results, and use the same moving averages to analyze both the charts. If you are trading on an hourly chart using a 9-period and 21-period moving average, use the same set-up to analyze a daily chart.
5. It will be difficult for the price to cross above a falling moving average as it will act as a strong resistance for any price rise. Similarly, it will be difficult for price to cross below the rising moving average, as it will act as a strong support for any decline in prices.
6. Once the entry is made based on moving average signals, the exit may be done based on other tools. The reason is that by the time the moving average gives an exit signal, a large part of the profit is lost. You could base your exit on a trailing stop loss (explained in Chapter 30 "Money and Risk Management").

Typical Price

The typical price is calculated by adding the previous period's high, low and closing prices together, and then dividing by three. This is also known as pivot point. The typical price indicator measures the average of the high, low, and closing prices for the period using a simple, single-line

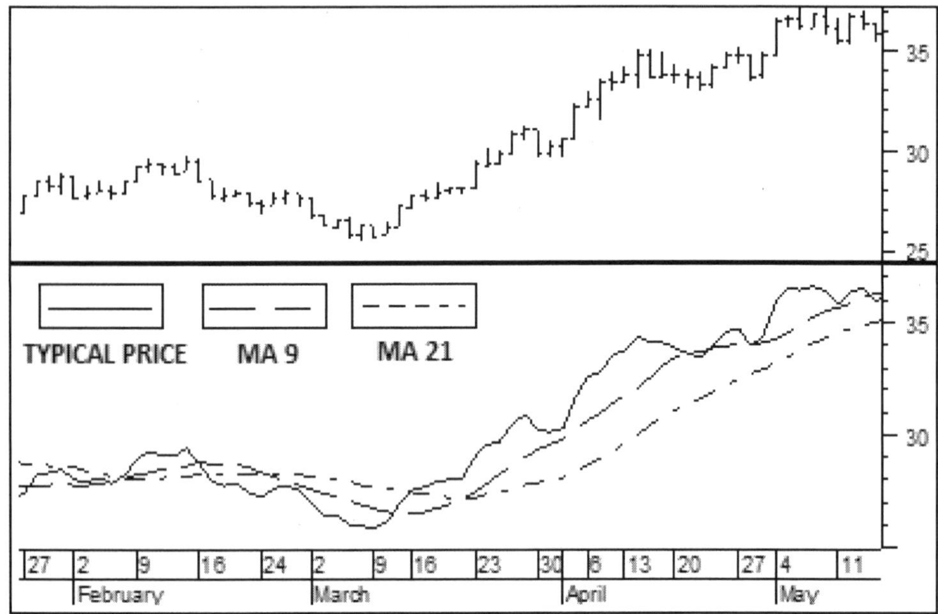

Figure 22.8: **Typical price**

plot. You can use it for your analysis in place of a price chart to incorporate the price movement of the whole period rather than just depending on the closing price. Figure 22.8 depicts the typical price indicator with two moving averages.

The most easily traded strategy is to buy when the typical price line crosses the moving average to the upside, and sell when it crosses the moving average to the downside.

A Note about Pivot Points

Pivot points are levels of major support or resistance, calculated from the previous period's high, low and close prices. The primary pivot point is an average of the previous period's high, low and close prices, and calculated by adding the three price figures and dividing the sum by three.

Pivot point = (H + L + C) / 3

Using this pivot point, the major support and resistance levels are calculated.

Pivot point (P) = (H + L + C) / 3
First resistance level (R1) = (2 x P) - L
First support level (S1) = (2 x P) – H
Second resistance level (R2) = P + (R1 - S1)
Second support level (S2) = P - (R1 - S1).

Pivot point (P), first support (S1) and first resistance (R1) are the three most important levels. The other variation of pivot point is to add today's open price in the calculation.

Pivot = [Today's Open + Yesterday's (H + L + C) /4]

The above are the most widely used pivot points by traders. There are numerous ways you can calculate your own pivot point and test those levels in trading.

If the market opens above the pivot point, it indicates bullish sentiment for that particular day. If the market opens below the pivot point, it indicates bearish sentiment. All support and resistance trading strategies apply to pivot levels. Remember that pivot trading is limited to the current trading day and you will have to calculate new levels for the next trading day. For short-term traders, the best way to use pivot (typical price indicator) is to plot a typical price line with 3- or 5-period moving average and trade on crossovers of the pivot and the moving average.

Envelope

Envelope is an extension of the moving average study. The construction is fairly simple. First, a moving average is plotted and then it is shifted up and down by a fixed percentage. This creates a band with an upper and a lower line running parallel to the middle line or the moving average (*see* Figure 22.9). For example, if a 5% envelop is constructed, it would display an upper line that is 5% above moving average and a lower line that is 5% below moving average.

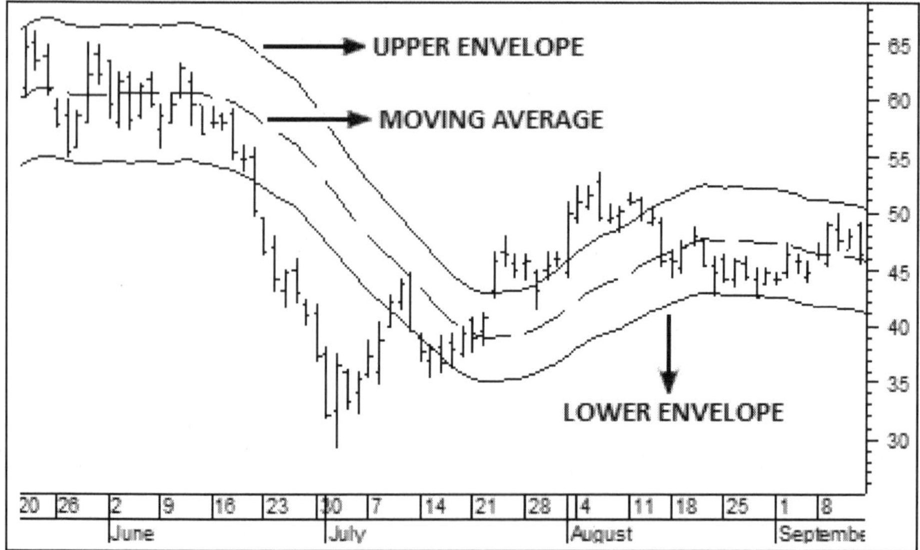

Figure 22.9: **Envelope**

All parameters of constructing an envelope are essentially user specific, and you will decide the type of moving average, period and the shift percentage depending on your trading style. If you had been trading with a simple moving average, use the same for constructing the envelope. For intraday traders, a short period moving average would be appropriate whereas long-term traders should use a longer period moving average. The percentage by which the envelope will deviate from the moving average will depend on the security being traded. The simple way to select it is to adjust the percentage until a minimum 90% of prices are within the envelope.

Trading Envelope

Envelope should be used with caution while trading and the signals should be confirmed before taking an entry:

1. Go long when the price starts to rise from the lower band.
2. Go short when the price starts to fall from the upper band.

In both the above trades, look for the strength of price reversal.

3. If prices continuously stay close to the upper band and are accompanied by higher lows, it indicates strong buying pressure. Go long keeping the last low as the stop loss level.
4. If prices continuously stay close to the lower band and are accompanied by lower highs, it indicates strong selling pressure. Go short keeping the last high as the stop loss level.
5. Use all the moving average trading strategies whenever applicable.

Bollinger Bands

Bollinger bands are advanced forms of the envelope (*see* Figure 22.10). The weakness of the envelope is that it does not adjust to volatility and the trader has to keep changing the shift percentage with the change in

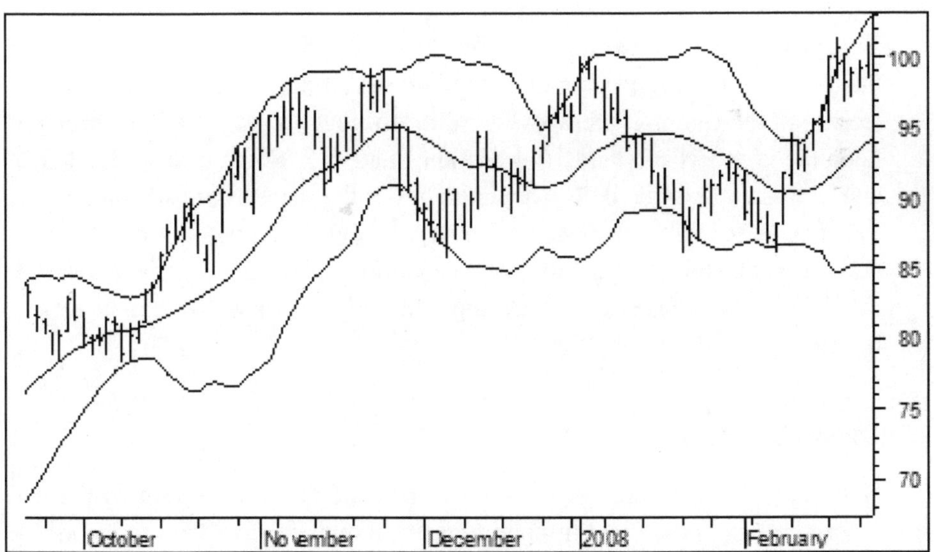

Figure 22.10: **Bollinger bands**

volatility. This is not practically possible for a trader, thereby reducing the relevance of the envelope. To overcome this shortcoming, John Bollinger developed Bollinger bands and improved upon the envelope by making it dynamic and adaptive to volatility by using standard deviation. Standard deviation is a statistical measure of price volatility and measures how widely closing prices have dispersed from the average price.

Construction

Bollinger bands consist of a 20-day simple moving average with upper and lower bands. The upper band is 2 standard deviations above the moving average, and the lower band is 2 standard deviations below the moving average. The standard deviation ensures that the bands react quickly to price movements and the periods of high and low volatility are easily identified by expansion and contraction of the bands.

Parameter Settings

Bollinger bands by default use the 20-period simple moving average based on the closing price and 2 standard deviations. You can adjust the length of the moving average according to your trading preference but keep the numbers of standard deviation fixed at 2. Some traders use 1.5 and 2.5 standard deviation depending on the length of the moving average. When using a 9-period moving average, 1.5 standard deviation may be tried, and while using a 50-period moving average, a 2.5 standard deviation may be used in calculations. Initially, just use the default settings.

Trading Strategies

Bollinger bands provide a good assessment of the price action as they incorporate both the volatility and trend. Although it provides some good trading opportunities on its own, it is best used in combination with other technical tools to harness its full potential.

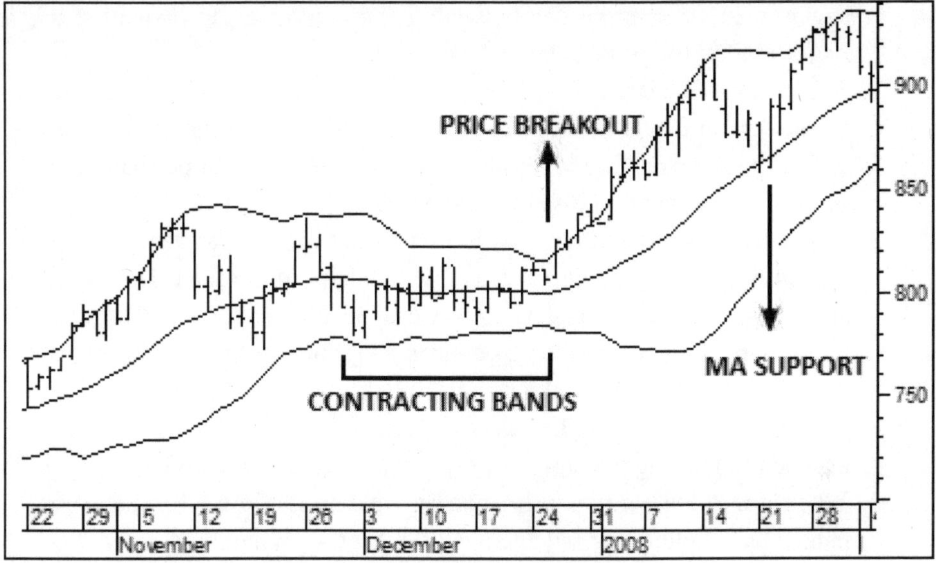

Figure 22.11: **Trading with Bollinger bands**

The following are important trading strategies:

1. When bands contract or tighten, it indicates a period of low volatility. In such a situation, a breakout is imminent and you can capture big profits by trading in the direction of the breakout. In Figure 22.11, after a period of low volatility indicated by contracting bands, the price has given an upside breakout.

   The upside breakout is confirmed when the price crossed the upper band and closed outside it. The stock continued to trade at the upper band in the next trading session indicating the continuation of the uptrend. A clear symmetrical triangle chart pattern also gave an upside breakout at the same time, giving a second confirmation of an uptrend. This is a strong signal for taking long trades.

   An extreme contraction of bands is termed as squeeze if the bands are closest to each other in the recent past. The breakout after a squeeze is very strong, and usually a new trend develops after a breakout.

   Bollinger bands that are far apart show a period of high volatility. High volatility is associated with major reversal levels. Therefore, the exceptionally increased gap between bands serves as an indication of major market top or bottom being formed.

2 Support and Resistance — The upper band acts as the resistance and the lower band acts as the support for the price when the markets are in a trading range. Sell when the price is close to the upper band and buy when the price is close to the lower band.

3 When prices are continuously running close to the upper band accompanied by a rising moving average, it indicates an uptrend. Do not go short unless clear reversal signals are available. In such a condition, the moving average will act as a strong support for any fall in prices. Therefore, go long when the price comes close to the moving average. Check momentum oscillators for confirmation of oversold levels around the moving average.

4. When prices are continuously running close to the lower band accompanied by a falling moving average, it indicates a downtrend. Do not go long unless clear reversal signals are available. In such a condition, the moving average will act as a strong resistance for any rise in prices, so go short when the price comes close to the moving average. Check momentum oscillators for confirmation of overbought levels around the moving average.

5. Double Top Sell — When you spot a double top formation on a price chart, check the position of the two highs in relation to the upper band (*see* Figure 22.12). If the first high is outside the upper band but the second one forms inside the band, it is a double top sell signal. The sell signal is confirmed when the price falls below the moving average.

6. Double Bottom Buy — When you spot a double bottom formation on a price chart, check the formation of the two lows in relation to the lower band. If the first low is outside the lower band but the second one forms inside the band, it is a double bottom buy signal. The buy signal is confirmed when the price rises above the moving average.

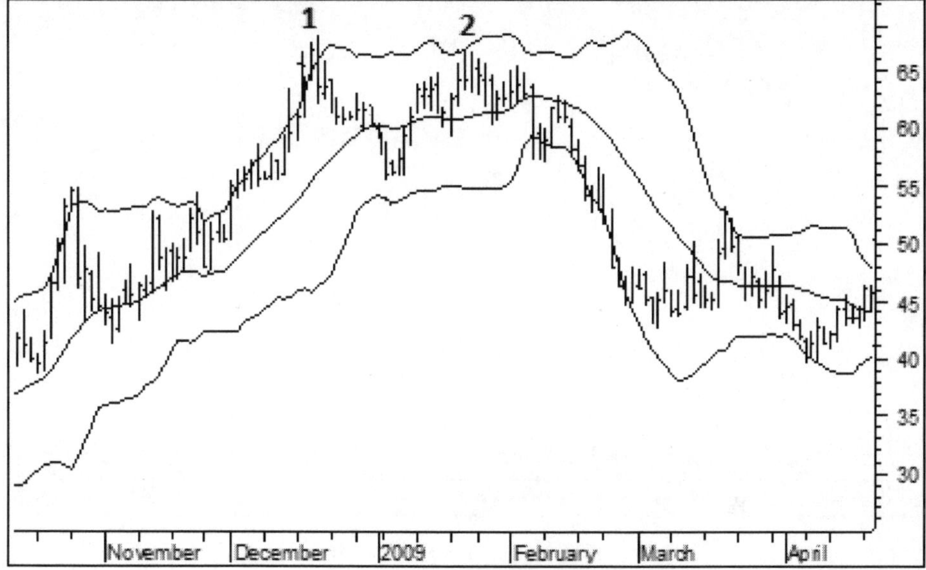

Figure 22.12: **Double top sell**

Option Strategies

1. Buy options when Bollinger bands are too tight and closest to each other in the recent past.
2. Sell options when Bollinger bands are too wide and have the largest difference in the recent past.
3. When the bands contract and run close to each other, employ a strangle option strategy.

Parabolic SAR

In trending markets, when you have a position in the direction of the trend, there may be confusion about the right exit level. If you exit early, you may miss a chance to profit from the continuing trend. If you wait too long to exit, the markets may change direction and you may lose a big part of your profit. Parabolic SAR (Stop and reversal) is a good indicator to be used as trailing stops, and provides you with clear exit levels

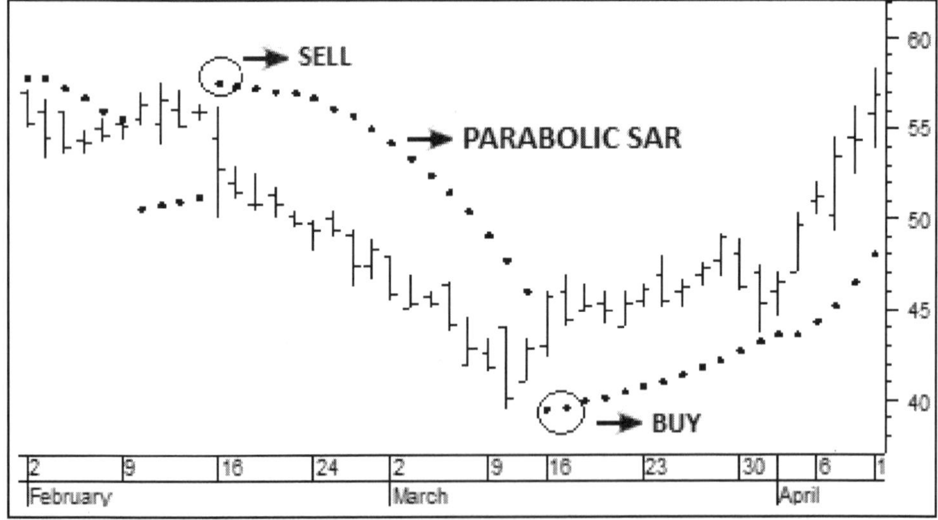

Figure 22.13: **Parabolic SAR**

when a security's trend reverses. Parabolic SAR was developed by Welles Wilder primarily to be used as a trailing price stop for open long and short positions (*see* Figure 22.13).

The interpretation of Parabolic SAR is simple:

- **Exiting Long Positions:** When the dotted line is below the price, hold on to your long position. When price comes below the dotted line, close your long positions.
- **Exiting Short Positions:** When the dotted line is above the price, hold on to your short positions. When price comes above the dotted line, close your short positions.

At the beginning of a trend, Parabolic SAR creates a greater distance between the price and the trailing stop. However, as the trend develops, the distance between the price and the indicator gets smaller, providing you with tighter stop-loss levels.

You can also use parabolic SAR for taking up new positions, but remember to first understand the trend of the market. If the market is in a trading range, Parabolic SAR will keep fluctuating up and down based on the price movement, repeatedly triggering your stop loss. Parabolic SAR is a trend following indicator, so never use it in trading markets. If the markets are trending, buy when the indicator is below the price and sell when the indicator is above the price.

There are two parameters specified at the time of plotting — step and maximum step. The values as recommended by Wilder are 0.02 for step and 0.20 for maximum step. Your charting software will use these values for calculation as default settings. The higher the step is set, the more sensitive the indicator will be to price changes. The indicator will fluctuate above and below the price too often if the step is set too high. The maximum step adjusts the parabolic SAR as the price moves. The lower the maximum step is set, the further the trailing stops will be from the price.

Chapter 23

Oscillators

TRENDING MARKETS PROVIDE BIG PROFIT OPPORTUNITIES from even a small number of trades. However, there are two aspects that traders have to face. First, how to trade when the markets are not trending and, second, where exactly to take a position even while trading in the direction of the trend. Oscillators provide a solution to both these points.

Oscillators are extensively used to trade non-trending securities by displaying overbought and oversold levels. They are also used to find an entry point to trade in the direction of the trend in trending securities.

Oscillators are calculated by different methods, but the interpretation is almost the same for all of them. Therefore, only two oscillators, MACD and RSI, are explained in detail in this chapter. For the other oscillators, only those aspects are explained in detail which are relevant but not covered in these two.

The default calculation settings in charting software are those that have been originally used by the creator of the indicator. During your initial trading days, do not try to experiment with these settings; work on the default ones. You can experiment with different settings once you have gained enough experience in using oscillators.

Centred Oscillators

Moving Average Convergence Divergence (MACD)

Moving average convergence divergence or MACD, was developed by Gerald Appel. MACD is unique in the sense that it incorporates characteristics of both the leading as well as lagging indicators (*see* Figure 23.1). It is one of the simplest and most reliable indicators available to traders.

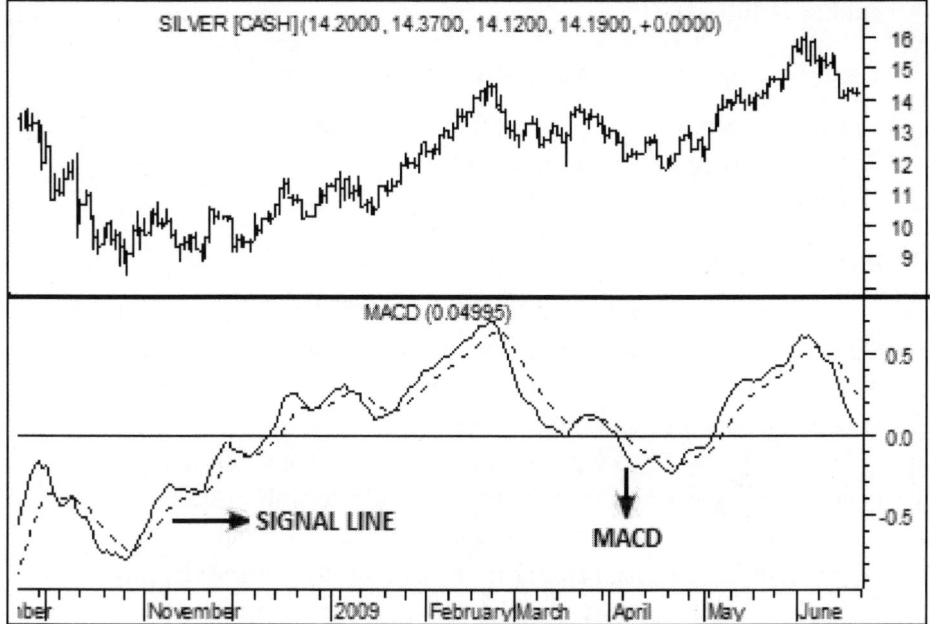

Figure 23.1: **MACD**

MACD is a refinement of the two moving average techniques and is calculated by subtracting the 26-period exponential moving average (EMA) from the 12-period EMA. Both the EMAs are based on closing prices. A signal line is plotted with the MACD, which is simply a 9-period EMA of the MACD.

MACD is plotted on a scale that indicates the positive and negative values of MACD. A centre line is drawn at zero level and MACD oscillates above and below this centre line. In a daily chart for example, A positive MACD means that the 12-day EMA is above the 26-day EMA. A negative MACD means that the 12-day EMA is below the 26-day EMA.

When MACD is positive and rising, it indicates a widening of the gap between the 12-day EMA and the 26-day EMA, or in other words, the two averages are diverging. This is a sign of increasing bullish momentum. When MACD is negative and falling, it again indicates a widening of the gap between the falling 12-day EMA and the 26-day EMA. This is a sign of increasing bearish momentum.

Trading MACD

There are three ways of trading MACD:

1. Trading divergence.
2. Trading moving average crossover.
3. Trading centre line crossover.

Trading Divergence

Divergence is perhaps the most reliable of oscillator signals. Generally, the price and indicator move in tandem and make new highs or lows at almost the same time. However, divergence occurs when the price of the security and the indicator move in opposite directions.

Divergence is of two types — positive (bullish) and negative (bearish). Positive divergence occurs when the price of a security makes a new low while the indicator starts to rise upward without making any new low. Negative divergence happens when the price of the security makes a new high, but the indicator starts to fall without making any new high.

Figure 23.2 shows positive divergence. Go long whenever this occurs, keeping the break of the last low as the stop loss point.

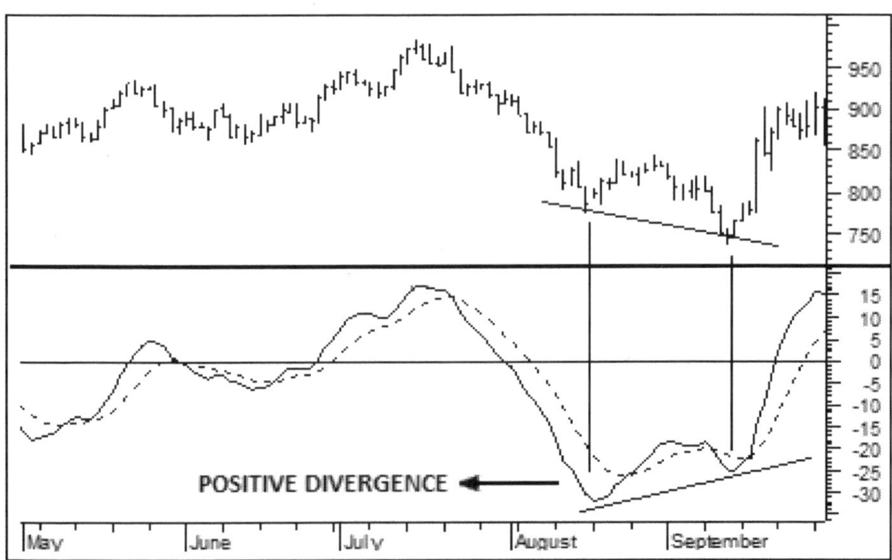

Figure 23.2: **Positive divergence**

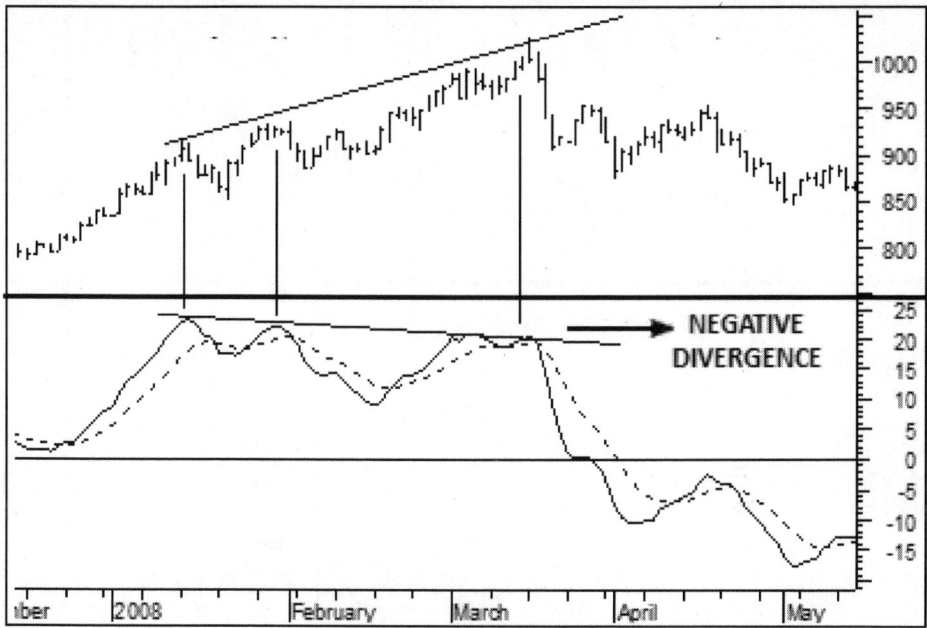

Figure 23.3: **Negative divergence**

Figure 23.3 shows negative divergence. Go short whenever this occurs keeping the break of the last high as the stop loss point.

Triple divergence: A triple divergence occurs where a divergence has failed and the price makes a third high after a negative divergence or a third low after positive divergence, but the indicator repeats its signal by making another lower high (in an up trend) or higher low (in a downtrend). The previous chart of negative divergence is also an example of triple divergence. Trade the triple divergence in the same way as divergence. You can, in fact, increase the trade size, as this is an even stronger signal than the original divergence.

Bullish Moving Average Crossover

This occurs when the MACD line crosses the signal line to the upside. This signal is best used when the security is in an uptrend. Go long whenever the crossover occurs (*see* Figure 23.4).

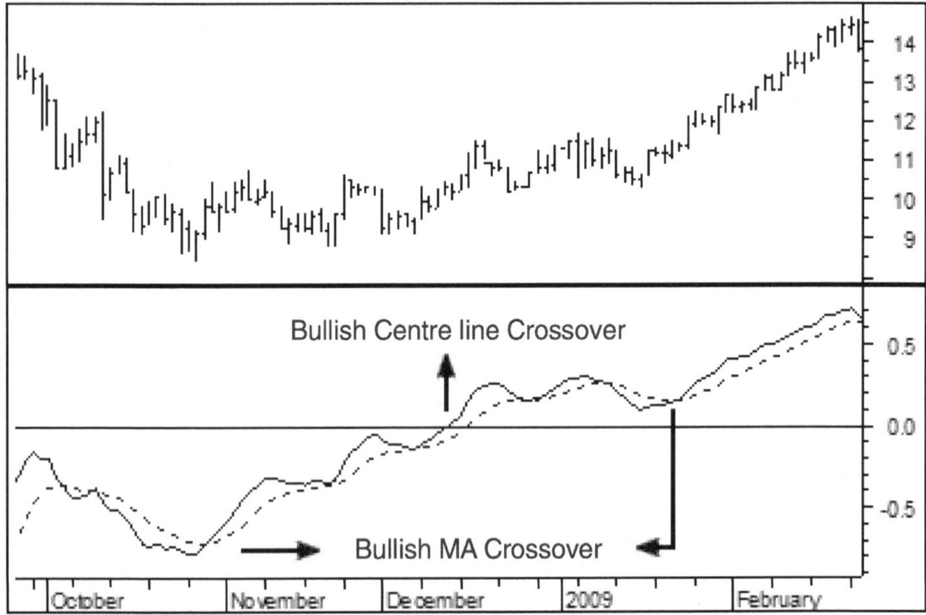

Figure 23.4: **Bullish centre line crossover**

Bullish Centre Line Crossover

This occurs when the MACD crosses the zero line to the upside and moves into positive territory. This should be used more as a reference point as it indicates that the price has an upward bias and a further rise can be expected (*see* Figure 23.4).

A bullish crossover when the MACD is in positive territory is a better signal to go long. If bullish centreline crossover happens after you have taken a long position, you can expect further price rice and look for averaging opportunities. Also, check if the price is making higher highs and higher lows, as that is another confirmation of bullish sentiment.

Bearish Moving Average Crossover

This occurs when the MACD line crosses the signal line to the downside. This signal is best used when the security is in a downtrend. Go short whenever the crossover occurs (Figure 23.5).

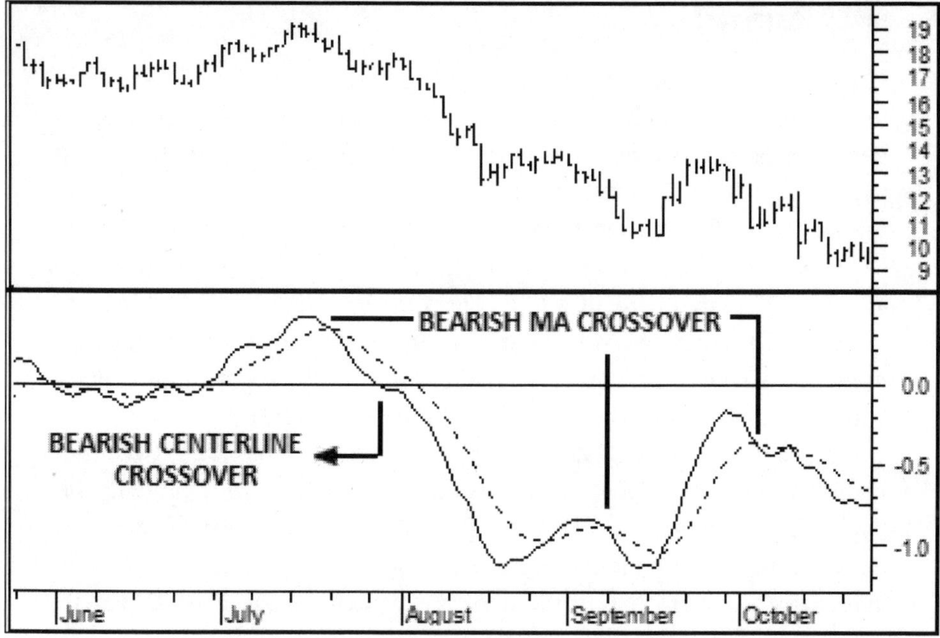

Figure 23.5: **Bearish centre line crossover**

Bearish Centre Line Crossover

This occurs when the MACD crosses the zero line to the downside and moves into the negative territory. This should be used more as a reference point as it indicates that the price has a downward bias and a further fall can be expected (*see* Figure 23.5).

A bearish crossover when the MACD is in negative territory is a better signal to go short. If a bearish centre line crossover happens after you have taken a short position, you can expect the price to fall further and look for averaging opportunities. Also, check if the price is making lower highs and lower lows, as that is another confirmation of bearish sentiment.

MACD Histogram

Histogram is an indicator based on MACD (*see* Figure 23.6). Therefore, in a sense, it is an indicator of an indicator. It is simply a graphic representation of the difference between the main MACD line and the nine-period signal line. This difference is then plotted on a scale to form a histogram, indicated as a series of vertical lines. The scale is the same as the MACD scale, with the zero line as the centre line. Histogram oscillates above and below this centre line. The zero level means that there is no difference between the MACD and the signal line. This can only happen at the crossover point; that is why whenever the crossover of the MACD and signal line occurs, the histogram will be at zero line.

The best use of the histogram is to look for divergence between the histogram and the price. Another method is to look for a divergence between the histogram and the MACD as shown in the chart. Divergence between the MACD and the MACD-histogram is used to predict moving average crossovers. A positive divergence between the MACD and the

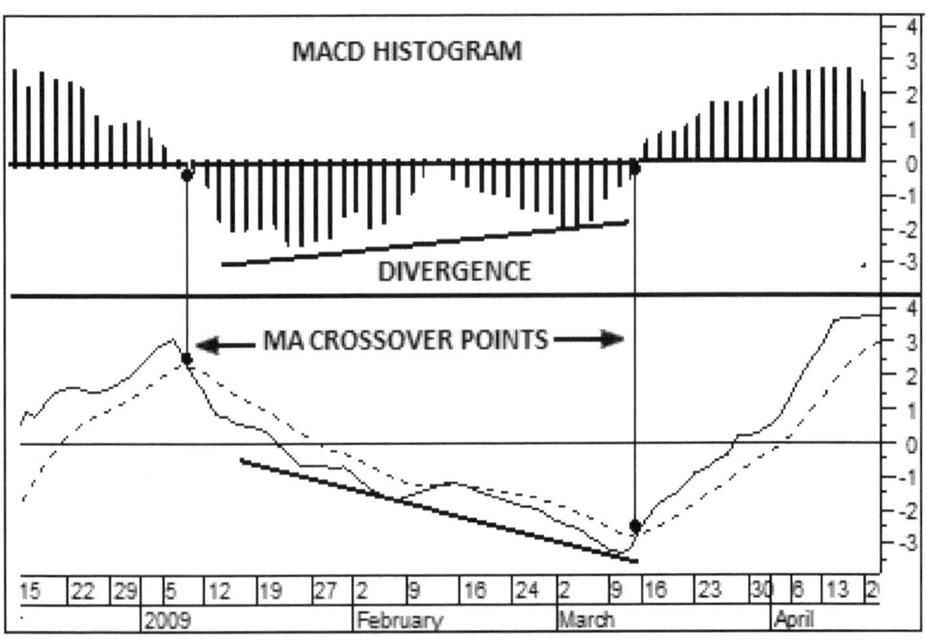

Figure 23.6: **MACD histogram**

histogram indicates that the MACD is strengthening and a bullish moving average crossover is likely. A negative divergence between the MACD and the histogram indicates that the MACD is weakening, and a bearish moving average crossover is likely. It is advisable to trade the longer and sharper divergence and avoid the weak ones.

Price Rate of Change (ROC)

Price rate of change is a momentum indicator that displays the current closing price relative to the closing price 12-periods ago (*see* Figure 23.7). It is then converted into percentage and plotted as an oscillator that fluctuates above and below the zero line.

If the security's price closes higher than it did 12 periods ago, the ROC will be above the zero line, and if the security's price closes lower than it did 12-periods ago, the ROC will be below the zero line.

Although the default time-frame is a 12-period, you can change the settings to 10, 25 or any other number you prefer, but do so only after enough experience.

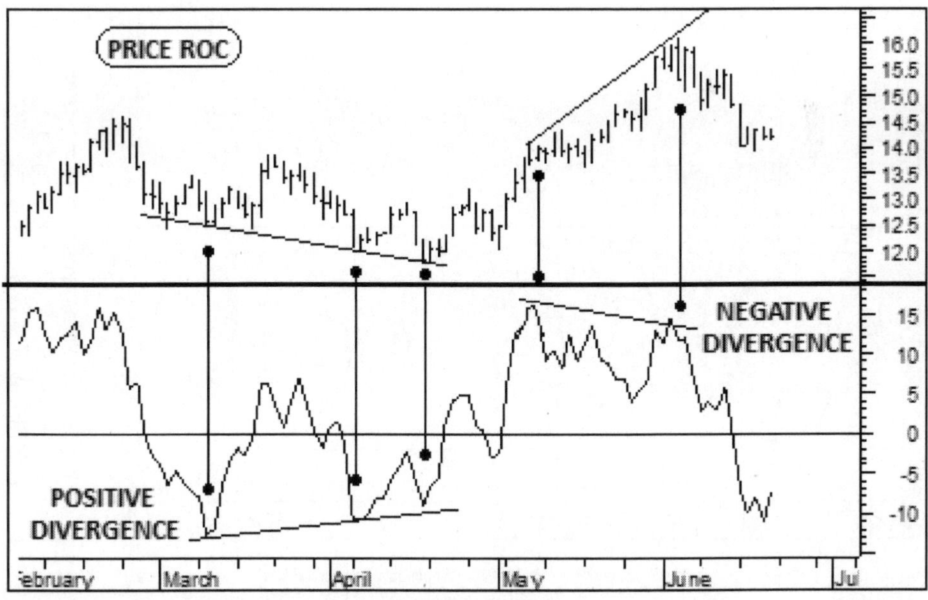

Figure 23.7: **Price ROC**

Trading ROC

1. **Divergence:** Buy after a positive divergence and sell after a negative divergence.
2. **Zero Line Crossovers:** Buy when the ROC crosses the zero line to the upside and sell when it crosses it to the downside.

Look for higher highs and higher lows on the ROC when it is below the zero line as a good entry for long positions. Correspondingly, look for lower highs and lower lows on the ROC when it is above the zero line as a good entry for short positions.

Banded Oscillators

Relative Strength Index (RSI)

RSI was developed by Welles Wilder in 1978, but it is still the most popular and extremely useful momentum oscillator.

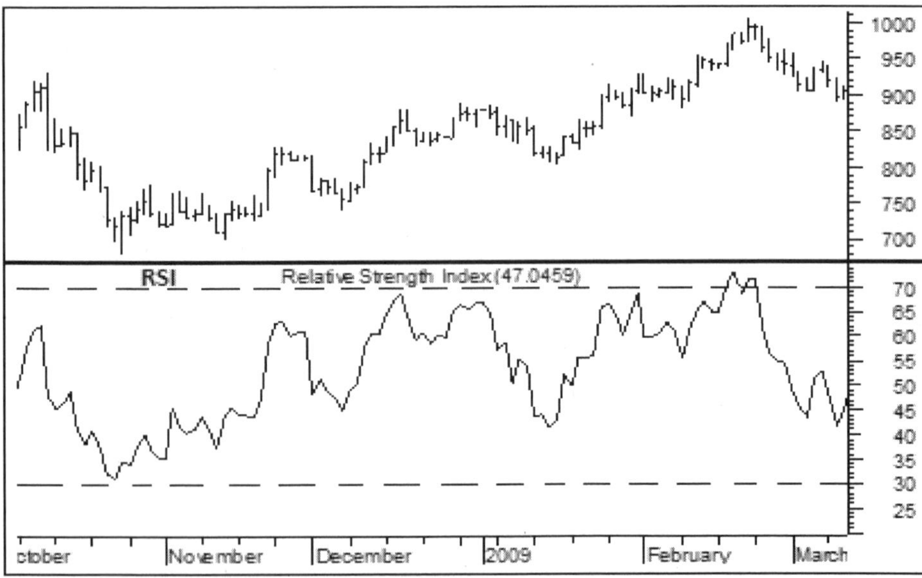

Figure 23.8: **Relative Strength Index (RSI)**

The basic concept behind RSI is to compare the magnitude of the recent gains (higher closing than the previous one) to the recent losses (lower closing than the previous one) to determine the overbought and oversold levels of a security. Wilder used 14-periods in the calculation, which is the default period setting in the charting software. If you are analyzing hourly charts, the default will be 14 hours, and if you are analyzing daily charts, it will be 14 days. RSI is plotted on a scale of zero to 100 and oscillates between these set limits. Figure 23.8 depicts the RSI indicator plotted below the price chart.

RSI Trading Strategies

RSI can be used to trade both non-trending as well as trending securities markets.

Non-trending or Ranged Markets

- **Overbought and Oversold Levels:** Readings above 70 are considered overbought, and below 30 are considered oversold. Whenever RSI is between 70 and 100, the security is supposed to be too heavily bought and ready for downward correction. Whenever RSI is between 30 and 0, the security is supposed to be too heavily sold and ready for upward correction.
- **RSI below 30:** It indicates an oversold zone and you can go long. However, to reduce the risk, it is better to enter when the price starts to move up after making a low, or when the RSI rises above the 30 levels.
- **RSI above 70:** It indicates an overbought zone and you can go short. However, to reduce the risk, it is better to enter when the price starts to move down after making a high, or when the RSI falls below the 70 levels.

Divergence

Divergence is perhaps the most reliable of oscillator signals. Generally, the price and indicator move in tandem and make new highs or lows at almost the same time. However, divergence occurs when the price of the security and the indicator move in opposite directions.

Divergence is of two types — positive (bullish) and negative (bearish). Positive divergence occurs when the price of a security makes a new low while the indicator starts to rise upward without making any new low. Negative divergence happens when the price of the security makes a new high, but the indicator starts to fall without making any new high.

Figure 23.9 depicts positive divergence. Go long whenever this occurs keeping the break of the last price low as a stop loss level. The signal is stronger if divergence occurs after an oversold reading on RSI.

Figure 23.10 depicts negative divergence. Go short whenever this occurs keeping the break of the last price high as a stop loss level. The signal is considered stronger if the divergence occurs after an overbought reading on RSI.

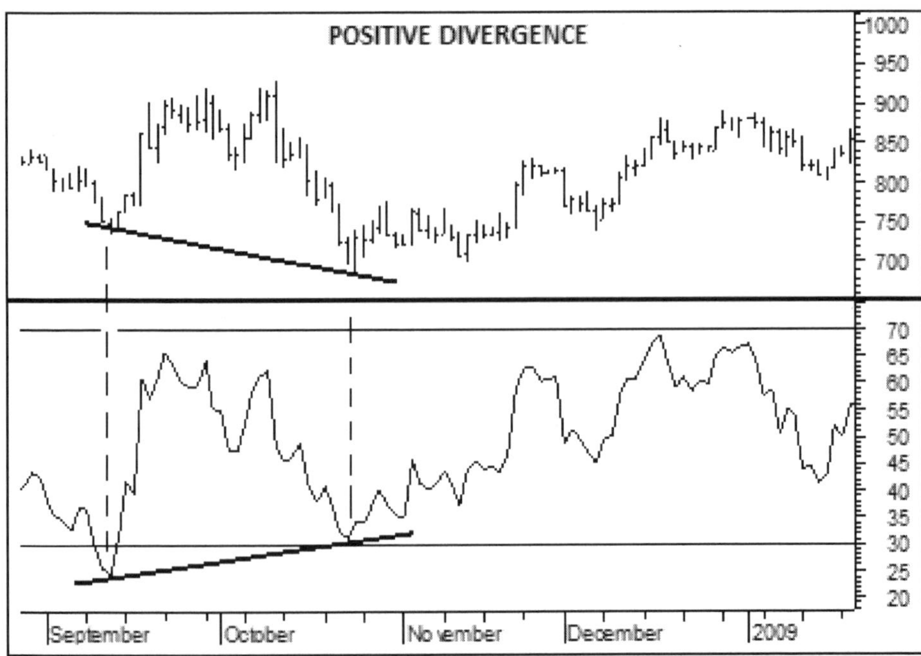

Figure 23.9: **Positive divergence**

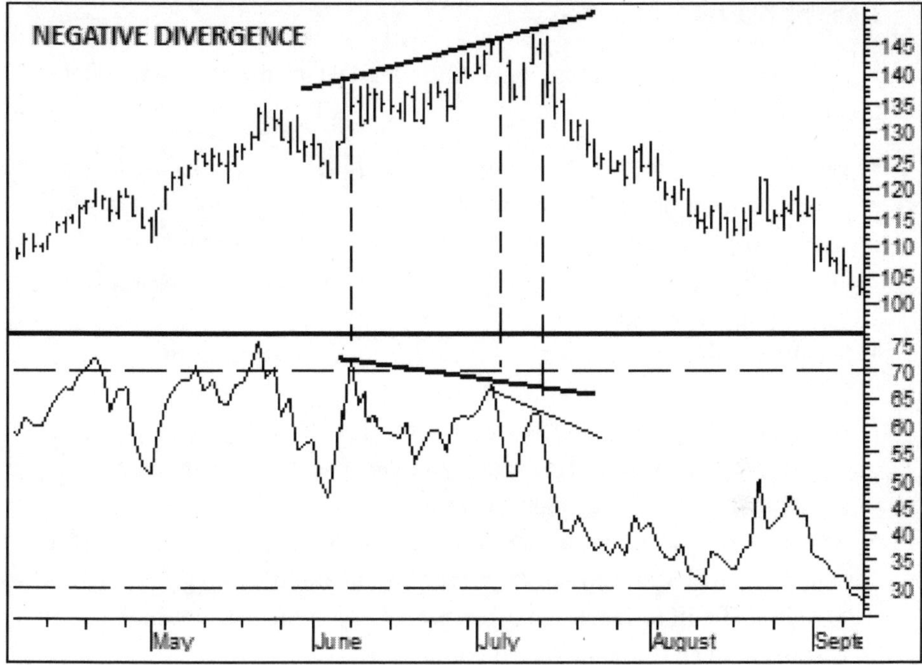

Figure 23.10: **Negative divergence**

Triple Divergence: A triple divergence occurs where a divergence has failed and the price makes a third high after negative divergence, or a third low after positive divergence, but the indicator repeats its signal by making another lower high (in an uptrend) or higher low (in a downtrend). The previous chart of negative divergence (*see* Figure 23.10) is also an example of triple divergence. Trade the triple divergence in the same way as divergence. You can, in fact, increase the trade size as this is an even stronger signal than the original divergence.

Centre Line Crossover

Centre line crossover should be used as an exit from a trade rather than for fresh entry. If you have a long position, you should look for an exit opportunity if the RSI crosses the centre line to the downside. If you have a short position, you should look for exit opportunity if the RSI crosses the centre line to the upside.

Trending Market

When a security is trending, only trade signals in the direction of the trend.

- **Uptrend:** Modify the oversold levels in an uptrend to 40, as the buying pressure in an uptrend will not allow for a deep correction. Go long when the RSI falls below 40. Never trade on an overbought signal in an uptrend. However, you can use negative divergence to book profits on existing long positions.
- **Downtrend:** Modify the overbought levels in a downtrend to 60 as the selling pressure in a downtrend will not allow for a strong pullback. Go short when the RSI rises above 60. Never trade on an oversold signal in a downtrend. However, you can use positive divergence to book profits on existing short positions.
- **Identification of Shift from Trading Market to Trending Situation through the RSI:** When the RSI starts to spend more time in the overbought zone and finds it difficult to reach the oversold zone, it indicates that the market is shifting to an uptrend. Avoid taking short positions.

When the RSI starts to spend more time in the oversold zone and finds it difficult to reach the overbought zone, it indicates that the market is shifting to a downtrend. Avoid taking long positions

RSI can also be analyzed just like a price chart. Look for support and resistance, trendlines, chart patterns, etc., and trade accordingly.

Stochastic

The Stochastic Oscillator was developed by George Lane in the late 1950s but is still the most widely used indicator, just like RSI (Figure 23.11).

A stochastic oscillator compares a security's current price to its high / low range over a selected number of periods, the most commonly used being 14 periods stochastic. In hourly charts, it will be 14 hours, in daily, 14 days etc. It is plotted on a scale from zero to 100.

The stochastic oscillator is indicated as %K. Don't be confused by the "%K" term; it's just the mathematical representation of ratio used in calculations. A 14-day period %K or 14-day period stochastic oscillator uses the most recent close, the highest high and the lowest low of the past 14 days and finally depicts where the latest close is placed compared to the range. The %K is equal to zero when the latest close is equal to the lowest low of 14-day period. It is equal to 100 when the latest close is equal to the highest high of 14-day period.

The stochastic oscillator or %K is plotted along with another line known as %D to form a complete stochastic indicator. %D, also known as trigger or signal line, is simply the 3-period moving average of %K. In the stochastic oscillator chart (Figure 23.11), the dotted line is the %D line.

As you can observe from Figure 23.11, the dotted line (%D line) moves close to the stochastic line (%K line). Since %D is a moving average, it reacts slowly and turns only after the %K line has turned.

This is a fast stochastic that is mostly used by short-term traders for analysis. Therefore, it can be termed as %K (fast) and %D (fast). Another version is the slow stochastic in which %K (slow) is the three-day

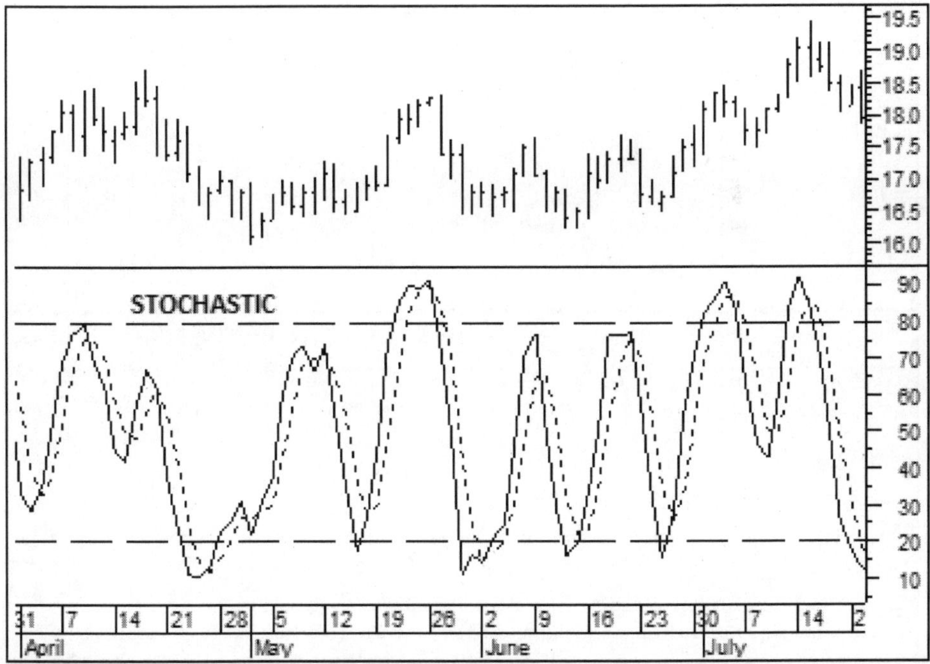

Figure 23.11: **Stochastic**

simple moving average of %K (fast), and %D (slow) is the 3-period moving average of the new slow %K. It may sound confusing but %K (slow) line is the same as %D (fast) line. As %K (slow) is nothing but moving average that slows down the reaction time, it is known as slow stochastic. Slow stochastic gives delayed signals but its advantage is fewer whipsaws, which helps a trader to avoid frequent stop losses.

Trading Stochastic

Divergence

This is the most reliable signal. You must wait for a positive or negative divergence to develop to get the best trading opportunity. To enter a long position, wait for a positive divergence to develop after the indicator moves below 20. To enter a short position, wait for a negative divergence to develop after the indicator moves above 80. Figure 23.12 shows a negative divergence.

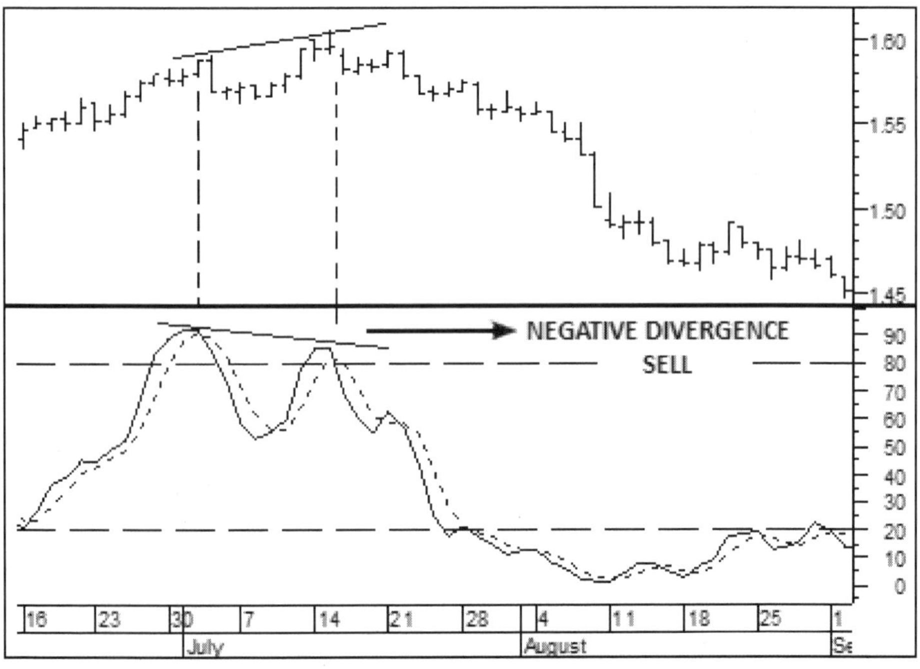

Figure 23.12: **Negative divergence**

Overbought and Oversold Levels

Readings above 80 are considered overbought, and below 20 are considered oversold. Whenever stochastic is between 80 and 100, the security is supposed to be too heavily bought and ready for downward correction. Whenever stochastic is between 20 and zero, the security is supposed to be too heavily sold and ready for upward correction.

- **Stochastic below 20:** It indicates an oversold zone but go long only when the price starts to move up after making a low and the stochastic rises above 20 levels.
- **Stochastic above 80:** It indicates an overbought zone but go short only when the price starts to move down after making a high and stochastic falls below 80.

Crossovers

Buy when the %K line crosses the %D line to the upside in an oversold zone, and sell when the %K line crosses the %D line to the downside in an overbought zone (*see* Figure 23.13).

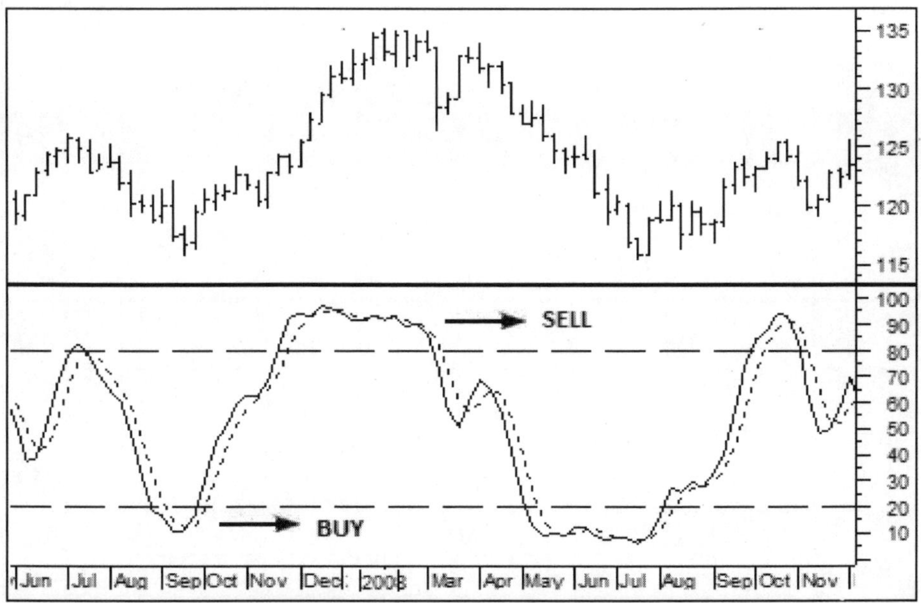

Figure 23.13: **Crossover in overbought and oversold zones**

Trading based purely on overbought / oversold levels and crossovers gives good results in non-trending securities. In trending securities, use them to trade in the direction of the trend. In an uptrend, buy on upside crossover no matter where it occurs on a scale, and in a downtrend, sell on a downside crossover no matter where it occurs. As with other indicators, use these signals with other tools like trendlines for getting a good entry point. Divergence can, however, be traded on its own and if supported by other tools, the trade size can be increased.

Williams %R

Williams %R is a momentum indicator developed by Larry Williams. The indicator is almost similar to stochastic except for a negative scale (*see* Figure 23.14). Williams %R is plotted using negative values ranging from zero to -100.

Values between zero and -20 are considered overbought and values between -80 to -100 are considered oversold.

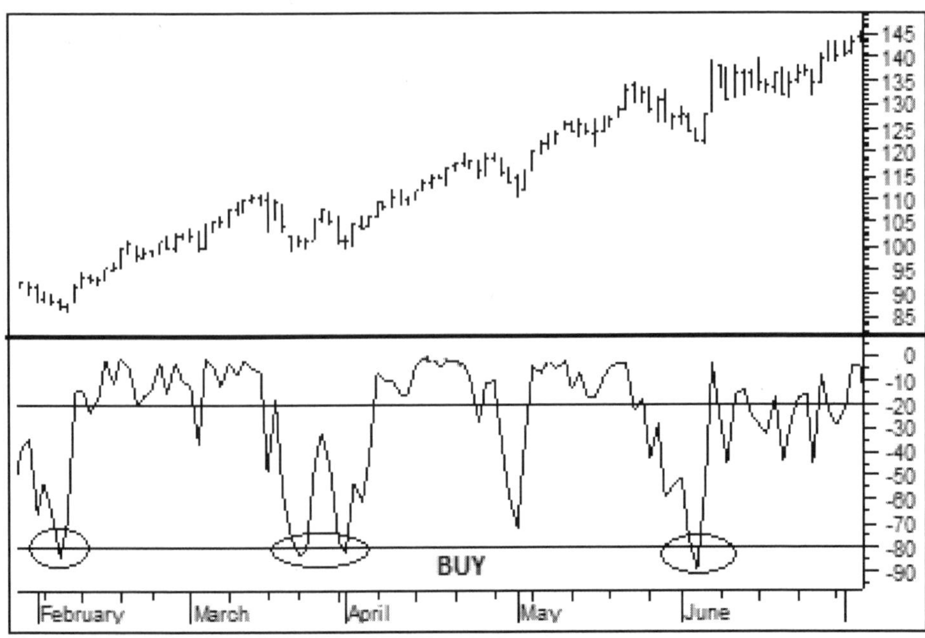

Figure 23.14: **Williams %R**

Williams %R reacts more quickly to price changes than stochastic and gives early signals of overbought and oversold levels. However, this makes it more prone to whipsaws and difficult to spot a clear divergence signal.

One of the best ways to trade Williams %R is to trade in the direction of the trend. In the previous chart, the trend is up which can also be easily judged from the fact that the %R indicator is spending most of the time in an overbought zone. Therefore, you must only trade long. Williams %R is one of the best indicators to use this strategy. Whenever it falls in the oversold zone and rises again, buy the security. Similarly, when the trend is down and the indicator moves to the overbought zone, sell the security.

Chande Momentum Oscillator

The Chande Momentum Oscillator (CMO) was developed by Tushar Chande. CMO is very similar to RSI except that it uses data for both gains and losses in the numerator for calculation, thereby directly measuring momentum (*see* Figure 23.15). Tushar Chande called it "pure

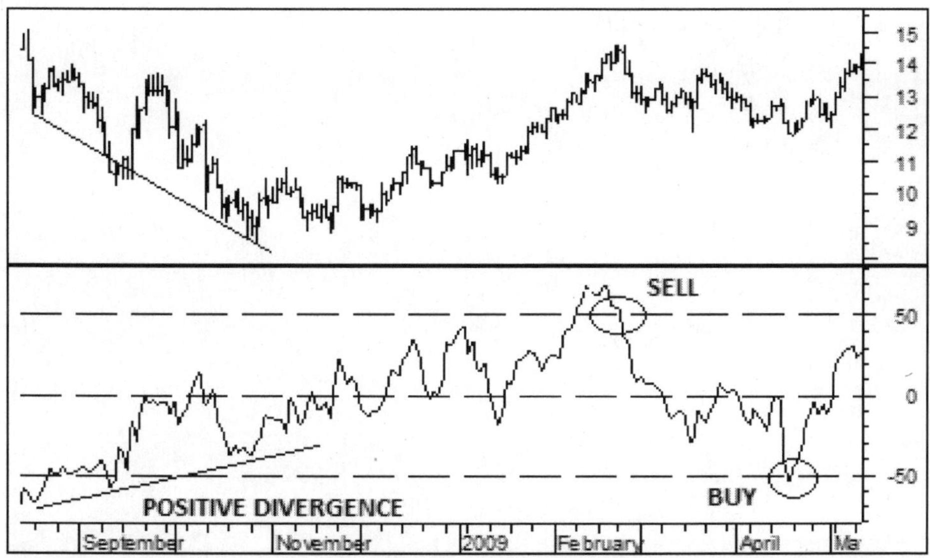

Figure 23.15: **Chande Momentum Oscillator**

momentum". The calculations are applied on unsmoothed data unlike RSI, and therefore, short-term extreme movements in price directly affect the indicator.

CMO is plotted on a scale of +100 and -100 and the default period is 20. At +50, the security is considered overbought, and at -50, it is considered oversold.

Trading CMO

Trading strategies for CMO are the same as other oscillators. Buy a security when it is oversold and sell it when it is overbought. If the markets are trending, trade only the signals pointing in the direction of the trend.

Divergence was not mentioned by Mr Chande in his original works but you can use it to identify entry positions. In the previous chart, there is a strong positive divergence after which the security's price moved up substantially.

A refinement of overbought / oversold entry and exit rules is to plot a moving average trigger line on the CMO. In a daily chart for example for a default 20-day CMO, a 9-day or 5-day moving average may serve as a good trigger line. Buy when the CMO crosses above the trigger line and sell when it crosses below.

Chapter 24

Trend Indicators

DIFFERENT MARKET CONDITIONS REQUIRE DIFFERENT ANALYSIS. Some tools are designed for trending markets and some for non-trending markets. Knowing whether a security is in a trending or non-trending phase helps a trader to employ relevant strategies.

There are two commonly used indicators to measure the strength of a trend and define whether the trend is strong or weak. These are Average directional index or ADX and Aroon. These indicators also depict whether the security is trending or in a trading range.

ADX

Average directional index or ADX was developed by Welles Wilder to measure the strength of a current trend. The ADX calculation is based on price range expansion and derived from two other indicators — the Positive Directional Indicator (+DI) which measures the force of up-moves, and the Negative Directional Indicator (-DI) which measures the force of down-moves (*see* Figure 24.1).

+DI and -DI indicators are combined and then the moving average is used to smoothen the data to get the final ADX line. Since ADX uses both +DI and -DI, it only indicates the strength of the trend, not the direction. Usually, all the three indicators, i.e., +DI, -DI and ADX are plotted in a single chart and called as Directional Movement Index or DMI.

The default setting is 14-periods but you can change the period settings according to your preference. Theoretically, the ADX oscillator fluctuates between 0 and 100; however, readings above 60 are quite rare.

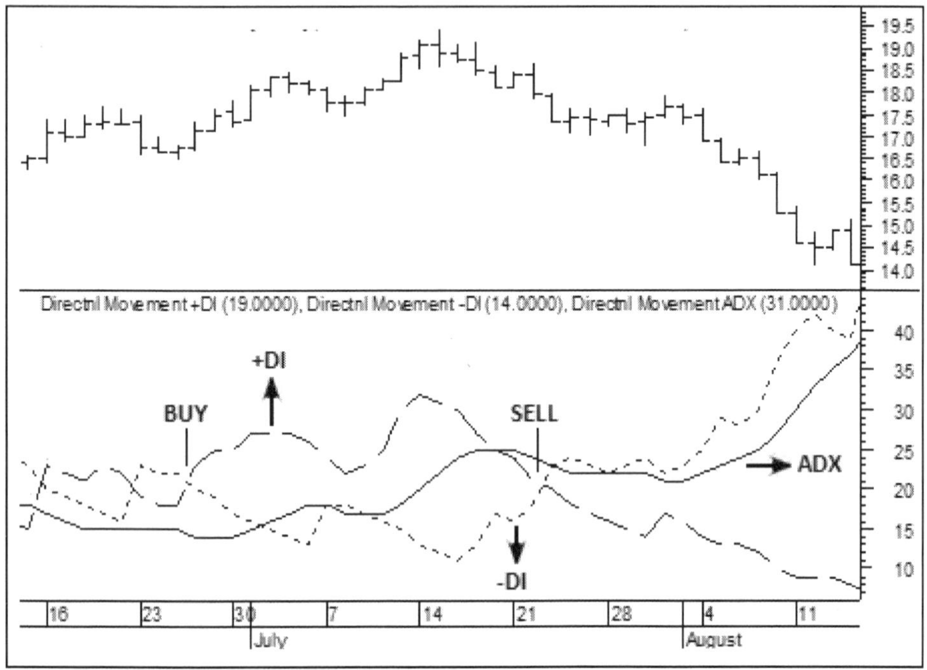

Figure 24.1: **Trading through ADX**

Significations

1. When ADX stays below 20, it indicates a non-trending market.
2. When ADX starts to move above 20, it indicates that the trend is gaining strength.
3. When ADX moves above 40, it indicates a strong trending market.
4. Rising ADX value indicates that the trend is gaining strength while falling ADX value indicates that the trend is losing strength.
5. When +DI is above -DI, look for "buy" signals from other tools and ignore the "sell" signals.
6. When -DI is above +DI, look for "sell" signals from other tools and ignore the "buy" signals.
7. When +DI crosses -DI to upside, it is a bullish signal. When -DI crosses +DI to the upside, it is a bearish signal. Use the extreme point rule to trade the crossovers.

The Extreme Point Rule — Extreme point is the high or low point on the day when the +DI and the -DI cross one another. When +DI crosses -DI to the upside, extreme point is the high of the day; when –DI crosses +DI to the upside, extreme point is the low of the day.

The extreme point is then used for taking the actual buy or sell position after the crossover. You should take a long position only when the price rises above the high extreme point price level. If the price fails to rise above the extreme point, you should not go for any new buy position. Similarly, trade for short positions, selling only when the price falls below the low extreme point.

If you have an open long position, wait until the price crosses the low extreme point after the crossover to book the loss and take a new "sell" position.

If you have an open short position, wait until the price crosses the high extreme point after the crossover to book loss and take a new "buy" position.

8. When +DI is above ADX but -DI is below ADX, go long and avoid short positions. Similarly, when -DI is above ADX but +DI is below ADX, go short and avoid long positions.
9. If you have long positions in a strong uptrend, look for opportunities to book profit when the ADX is above 40 and +DI falls below ADX. This is a sign that the uptrend may be weakening even though ADX still shows a strong trend.
10. If you have short positions in a strong downtrend, look for opportunities to book profit when the ADX is above 40 and -DI falls below ADX. This is a sign that the downtrend may be weakening even though ADX still shows a strong trend.

ADX is a slow indicator and you would probably get all signals through other tools much before they are provided by ADX. However, its signals are much more reliable especially when used in combination with other indicators. ADX is best used as a starting point to know about the ongoing trend. Once the trend and its strength are identified, other technical tools should be used for taking entry.

Aroon

Tushar Chande developed the Aroon indicator. It consists of two lines — one line is called "Aroon up" and the other line, "Aroon down" (*see* Figure 24.2. Aroon up measures the strength of the uptrend, while Aroon down measures the strength of the downtrend. Both Aroon up and the Aroon down fluctuate between zero and 100.

The default period to measure the strength is 14 period. Considering a daily chart, if the latest closing is the highest in the past 14-day sessions, then Aroon up will be 100. If the latest closing is the lowest in the past 14-day sessions, then Aroon down will be 100. When the security has not made a new high for 14 days, then Aroon up will be zero, and when the security has not made a new low for 14 days, then Aroon down will be zero. If the high and low of the period are in between, the Aroon up and Aroon down will be placed accordingly. You can change the period according to your preference.

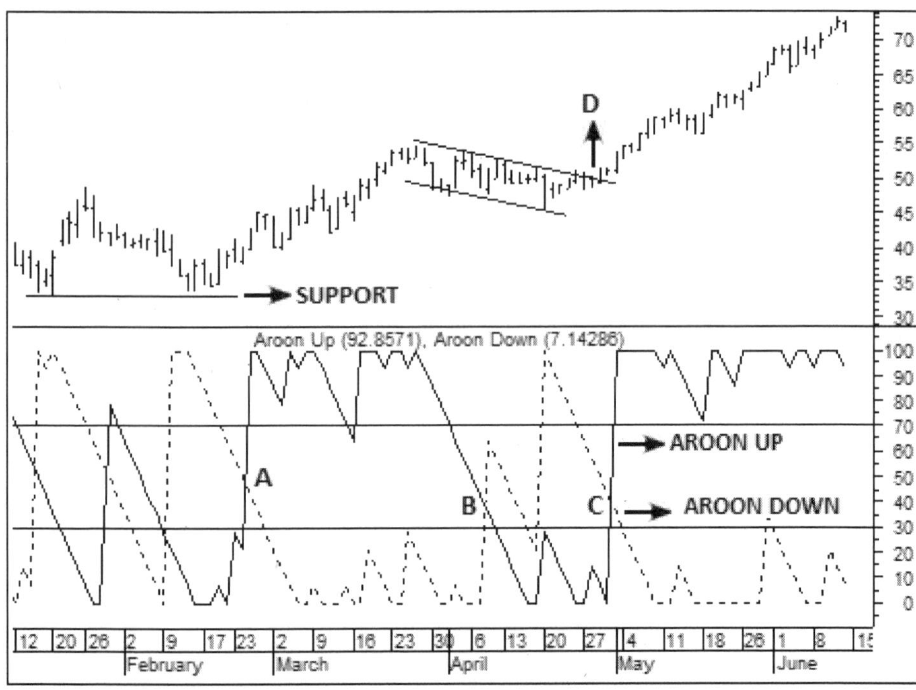

Figure 24.2: **Trading through Aroon**

Interpretation

When Aroon up is at 100, it indicates upside bias for price movement and an opportunity to take long positions. When Aroon down is at 100, it indicates downside bias for price and an opportunity to take short positions.

When Aroon up stays above 70 and Aroon down stays below 30, it indicates a strong uptrend. When Aroon down stays above 70 and Aroon up stays below 30, it indicates a strong downtrend.

As Aroon up and Aroon down fluctuate, they represent the gain or loss in the strength of the trend.

When Aroon up and Aroon down are close to each other and descending lower, it indicates that the price is consolidating and no strong trend is present.

Aroon up falling below 50 indicates that the current uptrend is weakening. Similarly, Aroon down falling below 50 indicates that the current downtrend is weakening.

Crossover of Aroon up and Aroon down between the levels of 30 and 70 confirm the formation of a trend. If Aroon up crosses Aroon down to upside, it is a confirmation of a new uptrend. When Aroon down crosses Aroon up to the upside, it is a confirmation of a new downtrend.

In non-trending markets, the Aroon indicator will give too many conflicting signals, but with combination of other tools, the false signals can be filtered.

Trading Signals from Figure 24.2

Point A: Buy at this point as Aroon up has crossed Aroon down to upside. Prior to point A, there have been strong "sell" signals but you should avoid taking entry until the price falls below the first low. This is just one way of filtering the random fluctuation. You can employ other indicators to confirm the signal provided by Aroon.

Point B: Crossover indicates that you should go short. However, after some time, Aroon down is not able to cross above 70 and starts to drop. Both Aroon up and Aroon down are running parallel and declining indicating a consolidation period and a non-trending market. You can close your position or wait by keeping a stop loss.

Point C and D: These two important signals have occurred simultaneously giving the best trading opportunity. The crossover at point C and range breakout at point D confirm the uptrend, and you can go long.

Chapter 25

Volume Indicators

THERE ARE DIFFERENT TYPES OF VOLUME INDICATORS, some based purely on volume while a majority includes the closing price and price range with volume in calculation.

On Balance Volume

On balance volume or OBV was developed by Joseph Granville and is among the first volume indicators to be used. OBV is a very simple indicator that compares volume to change in closing price (*see* Figure 25.1).

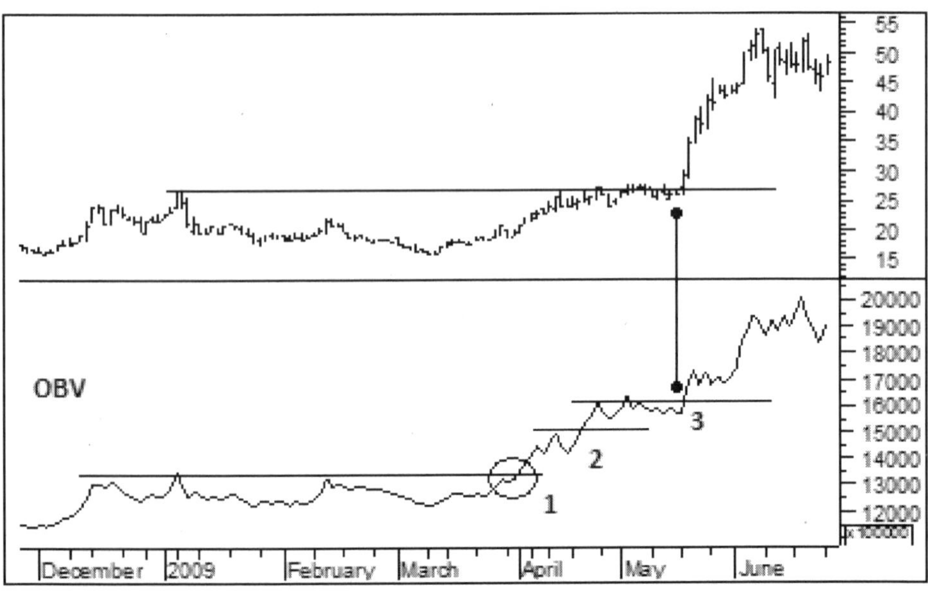

Figure 25.1: **OBV trading**

When the security closes higher than the previous close, all of the period's volume is considered up-volume and added to the total. When the security closes lower than the previous close, all of the period's volume is considered down-volume and subtracted from the total. A running total of the volume additions and subtractions forms the OBV line.

The underlying concept behind the OBV and other volume indicators is that changes in volume occur before price change. This helps to identify whether a security is being accumulated or distributed by a large number of investors.

The values on scale are not relevant and only the OBV slope is important.

Trading

1. An upward sloping OBV is used to confirm an uptrend. Until OBV keeps on making higher highs and higher lows, the uptrend should be considered intact.

   Go long and avoid short positions. Check momentum oscillators for oversold levels to take entry. Sell out-of-money put options and buy calls.
2. A downward sloping OBV is used to confirm a downtrend. Until OBV keeps on making lower highs and lower lows, the downtrend should be considered intact.

   Check momentum oscillators for overbought levels to take entry. Sell out-of-money call options and buy puts.
3. Negative Divergence: When the price makes new highs but OBV is falling, it indicates that the uptrend is about to end.

   Clear all long positions and enter short keeping the break of the last high as the stop loss point.
4. Positive Divergence: When the price makes new lows but OBV is rising, it indicates that the downtrend is about to end.

   Clear all short positions and enter long keeping the break of the last low as the stop loss point

Analyzing the chart (Figure 25.1)

1. This is the first "buy" signal given by OBV as it has broken the range and previous high. The price is still in the range and has not given any indication about a future up-move.

2. This is the second "buy" signal given by OBV as it starts to make a higher high. The price is at resistance and you would probably go short if trading purely on price movements. However, if analyzed carefully, it can be observed that the price is continuously hitting the resistance indicating that the upside breakout is likely.
3. This is the third "buy" signal given by OBV as it breaks the previous high. Immediately afterwards, there is a price breakout above the resistance.

Accumulation Distribution

The Accumulation Distribution Line was developed by Marc Chaikin and is quite similar to OBV (*see* Figure 25.2).

The difference is that while OBV uses the change in closing price from one period to the next, the accumulation distribution ignores the change from one period to the next, and uses price data for the given period only. The calculation looks into the location of the current close

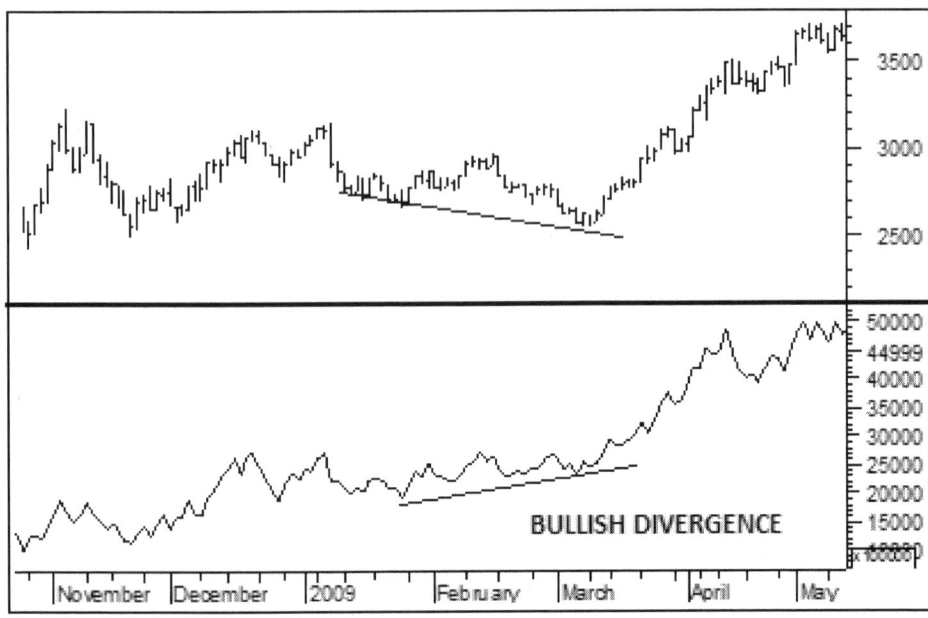

Figure 25.2: **Bullish divergence in accumulation distribution**

relative to the high and low or the range of the period which Chaikin described as CLV or close location value that ranges from minus 1 (close at the lowest point of the range) to plus 1 (close at the highest point of the range).

After defining CLV, its value is multiplied by volume in the analyzed period and the cumulative total forms the Accumulation Distribution Line. The scale is not important and only the slope of the line needs to be analyzed.

The analysis of accumulation distribution is the same as OBV. In Figure 25.2, the accumulation distribution line is continuously rising indicating that investors have started buying the security. The bullish divergence confirmed the "buy" signal.

Chaikin Money Flow

Chaikin Money Flow (CMF) was developed by Mark Chaikin and is based on the accumulation distribution line (*see* Figure 25.3).

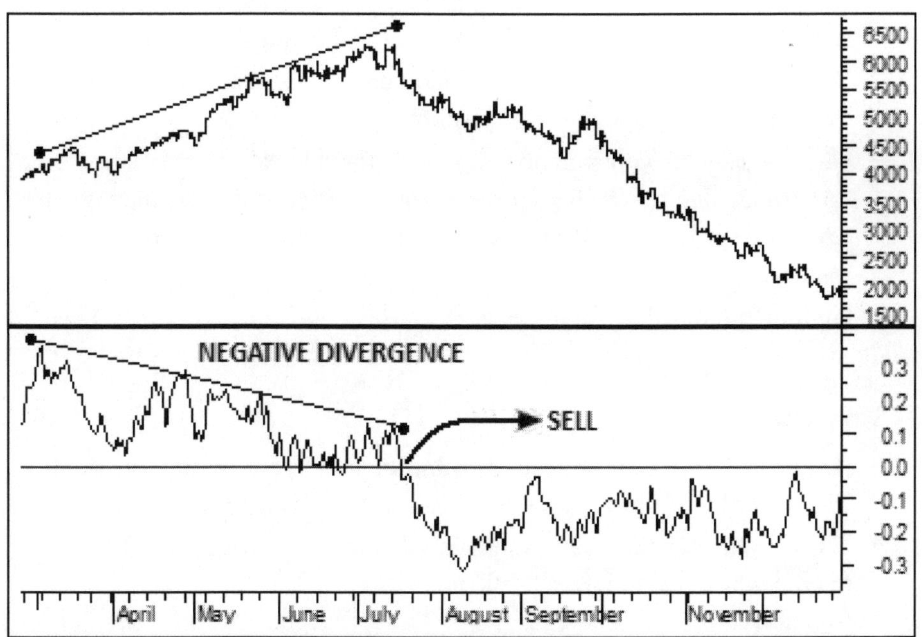

Figure 25.3: **CMF trading**

The basic concept behind the indicator is that the security is bullish if the prices close in the upper part of the period's high / low range consistently, accompanied with increasing volume. The security is bearish if the prices close in the lower part of the period's high / low range consistently, accompanied with increasing volume. The indicator is plotted on a scale with zero as the centreline, and oscillates up and down the centreline.

When prices consistently close in the upper half of their range on increased volume, then the indicator will be positive or above the zero line. When prices consistently close in the lower half of their range on increased volume, then the indicator will be negative or below the zero line.

Trading Strategies

Long Trades

1. Readings above zero indicate accumulation and strong buying pressure. The higher the reading, the stronger is the bullish sentiment.
2. When CMF is above zero, check momentum oscillators like RSI for oversold levels to take a "buy" position.
3. CMF is a good confirmation indicator for a break of resistance or downtrend line. If CMF is positive, buy at breakout immediately. If CMF is negative, wait for it to cross the centreline to the upside before going long.
4. Go long on bullish divergence.

Short Trades

- Readings below zero indicate distribution and strong selling pressure. The lower the reading, the stronger is the bearish sentiment.
- When CMF is below zero, check momentum oscillators like RSI for overbought levels to take a "sell" position.

- CMF is a good confirmation indicator for a break of support or upward sloping trendline. If CMF is negative, sell at breakout immediately. If CMF is positive, wait for it to cross the centreline to the downside before going short.
- Go short on bearish divergence.

In Figure 25.3, CMF is showing clear weakness and even though the price is rising, CMF is falling continuously. The price finally falls below the rising trendline giving a second "sell" signal. The break of centreline to the downside and CMF falling into negative territory is the final confirmation that the price is in downtrend.

Chaikin Oscillators

Chaikin Oscillator (*see* Figure 25.4) is based on the Accumulation Distribution Line. It is calculated by subtracting a 10-day period exponential moving average from a 3-day period exponential moving average of the Accumulation Distribution line.

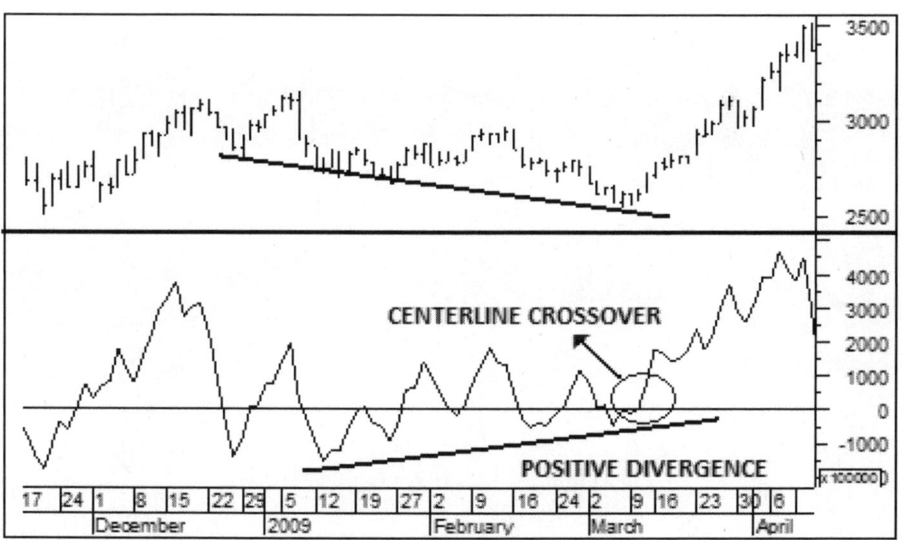

Figure 25.4: **Chaikin Oscillator**

Trading

1. Go long on positive divergence.
2. Go short on negative divergence

Centreline Crossover

1. Go long when the oscillator crosses the centreline to upside.
2. Go short when the oscillator crosses the centreline to downside.

You can use RSI with the Chaikin Oscillator to confirm the signals. When the oscillator is above zero, go long on RSI oversold levels. When the oscillator is below zero, go short on RSI overbought levels.

Chapter 26

Volatility Indicators

VOLATILITY IS A TERM USED TO DESCRIBE the magnitude of price fluctuations in a period. Many analysts are of the opinion that major tops are normally accompanied with high volatility, and major bottoms are formed with low volatility. However, in present times, the dynamics have changed and even major bottoms are likely to see huge volatility. Therefore, look for periods of high volatility as the indication that the major top or bottom is about to be formed, and reversal is likely.

Volatility indicators are not of much help to traders as the signals are rare and vague. The most trader-friendly volatility indicator is a Bollinger band that has been covered earlier.

There are two other commonly used indicators — Chaikin Volatility and Average True Range (ATR).

Chaikin Volatility Indicator

Developed by Marc Chaikin, the Chaikin Volatility indicator compares the range between the security's high and low prices and quantifies volatility as the widening of the range over selected periods. This is done in two steps — first, by calculating a moving average of the difference between the period's high and low prices, and second, by calculating the percent rate of change of that moving average.

The charting software uses 10-day periods for both, the moving average and the rate of change, as recommended by Chaikin.

There are two basic methods to interpret Chaikin's measure of volatility:

1. Market tops are generally accompanied by increased volatility while the bottoms are generally accompanied by decreased volatility. This is a commonly held belief of the volatility function.
2. The second interpretation of volatility by Chaikin is that a short-term increase in the volatility indicator points to an approaching market bottom while a longer term decrease in the volatility indicator points to an approaching market top.

Average True Range

Average True Range (ATR) was developed by Welles Wilder to measure the volatility of the security — *see* Figure 26.1. Most of Wilder's indicators were developed to trade commodities, and in his times, commodities used to be more volatile than stocks. Commodities are prone to gap-up and gap-down opening and circuits (when there is no trading due to the trading price limit being reached). A volatility indicator based on the high-low range of the same period fails to show the actual volatility created by the gaps or limit move, and would not show the true range of the price movement. To overcome this problem, Wilder used previous period's close and came up with three outcomes:

1. The distance from today's high to today's low.
2. The distance from yesterday's close to today's high.
3. The distance from yesterday's close to today's low.

From the above three, the greatest one was considered as the true range.

The average true range is the 14-period EMA of the true range.

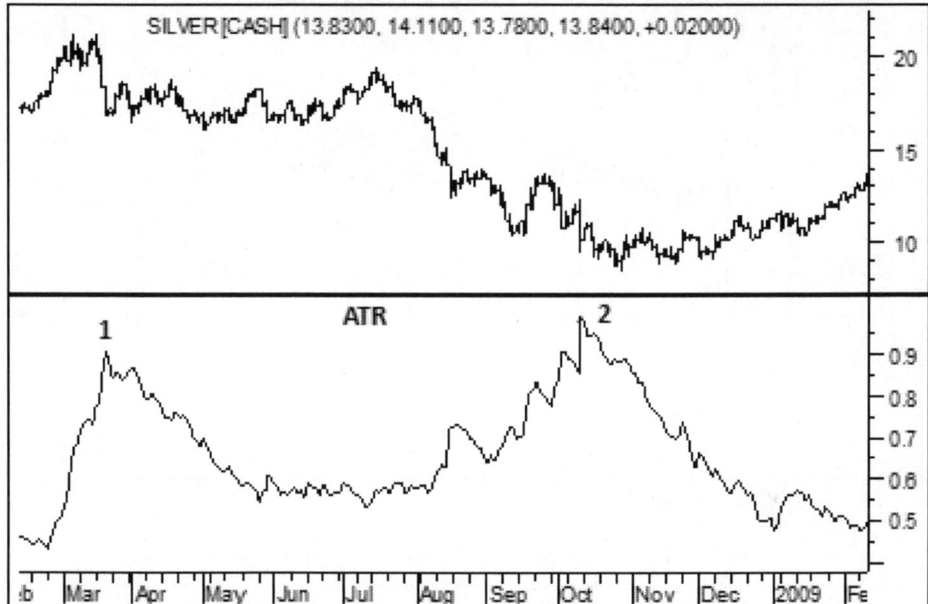

Figure 26.1: **Average true range**

Trading

High ATR levels indicate a likely end of the ongoing trend and warn of a major top or bottom formation. Low levels of ATR indicate a range-bound market. If the ATR moves in low levels for a long time, it is an indication of accumulation followed by an uptrend, or consolidation within a continuation pattern of an uptrend or downtrend.

In Figure 26.1, high 1 on ATR was formed close to the price top and high 2 was formed close to price bottom.

The advantage of ATR is that it takes into account the gaps caused in the security's price. The weakness is that you cannot do comparative analysis based on ATR levels for the same security as well as between different securities. This is because ATR depicts volatility in absolute levels, so a security with a price of ₹ 5 will have very low volatility levels compared to a ₹ 50 security.

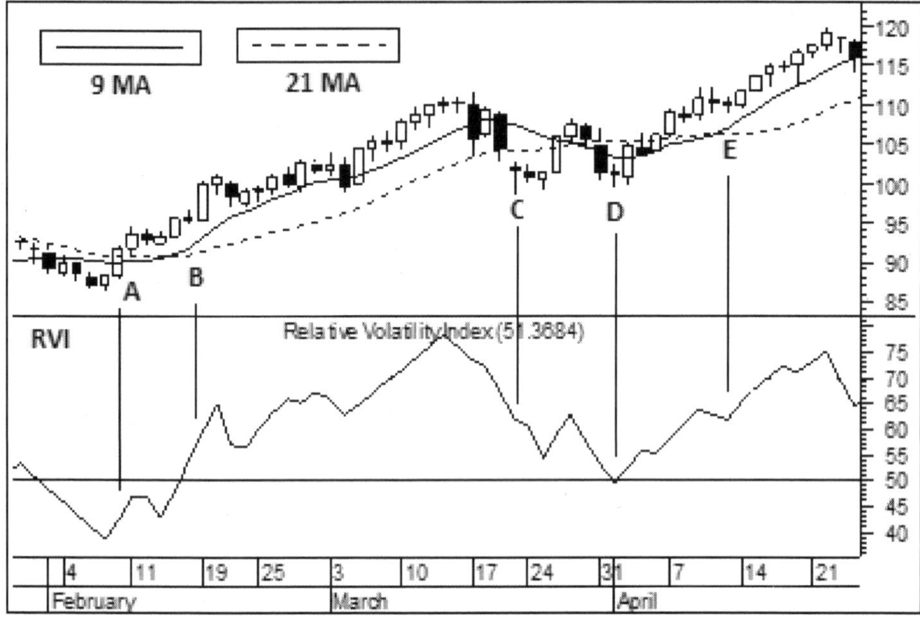

Figure 26.2: **Trading with Relative Volatility Index**

Relative Volatility Index

Developed by Donald Dorsey, the Relative Volatility Index (RVI) is similar to Relative Strength Index (RSI) except that it is used to measure volatility by incorporating standard deviation — *see* Figure 26.2. RVI uses an n-day standard deviation of the closing prices instead of a net day-to-day change.

Donald Dorsey made it clear that the Relative Volatility Index was designed as a confirmation for trading signals, especially moving averages crossover, and not as a standalone indicator.

Trading Signals from RVI

1. Use "buy" signals and enter long only when the RVI is above 50.
2. Use "sell" signals and enter short only when the RVI is below 50.
3. Close a long position if the RVI falls below 40.
4. Close a short position if the RVI rises above 60.

In the above chart (Figure 26.2):

- **Point A:** The price has crossed the moving average. A big bullish candle crossing and closing above the moving averages is the first "buy" signal. However, the RVI is still below 50 signalling caution.
- **Point B:** The moving average crossover has occurred and the RVI is above 50 giving a clear "buy" signal.
- **Point C:** The price has dropped below the moving averages but the RVI is not supporting the "sell" signal.
- **Point D:** The price has dropped below the moving averages for the second time accompanied by moving average crossover but the RVI has not dropped below 50 indicating caution while taking a short position.
- **Point E:** The price is above the moving averages; the moving average crossover has given a buy signal and is supported by the RVI placed above 50.

Conclusion

There are hundreds of indicators available to traders, but the major ones that have been covered are more than enough. In fact, you should minimise the number that you use, simply because you are bound to get conflicting signals by using more indicators. This will lead to confusion that will affect your trading adversely.

Limit your indicator count to three or four at the most, and create a combination that provides different information about the markets. For example, if you are using the RSI, there is no need to use any other momentum indicator like Williams %R as both basically provide the same input. Instead, you can combine the RSI with moving average and OBV to cover all aspects of the market. Remember that no combination has a cent percent success rate. You must find a combination that suits your trading style and enables you to make more profitable trades with minimal use of indicators.

The other aspects that you should consider are:

1. **Length:** The length specifies the amount of market data that is included in the indicator's calculations. A 10-hour moving average will consider the last ten hours or 10 hourly price data. Similarly, a 50-hour moving average will consider the last 50 hours or 50 hourly price data.

The length that you will use will again be dependent on your trading preference. However, analyzing the same indicator with different periods will again give you conflicting signals. So use one period for your trading purposes and the others for reference or confirmation.

Increasing the length of the indicator will slow the indicator, and decreasing the length will lead to too many false signals. Therefore, you will have to arrive at the optimal length by trial.

2. **Signal Line:** This is also known as trigger line and comes as an inbuilt feature in some indicators like stochastic. However, you can draw a signal line with indicators like RSI too, which will actually be a moving average of the RSI. For example, if you are using a 14-day RSI, a signal line can be constructed by plotting a 5-day period moving average of the RSI.

Indicators may seem exciting and many traders commit the mistake of becoming overly dependent on indicators for analysis. Use indicators in combination with other technical tools and never let indicators take precedence over price analysis tools like trendlines, chart patterns, etc. If an indicator is giving a "buy" signal but there is a bearish chart pattern or strong resistance, then avoid trading until clear signals are available. Just a few tried and tested simple indicators can provide you the required winning edge. Once you gain experience, you will be able to develop your own indicator, based on your market observation.

Chapter 27

Fibonacci Numbers

LET US TOUCH UPON SOME MATHEMATICS! Those of you who hate maths, do not flip the page just yet. You will find Fibonacci numbers interesting enough to learn more about it, and important enough to make this a part of your technical analysis study.

In the 12th century, Leonardo de Pisa, known to his friends as Fibonacci, discovered a fascinating mathematical sequence that came to be known as the Fibonacci numbers. Interestingly, these numbers were well-known in ancient India as early as 200 B.C., and first appeared under the name *maatraameru* (mountain of cadence), in *Chhandah-shastra*, the work of the Sanskrit grammarian Pingala.

Study the following sequence:

0, 1, 1, 2, 3, 5, 8, 13, 21, 34, 55, 89,144, 233 . . .

This sequence may seem to be a random placement of numbers, but there is a clear logic. Each successive number in the series is the sum of the two previous numbers.

0+1=1/ 1+1=2/ 1+2=3/ 2+3=5/ 3+5=8/ 5+8=13/ 8+13=21/ 13+21=34/
21+34=55 and so on.

The Fibonacci numbers have many mathematical properties, but the most fascinating thing about the Fibonacci numbers is their connection to nature. These numbers are seen in the arrangement of the pinecone rows, the growth of branches in trees, the chambers and appendages on many fruits and vegetables, arrangement of leaves on a stem, an uncurling fern, etc. Does it apply to our body? Let us observe our hands. We have 2 hands, each separated in 3 sections — 5 fingers on each hand separated in 3 sections by 2 knuckles, all Fibonacci numbers.

The other interesting aspect of this series is the quotient of two adjacent numbers. When you divide two consecutive numbers, it gives either 1.618033989 or 0.618033989. The ratios of successive Fibonacci numbers approach a value of 1.61803, which is the golden ratio known as *phi.* As the series proceeds, any given number is 1.618 times the preceding number, and 0.618% of the next number. The golden ratio is sometimes referred to as God's number due to its abundance in nature. Measure from your head to your feet, and divide that by the length from your belly button to your feet. The result will be around 1.618. The golden ratio is seemingly unavoidable and is found from the smallest to the largest structure in the universe.

This is a brief introduction to the Fibonacci numbers to indicate its importance. Those who have not been able to understand it needn't worry as one can use the Fibonacci sequence in technical analysis without having to necessarily understand it. Just remember that 0.618 is the ratio used in technical analysis along with 0.382 and 0.236. These ratios are converted into three percentages — 61.8%, 38.2% and 23.6% respectively, and used in analysis. The 50% level is also used and given equal importance although it is not really a Fibonacci ratio.

Use of Fibonacci in Technical Analysis

Fibonacci numbers are commonly used in technical analysis to determine the potential support, resistance, and price objectives in trending markets. Fibonacci analysis can be applied to short term as well as long-term price movements. However, there should be a noticeable up-move or a down-move in prices.

We have discussed the importance of trend and the advantages of following the trend. However, as it is obvious, the market does not move up or down in a straight line. In an uptrend, the market will often fall back during the course of the uptrend, and in a downtrend, the market will often rise. These retracements provide an excellent opportunity for traders to enter with new positions in the direction of the trend. However, there are some basic questions. How does one know how much the market will retrace? Once the retracement is over, how much further will the market move in the direction of the trend? When does one know that the market has changed trend and the retracement is actually the start of a new trend? What can be the probable range of future price moves?

The Fibonacci study provides one more tool to answer these questions — the Fibonacci ratios. The Fibonacci ratios provide clear levels as to how far the trend and counter-trend or retracement is likely to continue. When the Fibonacci percentages such as 23.6%, 38.2%, 50%, and 61.8% are applied to trending prices, they indicate the extent of retracement of the underlying trend and where a new high or low are likely to be formed.

There are three important Fibonacci studies used in technical analysis: retracements, arcs and fans.

Though these three studies are most common, there are more studies such as Fibonacci time zones, grid, etc. that you can study at a later stage. Retracements are the most widely used Fibonacci study; my advice is to start by studying the retracements first and see how effective they are.

Retracements

Retracements are movements that go against the trend. To use Fibonacci retracements, first find the ongoing trend and see if the prices have started to retrace. Then identify the top and bottom of the trend. This will be very subjective, so you must draw your own conclusion. Once you have found the range of the trend, Fibonacci levels of 23.6%, 38.2%,

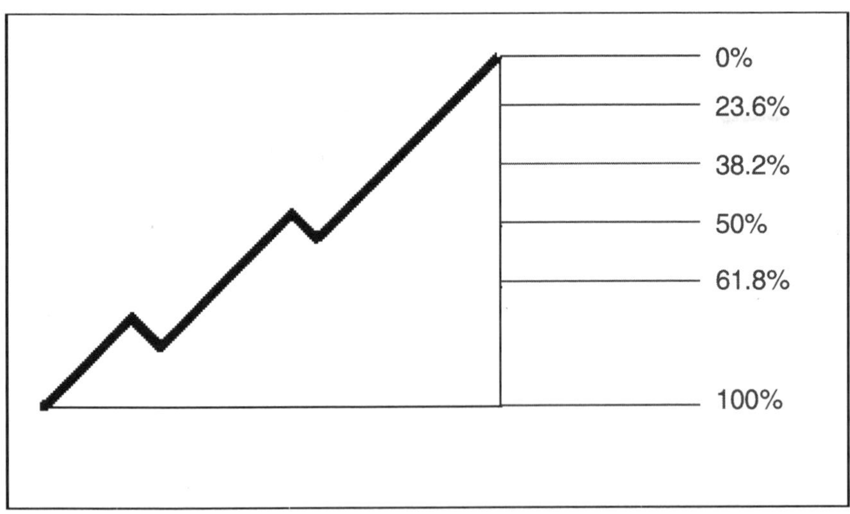

Figure 27.1: **Fibonacci Retracement Levels of 38.2%, 50% and 61.8%**

50%, and 61.8% will tell you the levels at which the price will find support or resistance (*see* Figure 27.1).

Taking an example, if gold has started a new uptrend from $800 and reached $900, the range of the trend is $100. Once gold starts to fall from $900, you can find Fibonacci retracement levels and use them as support since this is an uptrend. The first support level will be 23.6% of the range that will come to approximately $876. The second level will be 38.2% or $862 approximately. The third level will be 50% or $850 and the fourth level will be at 61.8% or $838 approximately. Therefore, applying the Fibonacci retracement study has provided four clear levels to watch for in a $100 move. In the same way, you can find retracement if the trend is down, and find Fibonacci resistance levels. In the charting software you are using, select the Fibonacci retracement study and connect the top of the trend to the bottom. The software will automatically show you the retracements level with horizontal lines. You can also draw further retracements like 161.8%, etc. if your analysis requires it.

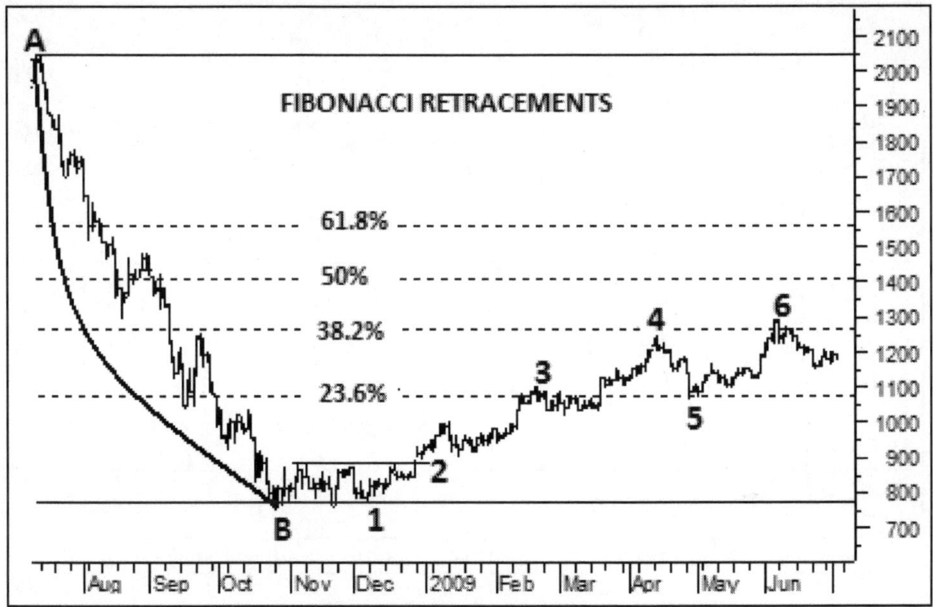

Figure 27.2: **Trading through Fibonacci retracements**

In Figure 27.2, the prices have been declining from point A to point B. The charting software will automatically draw the retracements levels for this price decline once you select the price range — in this example, from point A to B.

1. This is the first indication that the downtrend has weakened, as prices are not able to fall below the low created at point B.
2. The price has broken the small trading range to the upside. You can now enter a long position and look for retracements levels for further trades.
3. The first profit target and also the first resistance of 23.6% retracement is reached. Logically, the long position should be closed at this level. The price continues to trade at this level indicating that the resistance at the 23.6% level is weak and the upside breakout is likely. If you had cleared your long position, you can enter again with another long trade at this level. If you had taken a short position, place a stop loss just above the 23.6% level.

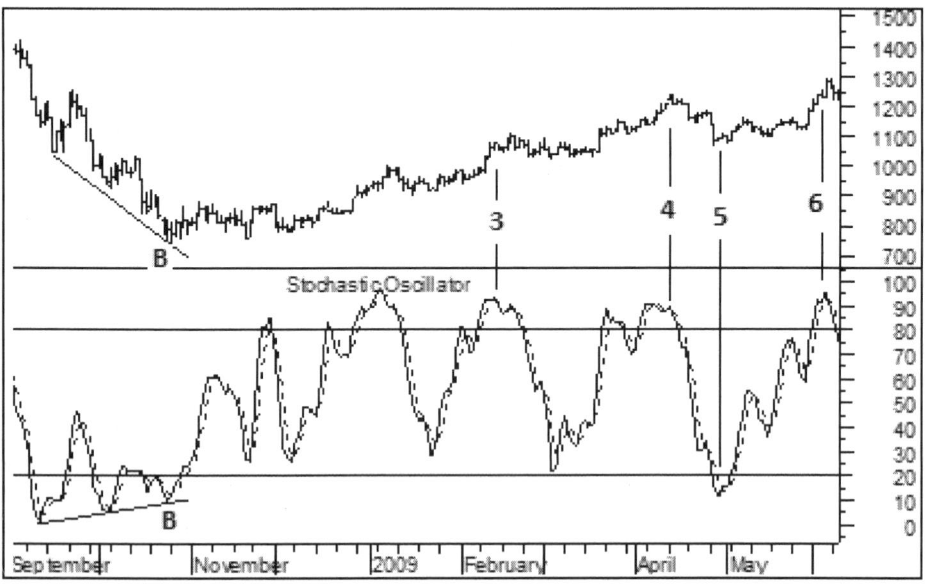

Figure 27.3: **Combining stochastic with Fibonacci retracement levels**

4. The price reaches the next resistance level of 38.2% retracement and finds resistance.
5. The price falls to 23.6% retracement and finds support.
6. The price again rises to 38.2% retracement and finds resistance.

As you can observe, Fibonacci retracement levels provide some of the best trading opportunities. When combined with other tools, the trading risks can be greatly reduced and rewards increased. Figure 27.3 shows the same trading points as mentioned above but with a stochastic indicator.

Stochastic had given a "buy" signal at point B itself, as there is a strong divergence. The next levels of Fibonacci retracement occurred at the overbought or oversold levels in stochastic providing very clear "buy" and "sell" levels.

Fibonacci Arcs and Fan

Fibonacci arcs and fans are price and time dependent unlike Fibonacci retracements. If you move ahead in time on the same price level, the arcs and fan lines will change. Arcs will also be placed differently on a semi-log and linear scale. Fibonacci arcs and fan lines are much less indicative and finding trading levels is difficult. You must observe arcs on multiple charts for a couple of months; use them only if they support your trading style and that too only as a supporting tool to other studies, never independently.

Fibonacci Arcs

Fibonacci arcs are curved lines that intersect the range of the trend at Fibonacci levels of 38.2%, 50% and 61.8% (Figure 27.4). These provide support and resistance levels and the range in which future price movement is likely to happen. Trading opportunity is present whenever the price approaches these curved lines. Figure 27.5 is the same as discussed in Fibonacci retracements. As you can observe, it is much less informative than retracements.

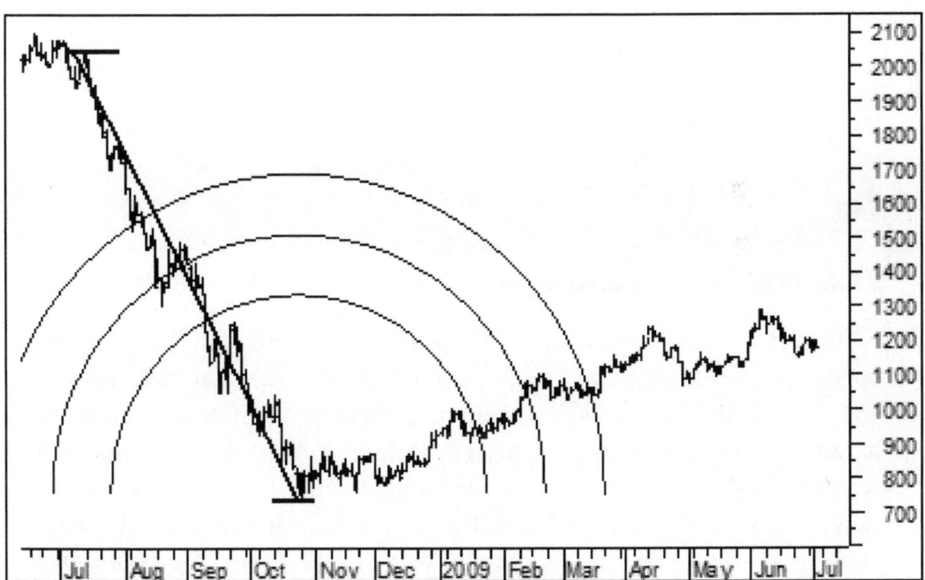

Figure 27.4: **Fibonacci arcs**

Fibonacci Fan

Fibonacci fan lines are diagonal lines drawn from the left-most point of the trend in a way that they intersect the trend range at Fibonacci levels 38.2%, 50% and 61.8% (*see* Figure 27.5).

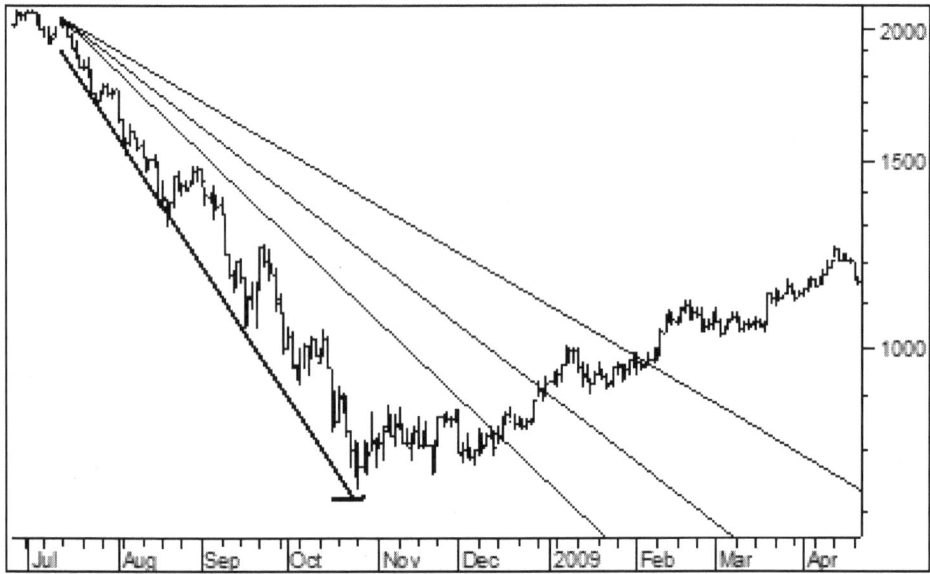

Figure 27.5: **Fibonacci fan lines**

Fibonacci Trading Strategies

Fibonacci retracement indicates levels from where the trend is likely to continue. In an uptrend, a "buy" position can be initiated at these levels, and in a downtrend, a "sell" position. Of course, the entry should be based on a combination with all other technical tools, as it will confirm whether these levels are a good entry point or not. Price movements between 0% to 38.2% and 61.8% to 100% Fibonacci levels give important clues to the future direction and offer a great opportunity for finding the big moves when looking for trades. A wait and watch approach should be applied around the 38.2% and 61.8% levels. If the market congests around these levels, trade using a breakout strategy. Enter only when the price moves past the range of that particular congestion zone.

If the trend is very strong, the price will not be able to cross 23.6% and will find support or resistance around this level. Most of the times, prices around the 38.2% retracement level provide good support or resistance and so this level provides the best trading opportunity. However, if the price goes to the 61.8% level, then it indicates that the trend is not that strong and chances of trend reversal are there. Here, an exit opportunity should be looked for in positions that were taken in an underlying trend direction. Once the price crosses the 61.8% level, then it indicates a clear weakening of the underlying trend and the start of a ranging market or a new trend.

If the indicators like RSI, Stochastic, etc., enter extreme oversold or overbought zones at the 23.6% or 38.2% retracement level, then it indicates that the retracement is over. Fresh positions can be initiated in the direction of the underlying trend. These indicators are very helpful but should only be used to trade in the direction of the trend in a trending market.

Draw long-term support / resistance and trendlines and see if they are close to any Fibonacci levels. Those levels will become more important for any new position. If the price crosses these levels with ease and good volume, then it indicates trend weakness.

Gaps and patterns, if present around the Fibonacci retracement levels, are very helpful in projecting the exact price targets.

There are hundreds of combinations that you can look for while analyzing, and only continuous observation and study will make you capable of finding the best level. All these trading aspects are very subjective and every trader may have different views, but ultimately all will be in profit if the positions are managed well.

Fibonacci numbers provide infinite ways to use them in financial markets for a research-minded person. For unknown reasons, major ratios drawn from Fibonacci numbers show a clear connection between trend and countertrend movement in markets. Once you get the knack of Fibonacci application, this will become a permanent part of your analysis.

Chapter 28

Elliott Wave

Introduction

Ralph Nelson Elliott (1871-1948) developed the Elliott wave analysis and almost all his studies on Elliott wave were published in 1946 in the book *Nature's Law — the Secret of the Universe*. Elliott wave is perhaps the most debated and subjective of all technical analysis studies. It generates extreme reactions from traders; they are either completely convinced or rubbish it completely.

Elliott wave creates scepticism in minds of the students because of two major reasons. The first is that the Elliott wave is so subjective that Elliott analysts rarely come to an agreement over a particular analysis. The second is that performing Elliott wave analysis in present price charts can be very frustrating due to the inherent complexities.

So, is it really worth learning about the Elliott wave? Yes, but only if you have enough time and patience. Elliott wave would require months of study and market observation for you to actually trade on it.

Elliott Wave Principle

According to Elliott, the financial markets do not behave in a chaotic manner but move in clear structure and patterns. The price movement on a chart may seem random at first, but these moves are based on human psychology and emotions. The structures and patterns in a price chart give an insight into mass psychology and how investors are behaving. If these are understood, it becomes easier to analyse the likely direction of future price moves. The mass psychology is very evident in financial markets because people trade on their beliefs. In a bear market, no amount of good news is able to stop the fall in prices. In a bull market, people will continue buying without any reason and the markets will continue rising, discounting all bad news and facts. Since Elliot wave analysis is based on how the masses behave, it is only successful in markets where public participation is high; an illiquid market cannot be analysed through Elliott wave analysis.

Elliott Wave Theory

Let us first relook at the important features of a trend. As we have seen, the prices may be in uptrend, downtrend or a non-trending phase. A trend can be seen in the smallest intraday movements to a larger monthly or yearly time-frame. In any trend, there are many smaller trends unfolding at the same time. The price rise or fall is not in a straight line. During the course of an uptrend, the price will fall often, and during a downtrend, the price will rise often. These are known as retracements. Elliott termed these price movements and counter-movements as waves.

According to Elliott, the price moves in a pattern of eight waves — five waves in the direction of the trend and three waves against it, also known as a 5-3 wave pattern. In an uptrend, a five-wave advance will be followed by a three-wave decline; in a downtrend, a five-wave decline will be followed by a three-wave advance. This 5-3 wave pattern is depicted in Figure 28.1.

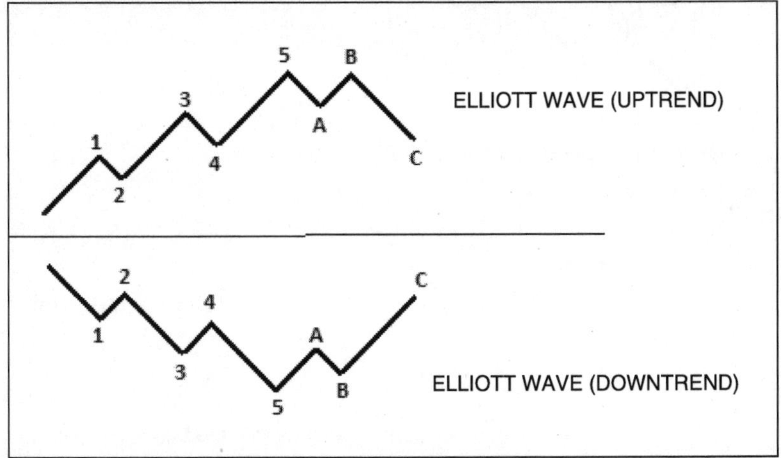

Figure 28.1: **Elliott Wave**

In financial markets, the price unfolds according to a basic pattern of 5-3 wave, to form a complete cycle of eight waves. Five-wave patterns are called Impulse waves and three-wave patterns are called Corrective waves. Remember that impulse waves are those that move in the direction of the underlying trend whereas corrective waves are retracements that go against the direction of the underlying trend.

Impulse waves are indicated by numbers 1-2-3-4-5 and corrective waves by letters A-B-C. Therefore, the complete cycle of eight waves will be 1-2-3-4-5-A-B-C (*see* Figure 28.2).

The impulse waves will always be a five-wave structure and the corrective wave will always be a three-wave structure.

To recap once again, one complete cycle consisting of eight waves is made up of two distinct phases — the impulse phase (also called motive phase) consisting of five sub-waves denoted by numbers 1-2-3-4-5 and the corrective phase whose sub-waves are denoted by letters A-B-C.

At the end of the eight-wave cycle, another similar cycle of eight waves starts. These A-B-C waves can also be wave 1-2-3 of the new trend, and instead of moving in the direction of the previous trend with another 5-wave structure, wave 4 and 5 will be formed.

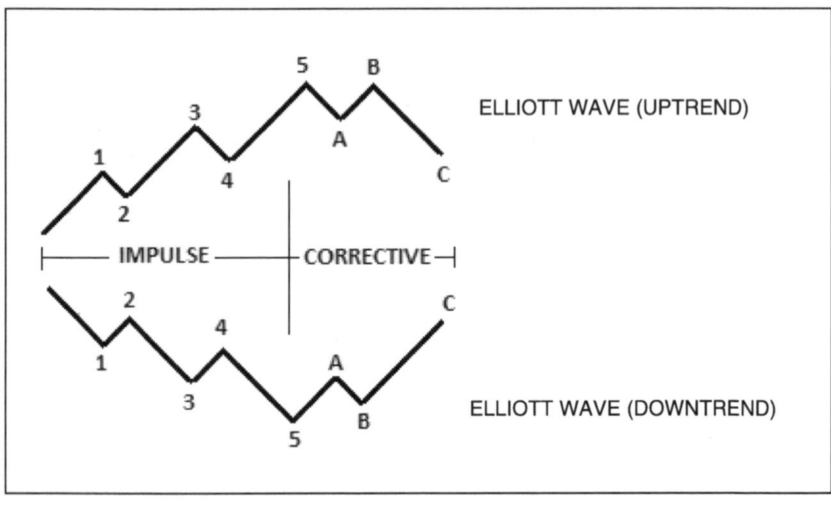

Figure 28.2: **Impulse and corrective waves within the Elliott Wave**

Why 5-3?

Elliott observed that the market's essential form was five-wave progress and three-wave correction.

A 5-3 pattern is the minimum requirement for achieving both fluctuation and progress. One wave does not allow fluctuation, which goes against the fact that every action has a reaction. The fewest sub-divisions to create fluctuation are three waves. However, three waves in both directions will not lead to progress. For the market to trend in one direction despite fluctuations, movements in the main trend must be at least five waves so that the distance covered is more than the three waves. This 5-3 formation is the best formation connected to a natural rhythm.

Waves within Waves

One of the important aspects of the Elliott Wave theory is that the market structure is fractal in nature. Fractals are structures that infinitely repeat themselves on an ever-smaller scale of observation. Elliott wave patterns have the same characteristic. A 5-3 wave structure can be sub-divided into smaller 5-3 wave structures. Similarly, a 5-3 wave structure will be a part of a larger wave having the same 5-3 wave structure. Therefore, we can count the Elliott wave on a long-term yearly market chart as well as short-term hourly market chart (*see* Figure 28.3).

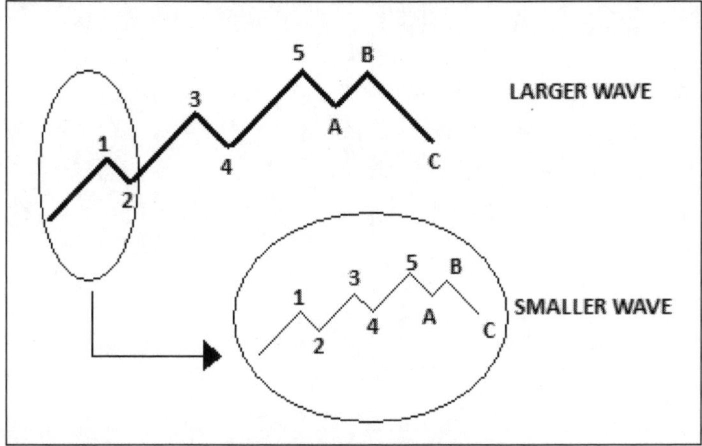

Figure 28.3: **Fractal nature of Elliott wave**

The basic Elliott sequence of "fives" corrected by "threes" remains constant no matter what degree of wave is being analyzed. Elliott wave pattern is not time dependent. Waves can be stretched or compressed in both time and price, but the underlying form remains constant. A price movement will always unfold in a 5-3 pattern.

The Wave Principle thus shows that waves of any degree always subdivide and re-subdivide into waves of lesser degrees, and simultaneously are a part of waves of higher degrees.

Within an impulse wave, Waves 1, 3 and 5 are impulse whereas Waves 2 and 4 are corrective. So Waves 1, 3 and 5 will again be a five-wave structure (1-2-3-4-5) whereas Waves 2 and 4 will be a three-wave structure (a-b-c), as explained in Figure 28.4.

The internal structure (or sub-wave count) of an impulse wave is 5-3-5-3-5, i.e., Waves 1, 3 and 5 are composed of 5 internal waves, and Waves 2 and 4 are composed of 3 internal waves.

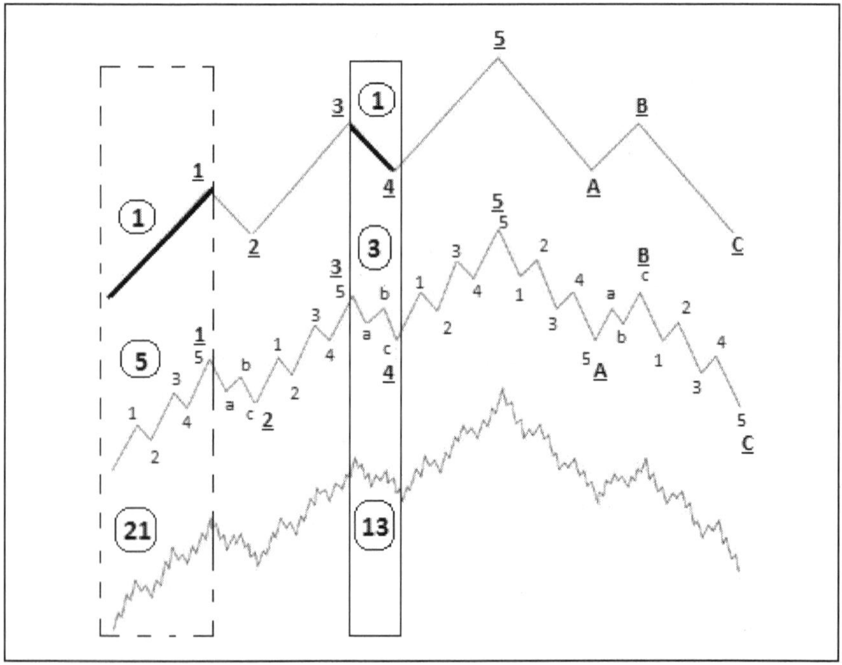

Figure 28.4: **Sub-divisions of an Elliott wave**

In the same way, in corrective wave A-B-C, Waves A and C are impulse waves as they are going in the direction of the trend, and Wave B is a corrective wave. So Waves A and C will be sub-divided into a five-wave structure (1-2-3-4-5) and Wave B will be sub-divided into a three-wave structure (a-b-c).

The internal structure of a corrective wave is 5-3-5, i.e., Waves A and C are composed of 5 internal waves, and Wave B is composed of 3 internal waves.

This way, impulse wave sub-divides into 5 waves which further sub-divide into 21 waves, and corrective wave sub-divides into 3 waves, which further sub-divide into 13 waves.

Therefore, wherever you start from, a complete cycle will have two waves — impulse and correction. The next sub-division will be eight waves (5+3), the next sub-division will have 34 waves (21+13), the next one will have 144 waves (89+55) and so on.

If you observe closely, you'll realize that all the numbers that have turned up are Fibonacci numbers. Fibonacci numbers and retracements levels are the foundation for Elliott wave analysis. As we have seen in the last chapter, Fibonacci numbers and golden ratio are Nature's building blocks. Financial market movements are governed by mass psychology, which too follows this natural rhythm.

I hope that by now, you have tried to locate the 5-3 wave structure. This is just the start to the long journey of Elliott wave analysis. It will take time before a clear picture starts to emerge, so have patience.

There are set rules and guidelines for Elliott wave analysis and the structures of wave formation. Correct labelling of waves is the foundation of wave analysis.

Rules for Wave Count

Elliott laid down three rules for a correct wave count and all must be applicable:

1. Wave 2 can never cross the start of Wave 1.
2. Wave 3 can never be the shortest impulse wave among Waves 1, 3 and 5.

3. Wave 4 can never enter the price area of Wave 1, i.e., Wave 4 cannot overlap Wave 1.

In addition to the above rules, there are certain guidelines that help in labelling waves:

1. The third wave is usually the longest wave, and it shows the greatest momentum.
2. If Wave 2 is a sharp correction, Wave 4 will tend to be a sideways correction, and if Wave 2 is sideways, Wave 4 will tend to be sharp. This is known as alteration.
3. Often, Wave 2 will be a deep retracement of the first wave, and retraces 61.8% or more of Wave 1.
4. Wave 4 is a small retracement, usually 23.6% to 31.8% of Wave 3.

There are more guidelines and exceptions that will be covered as you proceed further. As and when each topic is finished, keep on adding it to what you have learnt even if you have to study the whole wave chapter again.

Wave Classification

Since all waves sub-divide into smaller waves, a classification is used to label wave movement from the largest to the smallest time-frame. Elliott distinguished nine degrees of waves and classified them as Grand Super cycle, Super cycle, Cycle, Primary, Intermediate, Minor, Minute, Minuette and Sub-Minuette.

At the top is the family of cycle waves, which can take decades to complete. Primary and intermediate waves cover yearly and monthly time-frames. Minor waves and lower waves reflect daily and intraday market movements.

Cycle waves sub-divide into primary waves that in turn sub-divide into intermediate waves that in turn sub-divide into minor and sub-minor waves. You can thus precisely identify the position of a wave in the overall progression of the market,

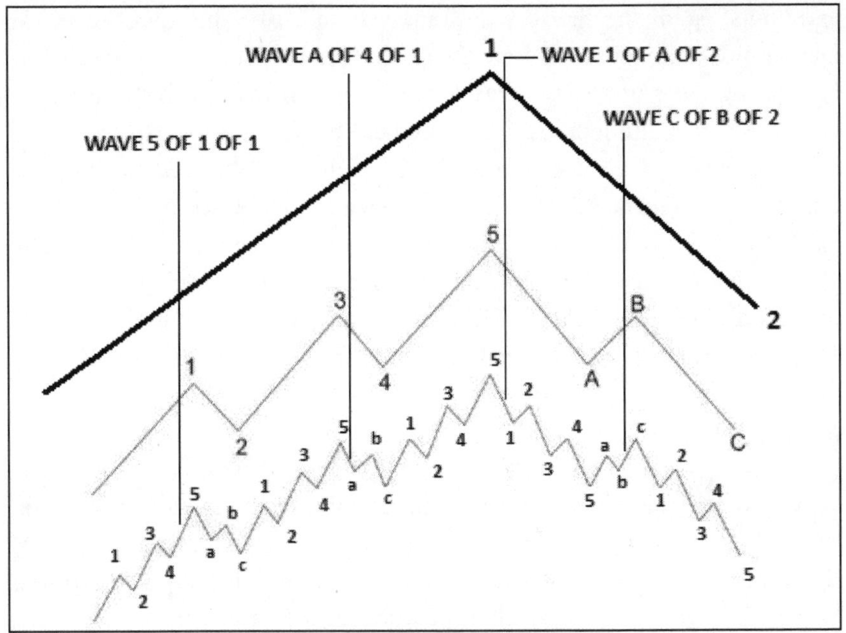

Figure 28.5: **Wave count methodology**

Wave Count in Multiple Degree Waves

The present price is a part of a wave, which is again a part of a higher degree wave. You will hear terms, like 2 of 5 of 5 or A of 2 of 1. These are just ways to represent where at present, price stands in waves of different degrees. If you are looking at a minor wave, wave 2 of 5 of 5 will mean that at present, minor wave 2 of primary wave 5 of intermediate wave 5 is running. Figure 28.5 will explain how you label waves when considering multiple degree waves.

Wave Characteristics

Wave 1

Wave 1 is always difficult to recognise. Traders consider this as a retracement of the previous trend and see it as a trading opportunity.

If the previous trend was bullish, this will be considered as a buying opportunity. Traders look for supports in charts, call options are bought and "puts" sold, the fundamental analysts talk of value that the instrument holds and tell investors about the long-term "buy" opportunity. Practically everyone is so confident of the bull market that short positions are feared and long positions are held without a stop loss.

If the previous trend was bearish, this will be considered as an opportunity to sell. The sentiments are negative and people see no hope for the market. Analysts talk of increasingly lower market levels and see no point in buying anything. Traders look for resistance levels to short. Put options are bought and calls sold. The economy does not look good, the earnings estimates are lowered and downgrades happen frequently.

Wave 2

Wave 2 strengthens the belief that the previous trend is still very strong. Wave 1 is taken as a correction of the previous trend, and as soon as Wave 2 starts, huge positions are built up making it a sharp correction of Wave 1. Anyone who has taken position in the direction of Wave 1 is ridiculed and asked to cut the position. If the previous trend was bullish, Wave 2 is considered as a continuation of the trend and new 'buy' orders are placed. If the previous trend was bearish, Wave 2 is considered as a continuation of the bear trend and new "sell" orders are placed.

Wave 2 corrects Wave 1 but will never cross the start of Wave 1. Usually Wave 2 will not retrace more than 61.8% of Wave 1. After that, the price will start moving in the direction of Wave 1 and mark the start of Wave 3.

Wave 3

Wave 3 is usually the most powerful wave. As Wave 3 continues and crosses the end of Wave 1, this is the first signal for the technical analyst that the trend is changing. If the previous trend was bullish, Wave 3 reduces the optimism, as the buy positions do not give profits. As soon as Wave 3 crosses the low of Wave 1, conventional technical analysts book losses and initiate fresh short positions. However, the general investors still do not believe that the bull trend has ended and hold on to their long positions. As Wave 3 proceeds further, the bullish sentiment goes away as more traders book losses on long positions. This is the time when bulls lose almost all their money if they are not careful.

If the previous trend was bearish, Wave 3 will help in reducing the pessimism. The news is still negative but the sentiments start to become positive. When Wave 3 crosses the high of Wave 1, conventional technical analysts book losses in short positions and initiate fresh long positions. As Wave 3 moves on, the bears realise that they are on the wrong side and this is the time when most of the bears that are not careful, lose all their profits, and may be more. Wave 3 usually exceeds Wave 1 by at least 1.618 times.

Wave 4

Wave 4 is perhaps the most clearly understood wave. Everyone has accepted the new trend and prices usually move sideways. Traders who had taken position at the start of Wave 3 book their profits, and those who had missed the opportunity to enter in Wave 3, look for entry levels. Elliott wave traders hold on to their positions or take new ones because of the potential that Wave 5 holds.

Wave 5

Wave 5 is the last phase of the five-wave move. The bullish or bearish trend is firmly in place. If this is a part of the bullish move, the news is universally positive and everyone is bullish. People who had missed the whole move enter here with "buy" positions. If this is a part of the bearish move, the news would be universally negative and pessimism will prevail. People liquidate all their "buy" positions and holdings, and bears have a great time.

Wave 5 is a very important wave. It is in Wave 5 that bullish or bearish sentiment is at its peak and people forget that the trend can change any time. In a bull move, people are absolutely confident and optimistic of the price rise whereas in a bear move, people are overtaken by panic and see it as the end of the market. Unfortunately, it is in Wave 5 where most of the investors either buy (close to the top) or liquidate their holdings after an endless wait (just close to the bottom).

Naturally, if such strong emotions are attached, the price moves may sometimes be so strong that they defy logic. If Wave 3 is not extended (explained later), the majority of the price rise or fall of the whole move may happen in Wave 5. In such a case, Wave 5 holds such potential that you can earn manifold returns within a span of days. Wave 5 of a bull move in the stock market is the time when small caps and penny stocks give returns that cannot be imagined or made in one's entire life by any legal means.

In Wave 5, most of the technical indicators will show divergence, and you as a technical trader, can come out after profiting from Wave 5. If Wave 5 has been an extended wave, you can look for harvesting the profit potential of Wave C.

Wave A

Just like Wave 1, Wave A is taken as a correction of Wave 5 and people are still confident of the previous trend continuing.

Wave B

Wave B corrects Wave A, but cannot cross the starting point of Wave A. People see it as a resumption of the trend. The fundamentals do not change much and most people trade in the direction of the trend.

Wave C

If Wave 5 has been a strong move, Wave C will also be a very sharp correction. Everyone realizes that the trend has changed and Wave C usually extends Wave A by 1.618 times.

Impulse Wave Extension

Extension is a common trait of an impulse wave. In an extension, the wave is abnormally elongated and its sub-waves are quite noticeable. As a rule, only one wave out of 1, 3 and 5 can be extended (*see* Figure 28.6).

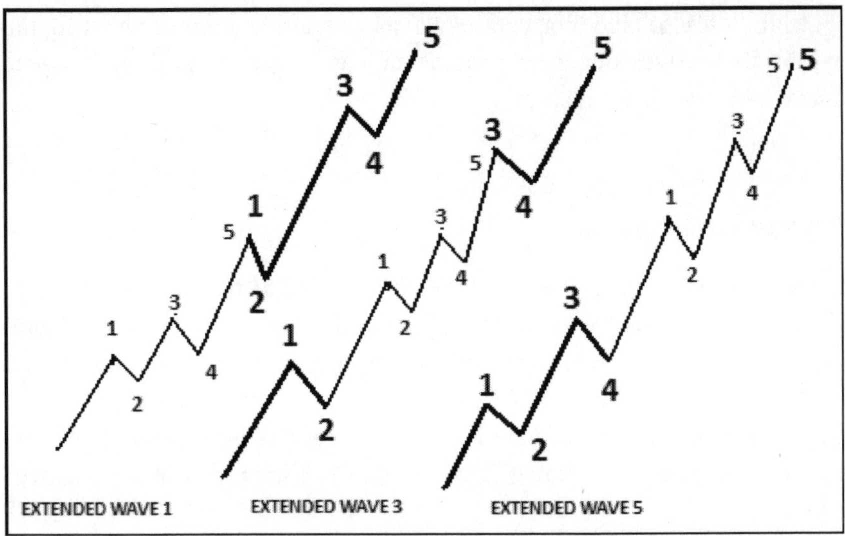

Figure 28.6: **Impulse Wave Extension**

Since only one wave can be an extended wave, it provides important leads on how the next impulse wave(s) are likely to behave. For example, if Wave 1 and Wave 3 are almost equal, then Wave 5 is very likely to be extended and will provide some excellent profit opportunities. Usually, Wave 1 is rarely extended whereas Wave 3 is most commonly an extended wave.

Wave 5 Failure

When Wave 3 is an exceptionally strong extended wave, Wave 5 fails to cross the high of Wave 3 which Elliott described as the failure of Wave 5.

Wave Patterns

Patterns are the foundation of the Elliott wave, and if you are able to recognize the patterns in a price chart, your wave analysis will be enhanced.

Both impulse and corrective waves contain a pattern or structure within themselves that help in understanding how far price is likely to move and in which direction.

Impulse Wave Patterns

Impulse waves are five wave patterns (1-2-3-4-5) that always move in the direction of the trend. Waves 1, 3 and 5 within an impulse are themselves impulse waves of a lower degree, which again sub-divide into a five-wave pattern. One of the impulse waves within an impulse wave is usually an extended wave, and in such a scenario, the other two are likely to be of an equal size. Waves 2 and 4 within an impulse wave are corrective waves.

Apart from an impulse, just two other five-wave patterns, the leading diagonal triangle and the ending diagonal triangle move in the direction of the main trend. These two diagonal triangles can be considered special type of impulse waves, and although rare, should be thoroughly understood.

1. **Normal impulse**: This is the most common impulse wave structure. Although it has been covered earlier, I will again mention the rules:

    - It is composed of five waves — three in the direction of the trend (1, 3, 5) and two counter-trend waves (2 and 4).The internal structure of an impulse is 5-3-5-3-5.
    - Wave 2 never moves beyond the start of Wave 1.
    - Wave 3 is never the shortest wave.
    - Wave 4 never overlaps the end of Wave 1.

    Guidelines

    - Waves 2 and 4 tend to alternate in form.
    - One of the waves out of 1, 3, or 5 is usually an extended wave (but not always).

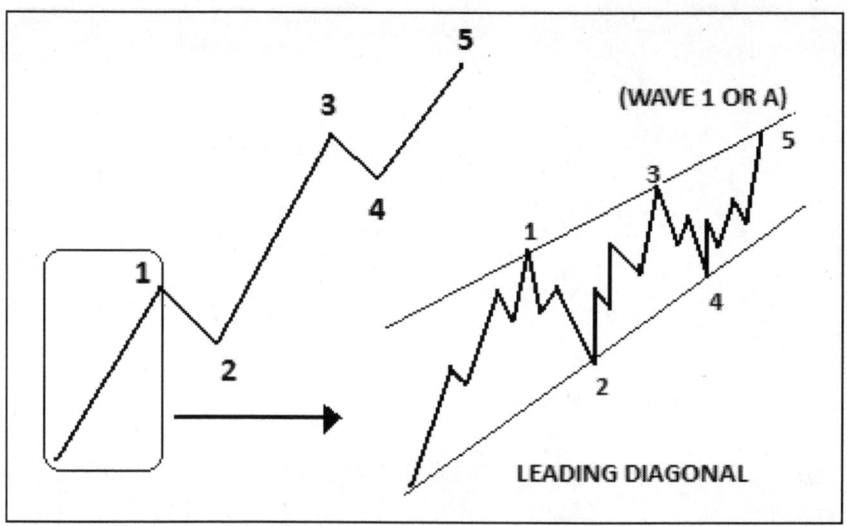

Figure 28.7: **Leading Diagonal**

2. **The Leading Diagonal**: The leading diagonal is a special impulse formation that takes a wedge shape within converging upper and lower trendlines. It occurs only in Wave 1 or Wave A (*see* Figure 28.7).

All the rules of impulse apply to formation of leading diagonal except one. In leading diagonal, Wave 4 overlaps Wave 1, i.e., Wave 4 enters the price area of Wave 1. The internal structure of a leading diagonal is 5-3-5-3-5.

Summary of leading diagonal:

- Wave 4 of leading diagonal often overlaps Wave 1.
- The internal structure is 5-3-5-3-5.
- The sub-waves move within two converging trendlines.
- The leading diagonal triangle usually occurs as part of Wave 1 of impulses or Wave A of corrective.

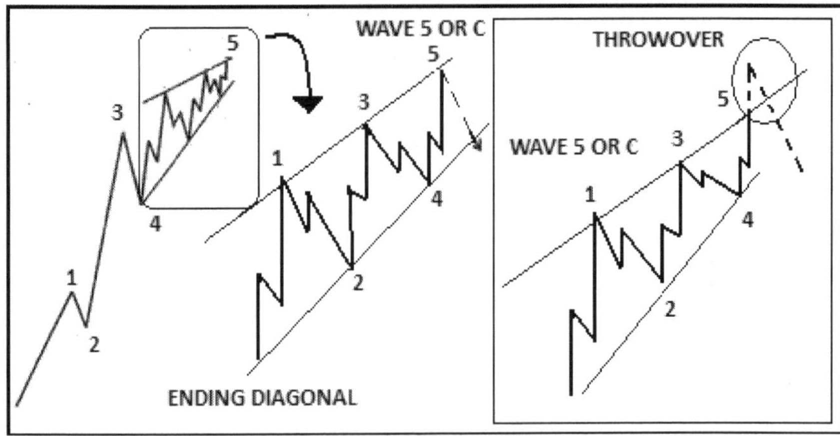

Figure 28.8: **Ending diagonal**

3. **Ending Diagonal:** The ending diagonal is another special form of impulse that occurs in Wave 5 or Wave C. Just like a leading diagonal, it takes a wedge shape within converging upper and lower trendlines (*see* Figure 28.8).

According to Elliott, it occurs when the price moves "too far, too fast". Ending diagonal typically marks the termination points of larger patterns, indicating exhaustion of the larger trend.

Just like in leading diagonal, the ending diagonal has overlapping Wave 4 and Wave 1. Wave 4 moves in the price area of Wave 1.

Ending diagonal has a different internal structure from impulse and leading diagonal. The internal structure of ending diagonal is 3-3-3-3 -3.

A rising diagonal is usually followed by a sharp decline, and a falling diagonal is usually followed by a strong up-move. In both the cases, the prices can retrace almost all the price moves of Wave 5 in a short time.

Ending diagonal triangles — extended 5th wave and failed 5th wave — all indicate a strong price reversal.

Sometimes, the fifth wave of the ending diagonal will spike sharply above the upper trendline of the triangle. Elliott called it as a "throw-over". Conventional technical traders would take it as a breakout of the triangle and trade accordingly as this is a very strong chart pattern. However, a trader should be careful when the ending diagonal triangle formation happens, as it signals an impending and sharp trend reversal. The throw-over is the final price move before the trend changes and this can only be judged by the Elliott wave.

Summary of ending diagonal:

- Wave 4 of the ending diagonal often overlaps Wave 1.
- The internal structure is 3-3-3-3-3.
- The sub-waves move within two converging trendlines.
- A throw-over can happen in which the price spike crosses the trendline in the direction of the trend for a short duration.
- The ending diagonal triangle usually occurs as part of a fifth wave extension.

Corrective Wave Patterns

Corrective waves are three-wave patterns that always move against the trend. Corrective waves have much more variations than the impulse waves which makes them difficult to identify in the initial stages of the formation. Corrective wave patterns broadly fall into four main categories:

- **Zigzags:** A pattern with a 5-3-5 internal structure that has three variations; single, double and triple.
- **Flats:** A pattern with a 3-3-5 internal structure that has three variations; regular, expanded and running.
- **Triangles:** A pattern with a 3-3-3-3-3 internal structure of four types, ascending, descending, contracting and expanding.
- **Double Threes and Triple Threes:** Combined structures of the above formations.

Zigzag

A zigzag is the corrective wave structure that shows a sharp reversal (*see* Figure 28.9). The zigzag pattern most commonly occurs as part of Wave 2 or Wave B. The reason is because in Wave 2 and Wave B, the previous trend is still considered strong and people rush to take positions. This makes a zigzag pattern a sharp move like an impulse. The internal structure of a zigzag is 5-3-5.

Characteristics

1. It is composed of three waves.
2. Waves A and C are impulses, Wave B is corrective.
3. Wave B is short and never retraces more than 61.8% of A.
4. Wave C must go beyond the end of A and is usually equal to Wave A in length.
5. The next most likely price lengths for Wave C are 61.8% and 161.8% of Wave A.

Important: If Wave C is much longer than 161.8% of A, and has a greater slope, then the pattern may be the beginning of an Impulse rather than a Zigzag pattern.

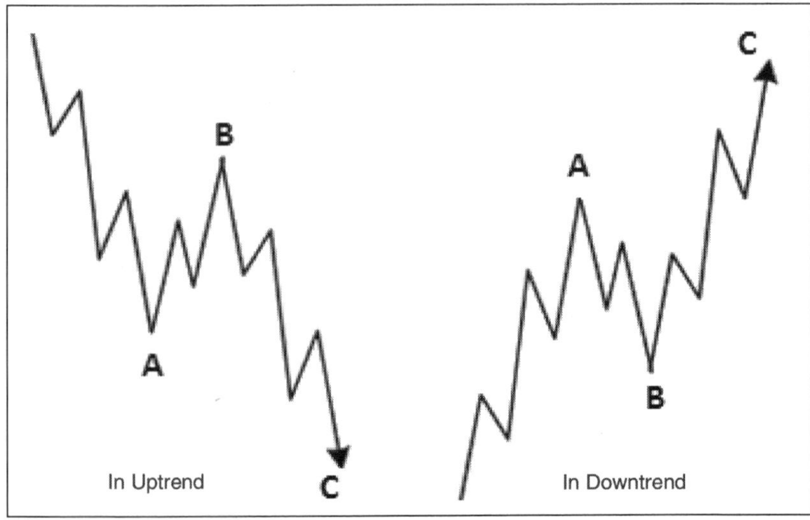

Figure 28.9: **Corrective wave zigzag pattern**

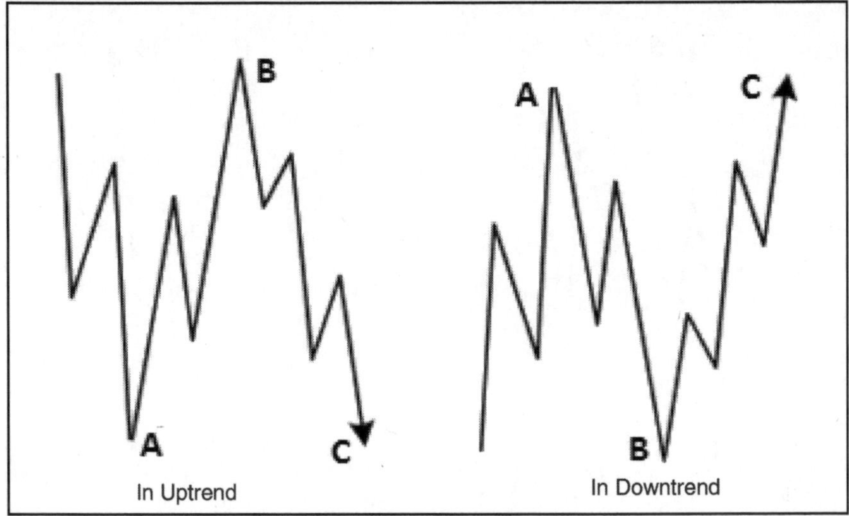

Figure 28.10: **Corrective wave flat pattern**

Flat

Flats are fairly common forms of corrective patterns and show a sideways movement — *see* Figure 28.10. Waves A and B of the Flat are both corrective patterns and Wave C is an impulsive pattern. Flats usually occur as part of Wave 4. The internal structure of a flat is 3-3-5.

Characteristics

1. It is composed of three waves.
2. Waves A and B are corrective, Wave C is an impulse.
3. Wave B ends near the start of Wave A.
4. Wave C does not cross the end of Wave A.
5. Normally, Wave C is at least equal to A.

Irregular

Irregular is a special type of Flat. In an irregular pattern, Wave B is extended and crosses the end of the previous impulsive wave — or the start

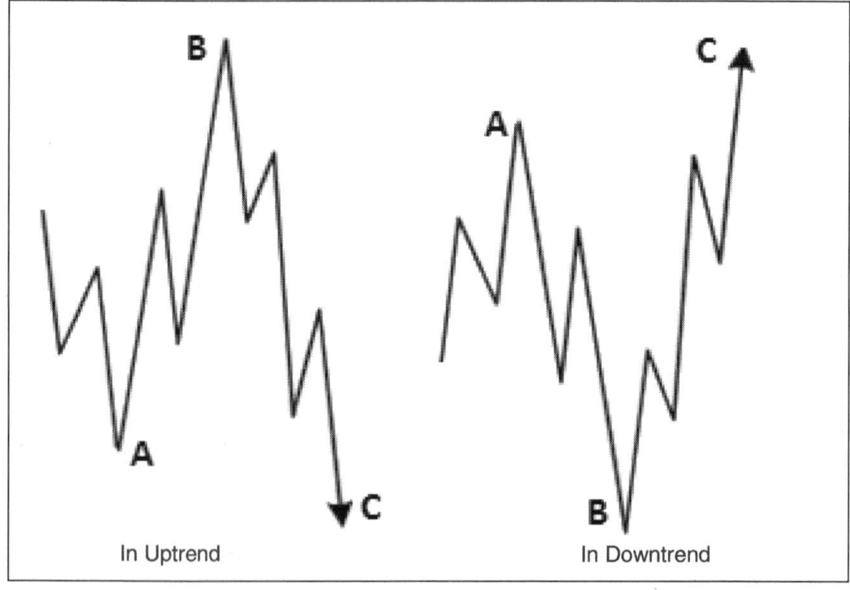

Figure 28.11: **Irregular pattern**

of Wave A (*see* Figure 28.11). The strong move of Wave B indicates that the market is likely to follow the direction of Wave B in future. It can occur in any corrective wave but is found mostly in Wave 2. The internal structure is 3-3-5.

Characteristics

1. It is a three-wave structure.
2. Wave B crosses the start of Wave A.
3. Wave C ends beyond the end of Wave A.

Triangles

Triangles are complex corrective wave patterns that are often formed in Wave 4 (*see* Figure 28.12). Unlike other corrective wave patterns, triangles are composed by 5 sub-waves marked a-b-c-d-e. All the five sub-waves are three-wave structures. The internal structure of a triangle is 3-3-3-3-3.

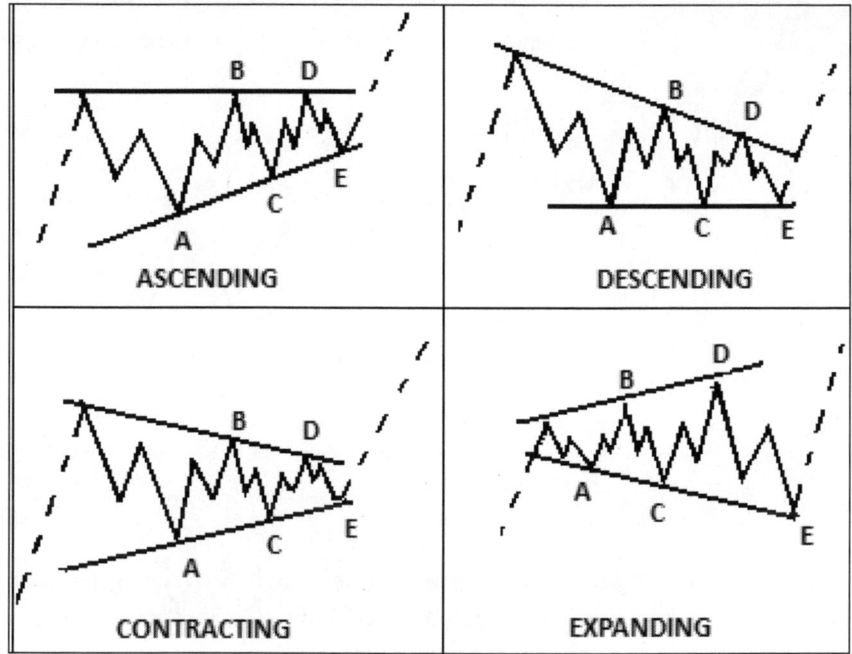

Figure 28.12: **Corrective triangle pattern**

There are four types of triangle formation; ascending, descending, expanding and contracting. Elliott wave theory uses the traditional technical analysis method for classifying and measuring triangles. Therefore, if you see a triangle in the fourth wave of an impulse wave, you can easily calculate the target price of the 5th wave and know where the whole impulse wave is likely to end. In the same way, if a triangle occurs in Wave B of an A-B-C correction, you can project the end of Wave C.

Double and Triple Three

The patterns that have been discussed until now sometimes add on within themselves or with each other to form another corrective wave pattern known as double and triple three (*see* Figure 28.13 and Figure 28.14). A double occurs when two patterns combine, and a triple when three patterns combine.

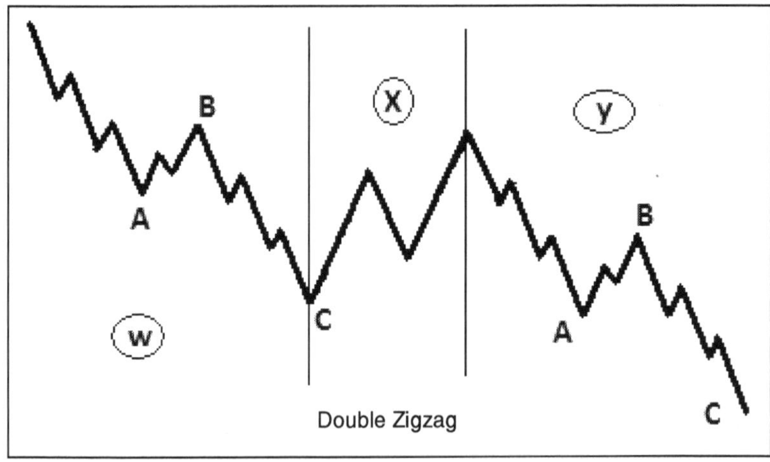

Figure 28.13: **Double zigzag**

The most common is a double zigzag in which two zigzag patterns combine to make a double zigzag pattern (Figure 28.13). Mostly it is the second wave that has zigzags as their sub-waves and it is rare in the 4th wave. In a double zigzag, two zigzag patterns are joined by an X wave and the pattern will be ABC-X-ABC. This X wave can be any of the three corrective wave patterns.

In the same way, triple zigzag contains three zigzag patterns joined by two X waves, and the pattern will be ABC-X-ABC-X-ABC.

The X wave is always composed of three sub-waves in all the double and triple three.

For convenience, the double zigzag is represented as W-X-Y instead of ABC-X-ABC. The first zigzag is labelled as W and the next as Y. Triple zigzag is represented by W-X-Y-X-Z instead of ABC-X-ABC-X-ABC. The first zigzag is labelled as W, the second as Y and the third as Z (*see* Figure 28.14).

If you wish to bring even more clarity, mark the second X wave as XX.

In double and triple three patterns, triangles usually appear only once as a final wave in the double and triple threes. Whenever the market starts to move in a double or triple correction, it is best to rely on conventional technical analysis tools like divergences and trendlines to look for an end of corrective wave pattern.

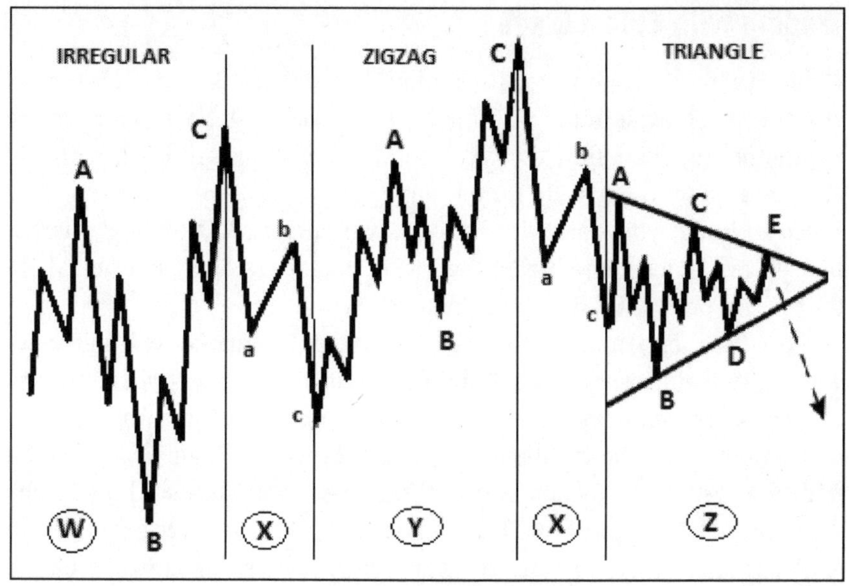

Figure 28.14: **Triple three**

A final revision of Elliott wave rules and guidelines:

1. Wave 1 can only be an impulse or leading diagonal.
2. Wave 2 is usually a zigzag.
3. Wave 2 usually takes a small amount of time compared to Wave 1.
4. Wave 2 generally retraces more than 61.8% of Wave 1
5. It is rare for Wave 3 to be shorter than Wave 1 by price.
6. Wave 4 will very often retrace about 38.2% of Wave 3.
7. Waves 2 and 4 usually alternate between zigzag and flat or between a triangle and a flat.
8. Wave 4 takes more time to complete than Wave 2.
9. If Wave 5 is extended, it will usually be about 161.8% of the price length of the start of Wave 1 and end of Wave 3. The other likely price targets for Wave 5 are 61.8% and 100% of Wave 1.
10. One of the Impulse waves is an extension.
11. The most likely wave to extend is the third wave of an Impulse.
12. A non-extended fifth wave of primary degree or lower usually has a lower volume than a third wave. However, the extended fifth wave shows more volume.

Trading with Elliott Wave

Elliott wave is a useful tool for finding low risk entry and high reward exit levels. Analyse multiple time-frame waves to get a clearer picture but the hourly chart should always be a part of the analysis. It is preferable to use a semi-log scale for trading.

How should you start with Elliott wave analysis? Look at the larger time-frame, at least one higher than what you are trading, and see where the present price is in the whole context.

Do not be too strong on the assumption that the market will move according to Elliott wave rules and guidelines. Most of the traders will try to force every intraday up and down move into an Elliott wave pattern that supports their belief about the market direction. Begin a wave count in that degree where the divisions are most obvious. Then see how far the wave count has progressed. Once that is clear, go to a lower degree wave and start analysing structures in detail. Keep a continuous watch on the market to see if the pattern or the wave that you had predicted is unfolding or not. If not, then re-analyse the waves. Be flexible about your analysis, relook and change it whenever required. This simple strategy will make your wave analysis strong and give more depth to your understanding about wave patterns.

Elliott wave is not about predicting one clear market direction but it is all about finding the most probable move. Try to find the most probable move from the patterns unfolding and trade accordingly.

Patterns are the first thing you must look for, starting from the easily distinguished 5-wave impulse to more complex corrective wave patterns. Elliott wave rules and guidelines should always be in your mind as the market unfolds so that you can be clear if the pattern is a correction or an impulse and if that pattern is itself forming in an impulse or a correction of a larger degree wave. Elliott wave rules and guidelines will also help you to confirm or reject the wave pattern as it unfolds.

It is a fact that Elliott wave cannot be traded at every level. The first clear trading opportunity comes in third wave when it crosses the high or low of Wave 1. The corrective wave patterns are complex and most of the traders don't trade during corrective waves. Even with limited scope of trading, Elliott wave provides some big profit opportunities due to the

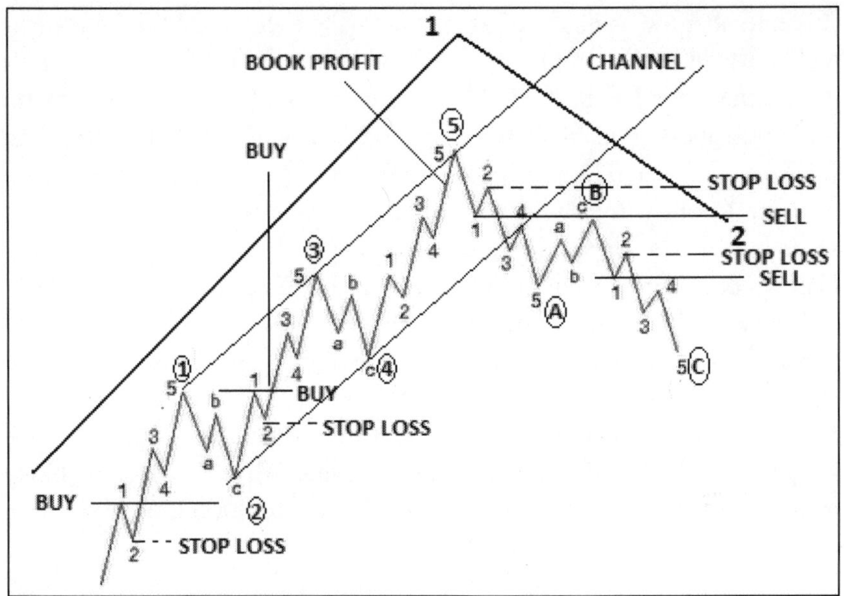

Figure 28.15: **Identifying entry and exit points in Elliott wave**

---

length of the move that can be cashed. By the time the third wave gives entry signals, conventional technical traders would have entered and closed many trades. If Elliott wave is used with other tools, you will know that the entry in Wave 3 can be very profitable if held for a longer time. If you are trading on just Elliott wave, you have to be very patient and wait for the right opportunity. Elliott wave is not for quick entry and exits.

Figure 28.15 indicates some of the good entry and exit points at crucial wave levels and channel points.

The best entry levels are provided when Wave 3 crosses the end of Wave 1. You can refine the entry by analysing the sub-waves and come up with even better levels. If you make an entry when Wave 3 crosses the end of Wave 1, keep a stop loss level close to the end of Wave 2.

The 3rd of the 3rd is one of the best entry levels when considering waves of two degrees. In the same way, exiting in the 5th of the 5th is the best exit level.

A low-risk entry strategy is to enter the market at the end of the intermediate corrective waves of the major impulse waves in the direction of the impulse.

Remember the principle of alternation - the second and the fourth corrective waves within an impulse wave will alternate in form and depth. If the second wave has retraced 61.8% or more of Wave 1, then the fourth wave will most probably retrace only 38.2% of Wave 3. If the second wave has corrected 38.2% or less of Wave 1, (a very rare occurrence), then the fourth wave should correct 61.8% or more of Wave 3. If the second wave is a simple corrective wave like a zigzag, the fourth wave is likely to be a complex corrective wave like a double three or a triangle.

I have explained the applicable Fibonacci ratios in wave count. Use those extensively in Elliott analysis. The end of Wave 3 and Wave 5 can be projected with a good level of accuracy using Fibonacci ratios. If Wave 3 is in extension, it will be equal to 1.618 or 2.618 times the price length of Wave 1. After Wave 3 is completed, Wave 5 will most likely be 0.618 times the length of the start of Wave 1 to the end of Wave 3. In case Wave 5 is extended, it will be 1.618 times.

Price Channel and Trendlines

Price channels and trendlines (*see* Figure 28.16) are very helpful technical analysis tools as you had learnt in Chapter 16 on "Trend". The technique to draw channels and trendlines is the same in Elliott wave too.

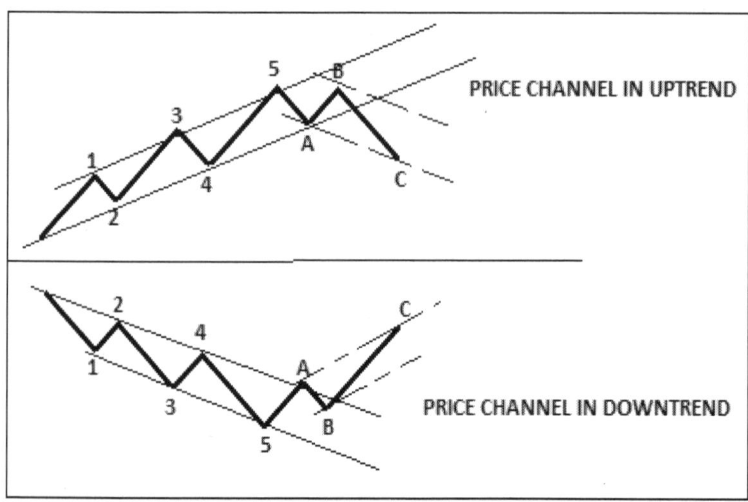

Figure 28.16: **Price channels and trendlines**

In Elliott wave, price channels can also be used to confirm the end of the third and the fifth waves in an impulse sequence. You have to wait for the first two waves in an impulse move to be complete before drawing a channel.

To project the end of Wave 3, draw a trendline connecting the start of Wave 1 and the end of Wave 2, then draw a parallel trendline touching the end of Wave 1. The third wave will most likely end close to this parallel trendline. Extend this channel and it can be used to project the Wave 5 target.

Another way to project the end of Wave 5 is to use new reference points that have been generated by completion of Wave 2 and 4. Draw a trendline connecting the ends of Waves 2 and 4, and then draw a parallel line connecting the ends of Waves 1 and 3. If Wave 3 is an extended wave, just draw a parallel line touching the end of Wave 1. This will cut through Wave 3 but is very helpful in projecting the Wave 5 target. You can also make use of two parallel lines touching the end of Waves 1 and 3. The fifth wave should complete close to one of these parallel trendlines.

Projecting the fifth wave of higher degree impulse wave can be done by constructing similar price channels for Wave 5 of sub-waves of a lower degree. Whenever the baseline is decisively broken, it is a clear indication that the impulse is completed. Baseline is the line drawn connecting the ends of Waves 2 and 4 or the start of Wave 1 and the end of Wave 4.

In the same way, use the trendlines to analyse the corrective waves. For example, a triangle will have two converging trendlines and when the price breaks a trendline in the direction of the previous impulse, it indicates the resumption of the trend and end of correction.

The corrective waves are much more difficult to judge than impulse. The complexity of corrective wave formation takes too much time to decipher the pattern. The easy way out is to wait until corrective waves end and confirm it by conventional technical analysis tools like trendlines, divergence in oscillators, candlestick patterns, etc. Since the market is in a trading phase in the corrective wave patterns, the breakout of trendline and taking position in overbought / oversold zone of oscillators like stochastic in direction of previous impulse trend can be a very good entry.

Fibonacci retracements provide important levels of end of corrective waves.

You will be disappointed if you are looking for an Elliott wave trading manual, because there cannot be any. Before you start trading with Elliott wave, it is important for you to again remember that it is very subjective. Therefore, you will have to develop your own trading methods based on the basic theory that you have learnt so far. Every Elliott wave trader has an individualistic approach to trading and if you blindly follow anybody, it may be disastrous as it is bound to clash with your trading style.

Chapter 29

Gann Studies

GANN STUDY WAS DEVELOPED BY WILLIAM DELBERT GANN (1878 – 1955). He was a mathematician and astrologer, and used all his knowledge of mathematics, astrology, astronomy and natural cycles to develop a trading system.

The basic structure of the Gann studies is based on the premise that the markets are cyclical in nature and geometrical in design, and involves looking at three crucial ingredients — price, time and pattern.

- **Price Study:** This included many of the modern day technical analysis tools like support and resistance lines, pivot points, etc.
- **Time Studies:** The time study was a complex mix of natural and social causes that reoccur at regular intervals.
- **Patterns:** The pattern study included reversal patterns based on bar charts and market swing points based on trendlines.

The majority of Gann study is based on Gann angles that are used to determine support and resistance, trend direction and strength, and probabilities of price reversal. Gann added his own observations to the trendline concept and stated that a true trendline should consider both the price and time. Gann angles (lines) are drawn using the relationship of time and price. The unique aspect of Gann is that just one price point is required to draw multiple lines which act as support or resistance whereas usual trendline analysis requires a minimum of two price points to connect a line. According to Gann, major highs or lows are the starting points for a trendline.

Gann Line

Gann Line represents a line drawn at the angle of 45 degrees from a major high or major low. This line is also called "one to one" (1x1) that means one unit change of the price within one unit of time.

The line having the slope of forty-five degrees represents a most stable long-term trend (ascending or descending). The slope value depends directly on your choice of units and scales for the time and price axis so it becomes too subjective. For example, according to your observation, a one week time-frame may take a distance of 2 mm on the horizontal x-axis, and this 2 mm may be set on y-axis for one dollar of price move.

When prices are above the ascending line, the market holds bull directions. If prices hold below the descending line, the market is in a clear bear trend. When prices break this trendline, it indicates a trend weakness. Gann grid represents trends built at the angle of 45 degrees.

Gann identified nine significant angles shown in Table 29.1. The 1 × 1 or 45 degree angle is the most important angle.

The relationship of time by price assumes a square grid. When translated into degrees, space taken by one unit of time on the x-axis is equal to space taken by one unit of price on the y-axis. Without this equality of time and price movement, the Gann studies cannot be done. On such a scaled chart, the 1 × 1 geometric angle, which for every one unit of time rises one point in price, is a 45-degree angle. The other Gann angles are depicted in Table 29.1

Table 29.1: Gann Angles

TIME	*X*	*PRICE*	=	*DEGREES*
1	X	8	=	82.50
1	X	4	=	75.00
1	X	3	=	71.25
1	X	2	=	63.75
1	X	1	=	45.00
2	X	1	=	26.25
3	X	1	=	18.75
4	X	1	=	15.00
8	X	1	=	7.50

Usually, a move after major tops or bottoms is extremely sharp and, therefore, lies in the 1 × 8 quadrant, which means it is moving 8 units of price per one unit of time. After some time, the sharpness is reduced and the market moves to a 1 × 4 line.

Each of the angles can provide support and resistance depending on the trend but 1 × 1 or a 45-degree angle provides major support or resistance. For example, in an uptrend, a major reversal is signalled when prices fall below the 1 × 1 angled trendline. The price can then be expected to touch the next trendline. In other words, as one angle is penetrated, expect prices to move and consolidate at the next angle.

Gann stressed on weekly charts for analysis so it is of no great help for traders. The market dynamics have changed completely from the times of Mr Gann, and price movements can remain too sharp or too shallow for extended periods. Otherwise too, till you are not able to trade profitably with price and volume charts, adding time will serve no purpose. Gann seems good for additional study but cannot be made a part of the analysis process, at least not in the initial years of trading.

Traders in their initial years of trading can ignore Gann, Fibonacci arc and Fibonacci fan, as they require a lot of time to understand and implement in trading. Even after so much of work, they are of little help to a trader.

Chapter 30

Money and Risk Management

- *Psychological management is the first step to managing risk.*
- *Risk management is the first step to managing money.*
- *Money management is the first step to making money.*

Trader's Life Cycle

The trading life of an individual can be divided into four distinct phases, just like a human life cycle. The first one is the child phase, the second is a teenager phase, the third is an adult phase and the fourth is the old age.

1. **Child Phase:** This is the initial phase in a trader's life cycle. Just as a child is curious about all the happenings and objects around, an individual is curious about financial markets. One wants to know what exactly is it that is being talked about in the media, in group discussions, etc. and gets hooked to the rags-to-riches and riches-to-rags stories. Inquiries about financial markets like how to trade, how much money can be made, where to find the broker, etc. are carried out. The child phase of a trader's lifecycle can start at 16 or 60, but is usually the shortest phase and can be over within days. A person will either ignore the financial markets or move a step ahead and invest.
2. **Teenager:** This is the second phase and it is action time after the initial curiosity. Most of the traders in this phase are like teenagers, hyperactive but with minimum experience. They start bonding with their own kind and with other traders who are trading in the market. Their views about markets keep on changing with every new input from fellow traders, TV commentaries, newspaper articles, etc. In this phase, a trader does not have a long-term view about market risks and what can be the repercussions of wrong trades. Trading is impulsive and con-

trolled by emotions. Traders think that whatever they did was right and never accept that they made a mistake. They believe that profits are always because of their intelligence, but losses are always because of some outside factor, which is not in their control.

This is the make or break phase for a trader. The teenagers have parental support and right advice, so their mistakes are taken care of. However, as a teenager in trading life, a person has no real well-wisher and one has to pay for the mistakes committed, literally. A trader may be trapped in this phase forever without realising that there is a better phase ahead.

3. **Adult Phase:** This is the third phase of a trader's life cycle associated with maturity and humbleness. Only fractions of traders reach the adult phase. Traders in this stage understand that one cannot fight with the market. They do not let their ego affect their trading and know that they can be as wrong or right as a first time trader is. Proper money and risk management techniques become an integral part of their trading. Neither do they boast about profits nor do they become woeful about losses. Traders in this phase are comfortable with their trading and make regular profits, ending the uncertainty of trading life.
4. **Old Age Phase:** This is the last phase. After living through hectic and active trading, traders retire; they get into academic research, philanthropy, travel around the world, etc. In short, they do what they had always wanted to do but could not, due to pressures of trading.

So why is it that most traders are not able to move out of the teenager stage? Why is it that even after spending countless hours watching the markets and many sleepless nights later, their trading account is still negative? The answer is simple; they do not implement money and risk management in trading.

As a trader, you will realize, or must have realized that you have no control over the market and it is impossible for anybody to predict price movements. However, you have absolute control over your trading account, and how you manage your money will decide your future as a trader.

Money management cannot be done without risk management, and risk management cannot be done without psychological management.

Psychological Management

Before you start trading, it is very important to understand your psychology. What is your personality? How do you handle situations? Are your actions impulsive or do you give due thought before doing something? Are you easily carried away by your emotions?

These questions may sound out-of-context, but they are the ones that decide how you are going to perform as a trader. Most of our actions are in some way controlled by emotions and unfortunately, so is our trading. You may spend hours on analysis and come up with the best entry and exit levels, but once you are ready to implement your analysis, your emotions will start to take over and analysis will be forgotten.

To illustrate, suppose you have bought a stock and it starts to rise. Your first reaction will be to book profit even if your target price is far away. This gives immediate satisfaction and removes all FEAR of losses that you experience with every tick down move. Now that you have booked the profit, the market still continues to rise and you are cursing yourself for coming out too soon. You calculate all the profit that you could have made. With every rise in prices, your frustration rises and you again buy the stock even though your original exit level has been reached. The other case may be that you do not book profit even though your target has been achieved. GREED has overpowered the analysis. The stock, after a few upticks, starts to fall and you continue waiting as your profits turn into losses.

Here is another situation; suppose you have bought the stock and it starts to fall. Your stop loss point is reached but you do not execute it because you HOPE that the market will rise. The stock continues falling and now making profit is no longer an issue; you hope to at least recover your capital. The stock continues falling; now you hope that it recovers to the extent where you can exit with a marginal loss.

The above example is just one in hundreds that a trader goes through. Trading is one of the most challenging jobs because it involves taking risk in an uncertain environment over which you have no control. Every price tick will make your emotions run high and all your actions will be based on them.

It is important to be aware of the following emotions that are a trader's enemy and must be controlled:

1. **Ego:** This is the biggest enemy. With ego, you live in a make-believe world of which you are the king. Nobody is better than you, and you are always right. Ego will not let you accept that you went wrong. Ego will make you fight the market over losing trades. Ego will compel you to enter the market immediately after a big loss because you want to get back your money. You will fight to impose your opinion about markets on other traders, and your next trade will be based on your opinion even if the market is giving different indications, because you have fought for it.

   You may have people supporting your ego before you started trading, but markets do not like egoistic traders, and the punishment is severe. Do not enter the market with an ego because the biggest emotional pain is bruising the ego and you may never be able to trade again. Be humble, not egoistic and arrogant. Accept that the market is all-supreme and will not move according to your wishes. If you are wrong, do not fight; just exit. If you are right, thank the market.
2. **Greed:** Greed is the emotion that makes you want increasingly more. No amount of profit is ever enough. Greed will dictate you to take positions much larger than your capacity, it will make you add to a losing trade, it will make you enter markets about which you have no idea, and it will make you act on tips and rumours.
3. **Hope:** Hope is your last resort when you have nothing else left. Hope will make you stick to a losing position and bring you to a point where only a miracle can save you. It will stop you from booking losses while they do not hurt. Hope will make you analyse markets with all possible tools and you will try to find the one that supports the market direction that you want. Hope, beyond a reasonable expectation, will finish your account in one trade.
4. **Fear:** Fear is a good emotion; it protects you from something that can hurt. It will be there with you before and after you take a position. Fear of the market is not bad but do not let it control your trading. The biggest fear will be fear of losing; it will stop you from taking a new position and compel you to exit a profitable one too soon.

5. **Anger:** Anger takes away all your sanity. You cannot afford to be angry while trading. Anger may be directed towards yourself, the broker, the market or anyone else. The reason could be anything — it may be because of trading or any personal issues — but whatever the reason for your anger, never trade if you are overcome by this emotion.
6. **Euphoria and Disappointment:** These two extreme emotions can be very distracting. While it is normal to feel joy after a good profit, or feel sad after a loss, but at extreme levels, they result in impulsive actions such as taking multiple positions one after the other and ignoring all risk-control strategies. If you are too euphoric or disappointed, the other emotions will control you easily. When you are feeling euphoric after a good profit, your ego will take over, and when you are feeling too disappointed after a loss, fear will not let you take a new position.

To avoid extreme emotions while trading, be realistic and logical. Do not let loss turn you into a pessimistic and fearful person; rather, see it as a learning opportunity to be used in future to make profits. Similarly, do not let profits turn you into an overconfident and arrogant person. Profits and losses are part of trading and both are equally likely to happen even after gaining years of trading experience.

Emotions are an integral part of being a human being; they cannot be ignored or completely overcome. However, the problem starts when emotions start controlling the way you trade. It is mandatory for every trader to be aware of the negative influence of emotions on trading and develop a strong mindset to control emotions. The following points will help in reducing the emotional impact on your trading:

1. **Develop a Trading System:** A trading system is simply a set of parameters and rules that govern your entry and exit positions. Once you have learnt all the technical tools, you will come up with your favourite ones that work for you. For example, you may develop a simple "buy" system when a 13-day moving average crosses above the 21-day moving average with an increase in volume. Once this happens, you will buy the security no matter what your emotions are and what other traders are saying. Remember that it is neither possible nor profitable to use too many tools; therefore, your trading system should be simple consisting of just three to four trading parameters. Stick to the system that you have developed, refine it with each trading experience and try

to remove the shortcomings. Look for a different trading system only when you are sure that the system has been given adequate time and energy, but still failed to generate expected profits. If you have to be a successful trader, you must devote your energy in finding trading techniques that work for you and not focus on individual trades as a benchmark for success or failure. You should keep the following points in mind while developing a trading system:

A. **Liquidity:** Your trading system should be developed and tested on markets with high liquidity. Equity indices, four major currency pairs, gold and crude oil in commodities are perfect for developing a trading system. If you are a stock trader, remember that no trading system can be developed for low volume and illiquid stocks. The same applies for rarely-traded commodities and currency pairs too.
B. **Risk Control:** Your system should have adequate measures to control risk. The stop loss level should be decided before entry into a trade, and it should be adhered to. The stop loss should not be too far away from the entry price, as the wide gap will finish your account within a few trades.
C. **System Should be Profitable:** You must include all costs associated with trading such as brokerage, taxes, etc. to look at system profitability.
D. **System Should be Consistent:** Your system should show consistent profits. It does not mean that you should get an increasing number of individual profits; rather, even if there are strings of losses, the profits should be able to cover all those losses within a set timeframe.

Almost all charting software now-a-days have the facility to create an automated trading system. Once you programme the system, the "buy" and "sell" will be indicated automatically whenever a particular condition is met. This is also known as mechanical trading. This helps you to back-test your system but do not rely too much on back-testing.

Paper trading or mock trading where you don't actually trade with money and just check your analysis on paper by calculating profit or loss on trades that you would have made, is a good option. However, you can avoid going through the process of paper trading as now you can even trade in as little as a single share. Slowly increase the traded quantity as you gain confidence over your system. Real trading will give you exact results and written records with all costs included.

The rules of a trading system will be based on your personality and lifestyle. If you tend to panic easily, you should not watch the markets after taking a position. Just place the orders and close the screen. You may make a rule that you will not trade during the first and last 15 minutes of the market opening and closing respectively, or when you are facing some personal problems. Ultimately, it comes down to trading on your strengths and avoiding it in your weak moments.

2. **Develop a Trading Plan:** Treat trading as a business, not as a part time job. Like any other business, trading in financial markets too requires a plan. A trading plan defines your goals, the strategies you need to achieve those goals, the risk you can afford to take, etc. The following are the important aspects for a trading plan:

   A. **Trading Objectives:** Ask yourself why you want to trade and what you expect to achieve out of it. If your answer is that you want to make a lot of money and enjoy the thrill of market movements, you probably should give up the idea of trading immediately. You need a clear outlook for trading and cannot afford to be vague. Moreover, there are a lot of ways to experience a thrill: bungee jumping, for one. You are, of course, going to trade for profits and making money, but it must be defined and not kept vague. For instance, you can have any target, such as a 2% weekly return, or making ₹ 1,000 in a month, depending on factors like your risk appetite, other sources of income, requirement of money for essential needs, etc. This way, you can compare actual trading results with planned ones and understand how you are doing and what needs to be done to make it better.

   B. **Which Markets to Trade in:** There are plenty of choices in respect of both the markets and instruments you wish to trade. You can trade for as long as the entire 24 hours! But this is not feasible to everyone. Don't be in an illusion that you can decide when to trade or not. It may be very difficult to control your urge to trade especially in the initial stages of trading. It is best to trade in just one or two securities initially; you can add more securities as you gain experience.

C. **Trade according to Your Personality:** Trade only those markets that suit your personality. The best way to know this is to start with a small account and avoid highly leveraged markets like derivatives in the initial stages of trading. This will give you time to understand your strengths and weaknesses and how you react to different situations. Don't trade when you are not mentally prepared as trading requires your complete attention. Don't use trading as a tool to escape from your problems; it can only aggravate your situation.

D. **Trading Expertise:** Your trading expertise will constantly evolve as you trade. At the initial stage, you must accept that with modest trading skills and experience, it is best to trade in moderation.

E. **Risk Level:** You must calculate your risk level and incorporate it into your trading plan. The maximum risk you can take in your trading portfolio, in a single position, or in a single day, must be worked out. Once the risk level is reached, exit from the market and stop trading. This will always keep your trading account active to trade another day rather than being wiped out in a few trades.

F. **Always Prepare before You Trade:** Don't trade without preparation; do your analysis and keep a watch on global markets.

G. **Analyse Your Trading Activity:** It is not enough to just close a trading position, you must also perform a post-trading analysis of your position to know which techniques to use further and which to discard.

"Plan your trade and trade your plan" is a well-known and wise saying. Your trading plan should be adhered to blindly while trading, but should be open to revision after the trade. As you grow as a trader, your trading plan will also see changes that will justify your skill level and psychological control.

3. **Discipline:** Discipline is an absolute must for every trader. You may work on charts, develop a system, make an excellent plan, but if you are not disciplined enough, all your hard work will be in vain. How disciplined you are in implementing your trading technique, rules and plan, will dictate how long you can sustain as a trader. Remember that trading is not like any other profession; years of experience can be nullified in a single loss. Therefore, it is discipline that will keep you

from being reckless and you will be able to enjoy the benefits of trading that no other profession provides.

4. **Patience:** If you are an impatient person, work hard to develop patience. Without patience, you cannot be successful. Don't be impatient to trade just as the market opens or when your system does not show any entry point. There is no opportunity that you can lose; markets have been there since ages and they will be there in future giving you opportunities repeatedly. Wait for the right time to make an entry. Once you have entered, remember that the position will take time to turn profitable; wait for the right exit price; don't get influenced by price movements.

Risk Management

Trading in the financial markets is all about risk and rewards. A risk-free trade does not exist, and with every entry, you are taking on the risk of losing money. With so much of associated risk, it becomes essential to manage risk if you have to survive as a trader.

Components of Risk Management

Stop loss

When a position goes the wrong way and starts to give you losses, it should be closed. Stop loss is nothing but closing a losing trade and booking the loss.

No amount of words can explain the importance of stop loss. When you book a loss, you are admitting that you were wrong and this requires controlling your ego. If you have courage to book losses, you will be part of that minority group that makes consistent profits. Ignoring indications from the market that you have made a wrong entry will eventually wipe out your trading account. There will be times when markets will turn in your favour just after booking the loss. Do not use this as an excuse to avoid initiating a stop loss order; just a single move by the market against you can end your trading career. The more you delay booking your losses, the larger they will become. It is not easy to recover losses;

you would require to clock a higher gain on the remaining amount of capital to arrive at the original level.

- If you lose 10% on a trade, you have to earn 11% on the next trade to get back to the original trading amount.
- If you lose 25%, you have to earn 33% on the next trade to get back to the original trading amount.
- If you lose 50%, you have to earn 100% on the next trade to get back to the original trading amount.

Needless to say, success can only come when you understand the huge risks involved by not using a stop loss. Deciding where to put the stop loss in your trade depends on your personal trading style and market conditions. A day trader may decide to restrict his loss to a maximum of 3% on a single trade whereas a long-term investor may put a stop loss at 10%. A highly volatile security requires a wide stop loss whereas a relatively stable security can be traded by keeping a tight stop loss. Support and resistance levels and trendlines provide good levels to place stop losses. Whatever be the case, it should be reasonable and in your comfort zone. Once you decide on a stop loss, place the order in the market and forget about it. Many traders make the mistake of moving the stop loss further and further with a hope that the market will turn any time.

Trailing Stop Loss: This is a very good technique to lock your profits. Once the position starts to turn profitable, you continuously move the stop loss with the market price. Here is an example. Let's say you have bought a ₹ 100 stock and put a ₹ 3 stop loss at 97. As the stock starts to rise, you keep on moving the stop loss higher so that it will always be ₹ 3 below the market price. When stock reaches ₹ 103, you move the stop loss to ₹ 100 and when stock reaches 110, move the stop loss to ₹ 107. This way, you will be able to continue with the profit as long as the price is moving up but will be out of the market if the stock price falls.

Appropriate Position Size

The size of your position should be very conservative. It is very easy to be swayed by the high profit potential of large positions especially in derivatives. If you have ₹ 1,000 in your trading account and you buy a thousand shares at a market price of ₹ 100 / share, you will lose all your money by just a ₹ 1 move against you. On the other hand, if you buy just hundred shares, you can be relaxed as it would require a ₹ 10 decline before you lose all your money. Of course, this situation would not arise as you would be placing a stop loss. Looking from this point of view, you can sustain 10 stop losses of ₹ 1 each if you buy hundred shares instead of thousand.

Psychological management and risk management constitute the largest part of money management. For investors, portfolio management is also an aspect that needs to be considered. The simple rule is to diversify the portfolio by investing in different instruments and sectors. You can have a couple of stocks from different sectors, commodity like gold, etc. as part of your portfolio.

Important Points in a Nutshell

1. **Never forget the plan:** You took a position based on some plan; don't forget it due to market volatility.
2. **Never overtrade:** You don't have to be in the market all the time. Overtrading leads to increased risk to your account and reduces your profit ratio. It also comes with an added cost burden as you pay commissions on each trade. You should not only know when to trade, but also when not to trade. Markets can be addictive and they will compel you to trade. If your system does not give any entry point, simply close the trading screen and move on to another activity.
3. **Never add to a losing position:** Taking more positions while the first one is still in a loss is a recipe for disaster. You might wonder how much further a market can go, but remember that a move can carry on for a much longer time than your account can handle.
4. **Add to the profitable position:** Once the position is in profit, look for opportunities to add more but in reduced quantities. For example, if you have bought 100 shares and you are in profit, buy 50 more. If market continues rising, buy another 25. Control the positions with trailing stop loss orders.
5. **Don't try to find logic:** There is no point in trying to find logic in price levels. For instance, expensive stocks will become more expensive and cheap stocks will get cheaper, or a seemingly illogical bull or

bear run may continue much longer than your logical mind can accept.

6. **Keep analysis simple:** Simple technical analysis tools work the best. Don't look for complex and difficult studies just because they seem fascinating.
7. **Don't chase the markets:** If you have missed the entry, do not chase the running market; you will get another opportunity soon. This works in the same way as the public bus. When you miss a bus, you wait at the bus stop because there is always another one.
8. **It is not worth being a contrarian in trending markets:** Being a rebel and doing things on your terms may sound good in discussions, but not in trading. Contrarian thinking works on very few trades and even in those, it sucks more of your energy than it pays.
9. **Follow the trend:** Make a rule to go with the trend and you are already a winner. Go long in bull markets and short in bear markets.
10. **All your analyses are probabilities:** Your analyses and predictions are just probabilities; don't make a mistake of thinking that markets will move accordingly. Expect the unexpected and trust the stop loss.
11. **Risk-reward ratio:** Keep a risk-reward ratio of at least 1:3. This implies that when you have a stop loss of ₹ 1, keep a minimum profit target of ₹ 3.
12. **Take a break:** Do not watch the market day in and day out. Take a break in order to return refreshed.
13. **Always trade with money you can afford to lose:** When you trade with money that is needed for your basic and necessary expenses, you are bound to make impulsive decisions based on emotions that can only lead to losses.
14. **Never trade with borrowed money:** Borrowing money to trade can only be termed as insanity. If you do that, you are ruined. This action will not just be limited to market losses but goes way beyond that and disturbs your personal and family life.
15. **Trade when the markets are calm:** In fast moving markets, you will never get a good price, and even if you do, placing a stop loss becomes all the more difficult. However, if you cannot stop yourself, be quick to enter and exit. If you wait to exit in high momentum moves, you may be trapped in a retracement that may be equally vicious.

16. **Avoid the opening and closing time of the market, at least in the beginning of your trading career.** Opening and closing time of the markets are more prone to volatility, and may provide wrong signals.
17. **Pamper yourself:** Trading is a tough job and when you make money, reward yourself for a job well done.
18. **Buy securities that show strength and sell those that show weakness:** Usually traders trade the other way round; they buy falling securities and sell the rising ones.

Happy trading!